PUNISHMENT AND DEMOCRACY

STUDIES IN CRIME AND PUBLIC POLICY
Michael Tonry and Norval Morris, *General Editors*

Police for the Future
David H. Bayley

Incapacitation: Penal Confinement and the Restraint of Crime
Franklin E. Zimring and Gordon Hawkins

The American Street Gang: Its Nature, Prevalence, and Control
Malcolm W. Klein

Sentencing Matters
Michael Tonry

The Habits of Legality: Criminal Justice and the Rule of Law
Francis A. Allen

Chinatown Gangs: Extortion, Enterprise, and Ethnicity
Ko-lin Chin

Responding to Troubled Youth
Cheryl L. Maxson and Malcolm W. Klein

Making Crime Pay: Law and Order in Contemporary American Politics
Katherine Beckett

Community Policing, Chicago Style
Wesley G. Skogan and Susan M. Hartnett

Crime Is Not the Problem: Lethal Violence in America
Franklin E. Zimring and Gordon Hawkins

Hate Crimes: Criminal Law & Identity Politics
James B. Jacobs and Kimberly Potter

Politics, Punishment, and Populism
Lord Windlesham

American Youth Violence
Franklin E. Zimring

Bad Kids: Race and the Transformation of the Juvenile Court
Barry C. Feld

Sentencing and Sanctions in Western Countries
Michael Tonry and Richard S. Frase

Punishment, Communication, and Community
R. A. Duff

*Punishment and Democracy: Three Strikes and
You're Out in California*
Franklin E. Zimring, Gordon Hawkins, and Sam Kamin

PUNISHMENT AND DEMOCRACY

Three Strikes and You're Out in California

Franklin E. Zimring
Gordon Hawkins
Sam Kamin

OXFORD
UNIVERSITY PRESS

2001

An Earl Warren Legal Institute Study

OXFORD

Oxford   New York

Athens   Auckland   Bangkok   Bogotá   Buenos Aires   Calcutta
Cape Town   Chennai   Dar es Salaam   Delhi   Florence   Hong Kong   Istanbul
Karachi   Kuala Lumpur   Madrid   Melbourne   Mexico City   Mumbai
Nairobi   Paris   São Paulo   Shanghai   Singapore   Taipei   Tokyo   Toronto   Warsaw

and associated companies in
Berlin   Ibadan

Copyright © 2001 by Oxford University Press, Inc.

Published by Oxford University Press, Inc.
198 Madison Avenue, New York, New York 10016

Oxford is a registered trademark of Oxford University Press.

Library of Congress Cataloging-in-Publication Data
Zimring, Franklin E.
Punishment and democracy : three strikes and you're out in California / Franklin E.
Zimring, Gordon Hawkins, and Sam Kamin.
p.   cm. — (Studies in crime and public policy)
ISBN 0-19-513686-1
1. Prison sentences—California. 2. Mandatory sentences—California. 3. Punishment in
crime deterrence—California. 4. Recidivism—California. 5. Crime prevention—California.
I. Hawkins, Gordon, 1919– II. Kamin, Sam. III. Title. IV. Series.
HV9305.C2 Z58   2000
364.6'5—dc21   00-036323

9 8 7 6 5 4 3 2 1

Printed in the United States of America
on acid-free paper

Acknowledgments

This is a large-scale project that depended on the help of many persons and organizations. Our first debts concern the study reported in part II of this volume. The Public Policy Institute of California provided financial support to the project, which was supplemented by funding from the Boalt Hall Fund at the University of California at Berkeley. The California Department of Justice provided both arrest records and criminal records for the members of our arrest sample. This was not a single-request, single-response type of cooperation but an ongoing relationship based on good humor and generosity. Kelly Kramer and John Dumbauld were the public officials we regularly bothered the most.

The research team at the Earl Warren Legal Institute included the authors and two skilled graduate students. Eric Carlson, then a second-year law student, designed the coding sheets and coded criminal records through the summer of 1998. James Allison, a doctoral student in the jurisprudence and social policy program, coded criminal records in the summer and fall of 1998 and served as our principal record auditor in 1999. Two outside researchers, doing independent work, served as collaborators: Elsa Chen of the Rand Corporation helped code cases for us and participated in our later design discussions. Samara Marion of Stanford, who is conducting a San Diego–based Three Strikes study, was a constant help with our San Diego analysis. James Rasmussen, the former head of criminal statistics at the California Department of Justice, was an important guide to problems with data retrieval.

The second major task of this project was to write a book much broader in scope than the initial empirical research. The new research staff for this adventure included Sarah Kermgard, a recent Berkeley graduate, and Amanda Packel, a first-year, then second-year, law student who served as a plenary project assistant as the manuscript grew into its final form.

Several colleagues read all or part of the book, including Peter

Greenwood of the Rand Corporation, Floyd Feeney of the University of California at Davis, Loic Wacquant of the University of California at Berkeley, José Canela-Cacho of the Earl Warren Legal Institute, Markus Dubber of the State University of New York at Buffalo, and our Boalt Hall colleagues Sanford Kadish and Meir Dan-Cohen.

At Boalt Hall, the usual dynamic duo carried this project along. Karen Chin was responsible for solving the many administrative problems that this enterprise presented; Toni Mendicino prepared and reprepared the manuscript and the graphics in this report.

Earlier versions of two sections of this book were published. Materials reported in chapter 1 were in volume 28 of the *Pacific Law Journal* (1996) and data from the study reported in part II of this volume were published by us as a monograph entitled *Crime and Punishment in California: The Impact of Three Strikes and You're Out* (Berkeley, Calif.: Institute of Government Studies Press, 1999).

Contents

Introduction   ix

Part I: Origins and Structure

1   Three Strikes Comes to California   3
2   The Largest Penal Experiment in American History   17

Part II: The Study

3   Building a Research Design   31
4   The Role of Recidivists in Urban California Crime   41
5   The Impact of Three Strikes on Criminal
    Punishment   63
6   Three Strikes as Crime Control   85

Part III: Impacts

7   The Jurisprudence of Imprisonment in California   109
8   Living with Three Strikes: Courts, Corrections, and
    the Political Process   125

Part IV: Implications

9   The Changing Politics of Criminal Punishment   151
10   Democracy and the Governance of
     Criminal Punishment   181
11   Legacies and Lessons   217

References   233

Index   239

Introduction

The "Three strikes and you're out" legislation adopted in California in 1994, was, at the same time, typical of recent American penal policy and decidedly unique. It is typical because of its orientation (long and mandatory terms of imprisonment), its devotion to symbolic gestures and slogans, and its willingness to displace discretion with binding general commitments to particular punishments. The California version was only 1 of 26 laws with that label passed in a three-year period during the 1990s, and the Three Strikes approach was only 1 of many punitive reforms of the 1990s.

What sets California's law apart from the other Three Strikes laws and every other penal law innovation of recent times is the extremity of its terms and the revolutionary nature of its ambitions. This statute was drafted by outsiders to have the maximum possible impact on criminal punishments. Whereas most penal laws are designed to deliver less drastic changes than they advertise—to bark louder than they bite—the California statute was designed to operate even more broadly than its specialized title would suggest. It was a law designed to bite louder than it barked.

The origin and impact of this legislation would have been an important subject no matter which state had adopted it, but the setting for the new law provided an even more compelling case for a major study. The state of California is one of the largest criminal justice systems in the free world. Its prisons and jails held almost a quarter of a million inmates before the new law took effect. The California prison system had grown more than fivefold in the 14 years prior to Three Strikes and already was larger than any prison system in the Western world. This was not only an extreme experiment but also one implemented in a very large and greatly expanded system.

This book reports our study of the origins, the impacts, and the implications of California's singular experiment in populist penal reform. Our coverage is divided into four segments: The first part of the book addresses the origin of the California law and the scale of its impact as a reform measure when compared to other examples of legislative criminal law reforms. Chapter 1 tells the history of the Three Strikes proposal and provides a summary of its terms. Chapter 2 argues that California's Three Strikes is the most important effort to achieve an abrupt increase in criminal punishments in modern times.

Part II of the book evaluates the effects of the California law on punishment policy and on crime rates. Chapter 3 describes and justifies the design of the research project conducted in San Diego, Los Angeles, and San Francisco. Chapter 4 reports the study's findings on the nature and prevalence of the crimes committed by the two target groups of the law—persons with one prior strike conviction and persons with two or more strike convictions. Chapter 5 examines the impact of the new law on the punishments received by those offenders with criminal records that subject them to mandatory prison terms under the law. Chapter 6 explains the logic of our test for the short-term deterrent impact of Three Strikes and demonstrates that the 1994 law could have had only a small fraction of the deterrent impact that has been attributed to it.

Part III addresses the broader impacts of Three Strikes in California in the 1990s. Chapter 7 examines how the 1994 legislation interacts with prior law to create a complicated and often inconsistent set of principles that guide the punishment of felons in California. Chapter 8 examines the impact of five years of operation of Three Strikes on the criminal and appellate courts, on the prison population, and on the politics of criminal justice reform.

The fourth and longest part of this book discusses some of the broad implications of the Three Strikes episode for American criminal justice. Chapter 9 uses Three Strikes as a case study in the evolving politics of criminal punishment in the United States. What has changed over the last generation? Why has this change taken place? What do our recent experiences tell us about future developments?

Chapter 10 bumps into the biggest set of questions that a study of Three Strikes should address—what is the proper role for citizens' preferences in structuring the governance of punishment in democratic systems? It is no accident that the longest chapter in this book concerns the most fundamental issue that the Three Strikes experience illuminates. Chapter 10 is a small down payment on a sustained inquiry of importance to the future of American criminal justice and of American government.

Chapter 11 returns to the particular topic of "Three strikes and you're out." It provides concluding emphasis on some of the legacies of the 1994 law in California and on key lessons about the governance of punishment that we have uncovered in this study.

The account of Three Strikes in these pages is incomplete in three important respects. First, whereas we discuss the proximate history of the California statute, we do not provide any history of earlier habitual-offender laws that have been present in European and Anglo-American legal systems for more than a century. This amnesia is based on two substantive judgments. First, we think Norval Morris's 1951 classic treatment, *The Habitual Criminal*, provides both the history and the perspective better than any chapter we could write. Second, our reading of the California statute convinced us that the earlier generations of habitual offender statutes were not a major influence on the logic or structure of the 1994 California law.

The second element missing from this book is the data and perspective that will be possible only after the statute has been part of California law and practice for decades. This is a study of short-term impact mounted and completed early in the career of the Three Strikes statute. The advantages of prompt study outweigh the liabilities, but there are important dimensions of the long-term impact of the statute that are unknowable at this writing.

The third key limitation of this book is the lack of any ethnographic study of the law at street level. We have assembled a statistical portrait of Three Strikes in the justice system, as well as of its effect on crime rates, that is missing elements of first-hand observation, which we hope social scientists will soon provide. That is, we hope that the methods and findings reported in these pages will provoke further study.

A single California statute might seem to be a narrow topic for a book, but narrowness of focus turned out to be the least of our problems in completing this study. One cannot hope to comprehend Three Strikes in California without learning a great deal about crime, about criminal justice, and about the continuing adventure of American democracy.

Part I

ORIGINS AND STRUCTURE

ONE

Three Strikes Comes to California

What makes the story of Three Strikes unusual in the annals of state government is that California's Three Strikes proposal was the ultimate "outside the beltway" legislation. It originated from marginal pressure groups without any powerful constituency in the legislative or executive branches of state government. Yet it became law without any significant amendment, compromise, or analysis. Was this a one-time fluke or a forerunner of how criminal justice policy will be made in the United States? This is the central issue we address in the following pages as we tell the story of how a radical proposal became widely supported legislation.

The path of the analysis is from the general to the specific. We begin with a capsule history of the Three Strikes initiative in California from a proposal to legislation to an initiative adopted by the voters. A second section will list a few of the objections that can be made to the penal approaches of the initiative. The third section takes more space to describe the two sets of "missing persons" in the California legislative process. Three Strikes swept through the lawmaking processes without any significant influence from powerful legislative or executive branch personnel. The legislative and initiative processes through which the proposal traveled were also almost entirely devoid of expert scrutiny from government specialists or from scholars. We regard this as an important part of the Three Strikes story, one that has not received much attention.

Our general conclusion is that Three Strikes was an extreme example of a populist preemption of criminal justice policy-making. No outside proposal would be likely to soon march through the legislative process untouched by human hands again. But the processes that left the state vulnerable to this blitzkrieg also produced structural changes in California's government that lessen the insulation between popular sentiment and specific criminal justice policy. This change may be much broader than Three Strikes, much more widespread than one state, and a partial explanation for large recent increases in the scale of penal confinement across the United States (Shogren 1995).

The Story Briefly Told

Penal laws that mandate aggravated penalties for recidivist offenders have a long history in the Anglo-American legal system. Special habitual-offender laws that could impose life imprisonment on a third felony conviction were common in England (Morris 1951) and the United States (Turner et al. 1995) through most of the twentieth century. But the reputation of these laws for enhancing community safety was not strong. Norval Morris's study of offenders sentenced under the English habitual-felon statute showed that most of these certified habitual felons usually committed crimes of minor social consequence and were distinguished from other criminals principally by their vulnerability to swift detection. Life terms for many of these petty thieves seemed like a progressive tax on stupidity. Although "three-time loser" laws remained on the statute books in many states, they were not widely used, nor were they an important issue in the modern politics of law and order until the 1990s.

The first conversion of habitual-criminal logic into the baseball parlance of "Three strikes and you're out" was passed in the state of Washington in 1993. Although the triggering threshold of three separate convictions was borrowed from the earlier habitual-felon model, the Washington law was designed to cover only selected, serious felonies, with a life sentence on the third conviction (Stiller 1995). An even narrower Three Strikes provision became part of the 1994 federal crime legislation (Vitiello 1997).

The California version of Three Strikes was first proposed by Mike Reynolds, a Fresno photographer and father of a murder victim (Morain 1994b). His version was broader than the other proposals being debated across the United States in three respects. First, significant sentencing enhancements were generated in this new package upon conviction for a second felony. So the Three Strikes label vastly understated the scope of the penalty enhancements. Second, the type of criminal record necessary to create eligibility for the 25-year-to-life sentence did not require violence. A conviction for residential burglary is a sufficient condition for Three Strikes. Because burglary is much more common than serious crimes of violence, many of those who become eligible for the extended sentences are burglars (Schiraldi 1994). Third, the third strike, which leads to a 25-year-to-life term, can be generated by conviction for any felony in the California Penal Code. In this sense, once the appropriate first two strikes occur, the California proposal is a return to the undifferentiated emphasis of the old-fashioned habitual-criminal legislation, except with mandatory language rather than explicit prosecutorial discretion and with enhancements for a second strike as well.

Each of these three expansions of coverage significantly multiplies the number of offenders in the California scheme, but together they operate exponentially. The serious-violence Three Strikes proposal that then-Governor Cuomo was discussing in New York would have involved a few hundred violent, three-time offenders per year (Egan 1994). The nationwide impact of the federal law was, at most, a few hundred offenders annually (Douglas 1994). The probable impact of the package in California might have been as much as 70 times as great. Nobody knew.

The campaign to put this initiative on the 1994 California ballot involved an alliance between two of the crime victim pressure groups in California: the California Correctional Peace Officer's Association (the prison guard union), which stood to benefit greatly by the expansion of the prison population; and the National Rifle Association, a gun owners' group that welcomes punitive sentencing programs as a method of addressing violent crimes without inconveniencing gun owners (Wilkie 1994). Before November 1993, this version of Three Strikes was not a significant part of mainstream politics in California (Morain 1994b).

Polly Klaas changed all that. This 12-year-old girl was abducted from her Petaluma home in October 1993 by a twice-convicted violent offender who had recently been paroled from the state prison system. For a month after she had been sexually assaulted and killed, Polly's fate was unknown and the anxiety and news coverage intensified. Then the ex-convict was apprehended and revealed the location of Polly's remains (Paddock and Warren 1993).

Violent crime had struck at the heart of a prosperous small town in Marin County. The victim was an idealized version of everybody's daughter or sister, an innocent young girl at a slumber party (Carman 1993). The offender was a violent recidivist of Willie Horton proportions (Price 1993). And the political timing was uncanny. A Republican governor with low approval ratings and a weak state economy was about to launch a reelection campaign (Jeffe 1994). Pete Wilson was anxious to seize the initiative in order to be portrayed as "getting tough" on crime (Stall 1994). The Democrats were then in control of the state legislature and were not about to give the vulnerable governor an opportunity to make crime a defining issue in his reelection campaign.

What followed was an extraordinary power realignment in the face of the upcoming election. The Democrats, unwilling to create a contest of wills in which the governor could claim to be distinctively tough on crime, responded to his call for new, enhanced punishment for recidivists. The legislaure considered a collection of five different proposals for increased sentences that ranged from specific programs targeted at repetitive violent offenders to a broad legislative version that was, word-for-word, Mike Reynolds's Three Strikes initiative in legislative form. Instead of choosing one of these five alternatives, the legislative leadership announced that it would pass whatever proposal the governor selected from the range of plans then under consideration (Richardson 1994b). By deferring in advance to the governor's choice, the Democrats' hope was that he would either back down from an unqualifed "get tough" stand or be politically neutralized if he persisted. But the willingness to pass even the extreme version of Three Strikes if the governor so demanded was an attempt to keep it from being a campaign issue that would divide the major political parties (Morain 1994b; Richardson 1994a). Give the governor whatever he demands, the strategy went, and he will have to find some other issue on which to run for reelection.

In March 1994, Governor Wilson reiterated his preference for legislative enactment of the copycat version of the Reynolds's Three Strikes program (Kershner 1994), a preference he had first announced at Polly Klaas's funeral (Skelton 1993). In doing this, the governor rejected a narrower bill that had been submitted by the California's District Attorneys Association (Hecht 1994; Morain 1994d; Weintraub 1994). In effect, the executive and legislative branches had swallowed whole the outside-the-beltway version of Three Strikes because the they were unwilling to concede the ground on "getting tough" to the other side in the political campaign to come. Three Strikes went mainstream in March 1994 through gubernatorial initiative and legislative enactment. The November passage of Initiative Number 184 became a political afterthought, of diminished practical import, and was overshadowed by the divisive Proposition 187 debate on immigration that was the most visible issue in the 1994 election.

The day after he rejected the Three Strikes proposal of the district attorneys of California because it was soft on crime, Governor Wilson also announced his own support for a one-strike proposal of life imprisonment for sex crimes and selected crimes of violence (Skelton 1993). This new wrinkle has since died a quiet death. But Pete Wilson was reelected handily, and the broad and mandatory language of

Reynolds's edition of "Three strikes and you're out" became one of the enduring legacies of California's 1994 political season.

A Critical Perspective

Before it is possible to comprehend any detailed criticism of California's Three Strikes scheme, the reader will need a basic tour of the provisions of the California law passed in 1994. Table 1.1 presents a simplified summary of the legislation. The table shows three key factors in determining the punishment of criminal offenders under Three Strikes: the defendant's prior record, the current offense, and the minimum punishment. The prior criminal record necessary to qualify for a second-strike sentence is one previous conviction for a "serious" or "violent" felony as defined in the statute. "Serious" strike offenses include residential burglary, but "violent" offenses for the purposes of this statute do not include most assaults and batteries. Separate provisions of the law include out-of-state and juvenile court adjudications as qualifying criminal records to be eligible for sentence enhancements.

The second column of the table indicates that any felony conviction triggers the mandatory penalties under the statute if the prior existence of a strike is present in the record. So that whereas only a restricted number of offenses can be strikes in a prior record, the current offense, which is called a second strike and third strike, is any felony, and that includes petty theft if a previous felony conviction was for a theft offense. Thus the "current-offense" definition of strike is quite different from the "prior-record" definition of strike.

The third element in table 1.1 is the minimum term provided by the Three Strikes statute. For second-strike offenses, this term is a doubling of the current-offense term, with further restrictions on minimum time served before release is permitted. For a third strike, the minimum term for any felony conviction is 25 years, and 80% of that term must be served before release is possible.

More than any other habitual-offender provision in the long history of such laws, the California version of Three Strikes is a penal practice without a theory. Twenty-five-year-to-life prison sentences are administered to persons convicted of minor felonies as a third strike, but only if the previous convictions were for violence or housebreaking. The requirement of a serious prior felony means that the habitual-felon logic of the earlier laws was not the exclusive basis

Table 1.1. Three Strikes Simplified.

	Required Prior Record	Current Qualifying Offense	Mandatory Prison Sentence
Second-strike enhancement	Conviction of "serious" or "violent" crime as defined in statute[a]	Any felony	Twice the current qualifying offense term, with no release before serving 80% of that term
Third-strike enhancement	Two convictions of "serious" or "violent" crime as defined in statute[a]	Any felony	25-years-to-life with no release before serving 80% of the 25-year term

[a] Special provisions deal with juvenile and out-of-state prior convictions.

Source: California Penal Code §667 (West Supplement 1996).

for the protracted term. If this were a statute aimed at the confirmed criminal, it would sweep even more broadly than it does.

Yet proportionality is also obviously not served in any consistent fashion by the new sentencing provisions. Any trivial felony by a twice-convicted burglar will call down a larger sentence for a third-time loser than a nonaggravated second-degree murder will generate for a non–Three Strikes defendant. In the early days of the new law, more 25-year-to-life terms under Three Strikes were handed down as a result of convictions for possession of marijuana than for murder, rape, and kidnaping combined (Butterfield 1996). Whereas previous attempts at habitual-criminal sanctions were dependant on prosecutorial discretion, California's Three Strikes law was supposed to be mandatory. Usually, the substitution of mandatory for discretionary charging and sentencing is justified by the need for consistency in serving the principles that produced the new penal law. But the hybrid version of Three Strikes has no principle to serve as bedrock. Adhering to the letter of the new law will not elevate any particular purpose of criminal sanctions in the penal treatment of recidivists because there is no principled basis for the new provision.

Indeed, some of the key provisions of the Three Strikes package seem to be in conflict with one another on basic questions. The enhancements provided after one prior conviction are proportional to the offense currently charged, so that the prior qualifying conviction doubles the base penalty for the new offense rather than supplanting it. The burglar and the armed robber will each serve more time in prison if this is a second strike, but they will not serve the same sentence. The seriousness of the current crime counts for much of the current sentence. Yet if the robber and burglar are in the docks with two prior strikes, the sentences to be imposed will be the same as long as the 25-years to life is more severe than three times the base penalty for the current offense.

The effect of separating penalties in response to whether a prior record contains a strike is to establish different penalty structures, depending not only on whether a special status felony conviction takes place but also on when the special status conviction occurs in a particular career. Table 1.2 shows the differing penal results for three defendants convicted of the same three offenses but in different sequence. Offender A faces no Three Strikes aggravation of the second felony sentence because the first felony conviction was not a listed felony. Offender A's third conviction generates a doubling of the burglary term because of the prior burglary conviction but does

Table 1.2. Sequence and Penalty Under California Three Strikes Law

	Offender A	Offender B	Offender C
First conviction	Theft	Burglary	Burglary
Second conviction	Burglary	Theft	Burglary
Third conviction	Burglary	Burglary	Theft
Sentence on second conviction	No Three Strikes enhancement	Twice the penalty for theft	Twice the penalty for burglary
Sentence on third conviction	Twice the penalty for burglary	Twice the penalty for burglary	25-years-to-life

not result in the highest level of Three Strikes liability. Offender B, by contrast, will face twice the theft sentence for the theft conviction because it follows a burglary conviction. But the theft conviction does not constitute a second strike, so Offender B's next conviction also carries the doubling of the burglary term only. Offender C faces twice the term for burglary at the second conviction and 25 years to life on the theft conviction because of the two prior Three Strikes convictions. When these three defendants are sentenced on their third conviction, they have identical criminal records in every respect but sequence. It is the defendant with the least serious current offense who receives the most severe prison sentence.

Is there any penological justification for these divergent results? Is Offender C's sequence evidence of larger public danger than from Offenders A and B? Is a burglary conviction followed by a theft conviction more dangerous than a theft conviction followed by a burglary conviction?

The Three Strikes provisions are silent on issues of principle, and it may be that the only general principle in the statute is to increase the seriousness of all punishments for those who had been convicted earlier of selected felonies. If the list of selected previous felonies had been confined to offenses of violence, it could be argued that the statute sought to isolate only dangerous felons, but the addition of house burglary waters the stock rather dramatically in that regard. And confirming a prediction of serious criminality with any felony conviction is a peculiar way to isolate the dangerous.

One searches in vain for consistent principles underlying Three Strikes other than harsher penal treatment for repeat offenders. The specific strategies in the statute were not subjected to scrutiny either before the law became effective or since. Those who support the law make claims for the appropriateness of the classifications in an indirect way, by attributing declines in California's reported crime rate to the new penal regime (Morain 1994c; Riccardi 1994). This proposal was unexamined at any stage in the political process (Vitiello 1997). The problem, in our view, was not the usual difficulty with new legislation, when nobody reads the fine print in legislative programs. For Three Strikes in California, nobody seems to have read the large print.

Missing Persons

The process that produced Three Strikes was the creation of a proposal outside ordinary government channels and its subsequent endorsement by the legislature and the governor. Months afterward, a favorable vote on Proposition 184 ratified the earlier enactment.

However, two things that did not occur in the legislative career of this law are of particular interest. First, the provisions of this package received little or no analytic attention from criminal justice professionals and academic experts prior to enactment. One reason that Three Strikes received little attention from practitioners and professors is that these experts were not consulted by anybody in government. Another reason for the absence of expert analysis was the short period of time between the post–Polly Klaas pressures for fast passage of a violent recidivist package and the March 1994 decision by Governor Wilson to demand line-by-line conformity to the proposed initiative. Both the haste and the pressure in this story are remarkable even for the far-from-careful, normal criminal legislation process. The Department of Corrections made some guesses about the impact of the proposals on the prison population (Welch 1994). Alternative violent-offender proposals were drafted by some legislators and by the California District Attorneys Association. No hearings or criminal justice impact studies were launched. The victim lobby groups, the prison guard union, and the National Rifle Association had no interest in legislative impact assessments and no competence to conduct such studies. The capacity of legislative staff and support personnel to conduct policy analysis had been reduced by budget cuts and staff reduction (Weiss 1991). In any event, the commitment of the legislative leadership to follow the governor's lead made independent judgments about the various different recidivist proposals beside the point (Gilliam 1994). The absence of interest in outside analysts' views on Three Strikes and its alternatives is one good reason that outside experts were quiet.

The second missing element in this story is the influence of political elites. The legislative process that passed Three Strikes into law in March 1994 was also remarkable in that neither the governor nor the legislature made any attempts to question or change the Three Strikes proposal (Gilliam 1994; Morain 1994b). This total lack of influence on the shape of major legislation is quite novel in California. In saying this, we do not mean that Edmund Burke would approve of the normal pattern for drafting and deliberating legislation in the Golden State. But one of the prerogatives of power is the capacity to shape the ways in which laws will be structured. The crafting by a lobby of a large, radical, and complex piece of legislation that sails through the legislature and the executive branches untouched by human hands is unusual even by standards of narrow political self-interest. For a Willie Brown–led legislative leadership to pledge itself to pass any bill selected by an adversary governor is by no means an everyday occurrence. For a governor from the political mainstream to reject a bill proposed by the state's district attorneys association because it was too soft on criminals in favor of a fringe group's alterative is also not a common event in the annals of state government. Which of these choices was the more cynical is a close question. Both Brown and Wilson knew much better than they acted. Neither is a likely candidate for the next edition of *Profiles in Courage*. But of these two stratagems, we regard the selection by Pete Wilson as the more important proximate cause of how Reynolds's proposal was swallowed whole by the legislative process. Willie Brown dared Governor Wilson, and the governor accepted that dare with a vengeance.

There is little doubt that the deficiencies of process mentioned earlier allowed some of the more problematic and internally inconsistent elements in Three Strikes to tiptoe onto the statute books in California. The critical question this raises is the extent to which the story of Three Strikes is a portent of the legislative future of criminal justice policy-making. Have we been talking about a one-time California fiasco or a visit from the political equivalent of Charles Dickens's Ghost of Christmas Yet to Come?

In our view, the Three Strikes story is a little of both. The one-time pressures involved were substantial. The 1994 campaign was a particularly mean political season in California and elsewhere (Kurtz

1994). The Polly Klaas episode was a one-time horror, and the prospect of the initiative put pressure on elected officials of a kind that does not exist in most states. The later attempts of Reynolds and others to push for life terms for first convictions for serious violence and 10-year prison sentences if 14-year-olds use guns in felonies did not capture the public's imagination or preempt the legislative process in the same way that Three Strikes had (Furillo 1996).

Two structural changes in the circumstances of criminal justice policy-making render the process vulnerable to populist domination. The first is the decline of expert influence on policy formation and evaluation. Criminal justice in the United States over the past generation has been experiencing two seemingly contradictory trends. On the one hand, the sheer amount of expertise available on questions of crime and punishment has expanded rapidly. There are well over 500 college and university criminal justice programs in the United States and bumper crops of new Ph.D.s each year (*College Blue Book* 1995). So we have more experts.

On the other hand, expert influence on the process and expert involvement in the process have declined. Let us give examples that involved professors of criminal law. When the young Gerald Caplan, currently dean of the McGeorge School of Law, marched off to Washington, D.C., to head the National Institute of Justice in the early 1970s, he was in a long tradition of legal academics intensely involved in the policy process. James Vorenberg of Harvard Law School had been the executive director of the 1966 President's Crime Commission. The Model Penal Code effort of the American Law Institute brought the best and the brightest in academic law into the process of substantive criminal law reform. But there is now a large gap between law professors and the legislative process, and not just in California. (One might title the complaint "From the Model Penal Code to Three Strikes in One Generation.") Part of the problem is that most academic lawyers are not much interested in criminal justice policy processes. Most of the problem is that there is no demand for what experts have to offer, which is information about the implications and consequences of policy choices.

The public seems to believe that analytic and statistical implications of policy choices in criminal justice are unimportant. And it is not just the academic expert who is a victim of declining influence. Deference to expertise in government is also an endangered species in the modern politics of criminal justice. In the 1950s and 1960s the allocation of power across branches of government in the American criminal justice system was protected by notions that those in the executive and judicial branches of government had special expertise in their jobs. Parole boards based decisions about prisoners' rehabilitation on special competence to predict future behavior, or so it was thought (Morris 1974). Judges and probation officers who wrote presentence reports were specially qualified to make sentencing decisions about individuals one at a time (Wechsler 1961). Prison wardens and correctional administrators had the wisdom and experience required to design and administer prison programs. Shared belief in specialized expertise became a support, not only for the hands-off doctrine that insulated correctional officials from judicial review, but also for a broader hands-off tendency that restrained legislatures from second-guessing the powers of the operating branches of the criminal justice system (Zimring and Hawkins 1991). Belief in expertise functions as a support of the division of labor and the division of power in functioning systems of criminal justice.

When citizens come to believe that there is no special expertise implicated in criminal justice decision making, separation of powers no longer allows the expert deference. If sentencing and selection for parole involved no special skill, no deference is due to the government actors that traditionally held power for these functions. Developments such as a decline in the belief in rehabilitation can thus undermine the standing of administrative and judicial actors. In the short run, the legislature may seem a more appropriate power holder. If punishment for crime is not a science, why not view making punishment policy solely as the sort of political act that democratically elected legislators are best suited to perform?

The modern politics of criminal justice involves rhetoric that imagines criminal sentencing as a zero-sum game between victims and offenders. If one prefers the victim, one believes that punishment should be increased. Those who oppose increasing punishments must, in this view, prefer offenders' interest to victims' interests. To live in this kind of world is to deny that expert opinion is of any real importance in making policy.

One reason for thinking the decline of belief in expertise is an important explanation for modern trends in the United States is that the shift to populist paradigms fits the timing of recent changes better than a theory of increased hostility toward criminals or fear of crime. Burglars have never been popular in the United States, and populist sentiments have always been hostile to convicted offenders. At any time in the twentieth century, a public choice between the interests of crime victims and the interests of criminal offenders would favor the former. Why were these sentiments not dominant in setting policy in the 1960s and 1970s?

It may be that the social authority accorded to criminal justice experts provided insulation between populist sentiments (always punitive) and criminal justice policies at the legislative, administrative, and judicial levels. This insulation prevented the direct domination of policy by antioffender sentiments that are consistently held by most citizens at most times. What has been changing in recent years is that the insulation that separated public sentiments and criminal justice decisions has been eaten away. Three Strikes was an extreme, but by no means isolated, example of the kind of law produced when very little mediates antioffender sentiments. The 1994 federal anti-crime legislation is another example of the direct reflection of public sentiments. At the federal level, the kind of expertise that used to write crime commission reports in the 1960s was considered a drawback to federal criminal justice administration in the 1990s. The deliberative and analytic style of Philip Heymann during his time as U.S. Deputy Attorney General was considered a problem by his critics (Freedman 1994). The ninth chapter of this book will further explore the changing politics of criminal punishment.

But one reason Three Strikes will cost so much to administer is that hard cost and benefit questions were not asked when alternative methods of controlling serious recidivists were before the legislature. This was a failure of governing politicians to do their jobs. Political leaders who hold government power must do more than reflect the sentiments of their constituents when important questions must be decided. Also, those who have expertise in criminal justice matters must raise their voices to be heard, disregarding the embarrassing fact that very few in the public are interested in what they have to say. The decline of expert authority is a social circumstance that makes responsible policy more difficult to achieve. It is not an excuse for abandoning the criminal justice system to populist preemption.

One central task in protecting criminal justice policy from sound-bite populism is to rebuild some conditions in decision making that insulate individual decisions from direct popular pressures. Some protection could come in the form of creating expert bodies, rather than legislatively fixed terms, to set the general guidelines for criminal sentencing; these bodies would protect the individual decisions of judges from the expectation that they should reflect popular sentiments and would redefine the political role of legislators, from reflecting the sentiments of their constituents to supporting measures that will rationally address the most important concerns of the public.

Chapter 10 will focus on details concerning the proper role of the branches of government in setting punishment policy. Let us close this introductory review with two preliminary cautions about our declared preferences. First, in pleading for the values of insulating decisions in criminal justice from popular sentiment, we are not suggesting a conflict between democratic and undemocratic systems but rather contrasting two different types of criminal justice decision making in a democracy. Indeed, more traditional forms of criminal justice decision making were more insulated from direct sentimental governance than Three Strikes and its ilk (see chapter 10).

Second, let us underscore the fact that no structures can protect us from excess without responsible behavior by individual actors in the face of political temptation. The sentencing commission is a mechanism that was designed to insulate the standards that govern sentencing decisions from direct political pressure (Tonry 1996). In Minnesota, where the first such commission was created, the mechanism has achieved this function (Zimring and Hawkins 1991). In the federal system, where a similar mechanism was designed for similar purposes, the new sentencing commission quickly acquired a reputation for blowing in the political winds (Zimring and Hawkins 1991). Mechanisms to deflect political pressure are a necessary, but not sufficient, condition for reversing the dominance of popular sentiments. The bedrock necessity is for political actors to subscribe to a culture of responsibility in regard to criminal justice, a value system that might unite those who hold political office in defending the institutions of criminal justice against outside attack.

No mechanism designed to insulate criminal justice will work well in the face of the sort of behavior of the governor and legislative leaders in the California of 1994. But perhaps the time is now ripe to suggest the creation of a culture of responsibility as a defense against the next panic. We earlier asked if Three Strikes was the Ghost of Christmas Yet to Come for American criminal justice. The hopeful undertone of this question relates to the fact that the harrowing vision of the future carried by that messenger was instrumental in persuading Ebenezer Scrooge to change his ways. Our hope is that the principal value of California's recent adventures with "Three strikes and you're out" will be as an object lesson in how criminal justice policy should not be made. The whole of this volume is in that respect a cautionary tale.

TWO

The Largest Penal Experiment in American History

The title of this chapter may seem a bit grandiose as a description of California's version of "Three strikes and you're out" legislation passed into law in March 1994. After all, the California legislation was only a mandatory version of habitual-criminal punishments that have been frequent elements in Anglo-American criminal law for quite some time (Morris 1951). And even the Three Strikes formulation itself was far from unique. The first incarnation of Three Strikes language was in Washington State in 1993, and no fewer than 26 criminal justice jurisdictions in the United States had passed some version by 1996 (Clark, Austin, and Henry 1997). What, then, is so special about California?

Three elements of the California initiative and legislation combine to make it a qualitatively different mandatory-sentencing regime. First, the scale of criminal justice in the state of California is by far the largest in the free world, much larger than the U.S. federal system. California's prisons incarcerate a larger volume of offenders than the penal systems of France and Germany combined (Zimring and Hawkins 1994). Therefore, any new wrinkle in criminal punishment will have a larger net effect in California than elsewhere because of the sheer size of the system. If California were to pass a Three Strikes law that was identical in all respects to legislation in other states, it would still have the largest impact. (Figure 2.1 compares prison systems in California with a variety of other states and nations).

Second, Three Strikes legislation is much larger in scope than other experiments with mandatory imprisonment because of the lavish levels of imprisonment provided for. In California, defendants with one residential burglary or violent felony conviction must receive prison terms double those mandated for the triggering offense and must also serve a significantly larger fraction of their total sentence prior to release after good time. The doubling of the nominal sentence and the increase from 50% to 80% in required time served effectively triple the penalty for the triggering offense. A 25-year-to-life mandatory sen-

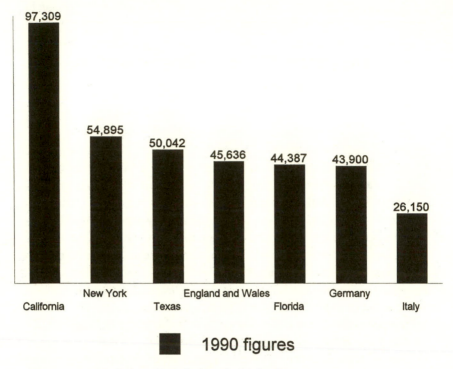

Figure 2.1. 1990 Prison Populations in Major Systems.
Source: Zimring and Hawkins 1994.

tence is the response to conviction for any felony under the California scheme for defendants with two prior convictions for strike offenses. The eventual arithmetic of long mandatory sentences is obvious if they are actually served. One 25-year sentence has five times as much eventual impact on the prison population as one mandatory 5-year sentence. Add in the rule that requires 80% of the sentence to be served, and the Three Strikes sentence is seven times the size of a 5-year mandatory sentence with no special provisions. With such a heavy impact at the individual level, the aggregate impact on the prison system can be quite large even with a relatively small number of 25-year-to-life sentences. Only 1,000 25-year-minimum sentences are the eventual equivalent of 25,000 prison-man-years, more than that which 10,000 two-year terms would generate.

The third item that widens the impact of California's Three Strikes is the breadth of that law's coverage. Only one prior qualifying felony is necessary before expanded and mandatory imprisonment is required; and Three Strikes is invoked by any triggering felony conviction (including petty theft if a prior felony conviction is present). Other Three Strikes statutes only aggravate penalties after two prior strike convictions and also require a serious felony theft conviction to trigger draconian third-strike penalties (see Clark, Austin, and Henry 1997). The expansion of coverage when only one prior strike is present is a very significant increase in the scope of the law by itself, and the coverage of any felony after a strike is also a major expansion by itself. The joint impact of these two extensions is to generate so much more coverage that the California approach can best be viewed as differing from other state laws with the same title not merely in scope but also in character. For example, the federal Three Strikes law is restricted to serious crimes only; most other jurisdictions' laws become effective only after two prior convictions (Clark, Austin, and Henry 1997). The California schema differs from these other laws not only in degree; it is also a different kind of criminal recidivist punishment policy than any other in the United States.

The quantitative impact of all the California differences can be seen from some statistics gathered on the early performance of Three Strikes laws. The compound effects of California's extension of the law to all felony convictions and to sentence enhancements after one qualifying prior can be seen in a published comparison of California with the state of Washington, the first jurisdiction to enact Three Strikes in 1993. By the end of 1996, California had sentenced 26,074 offenders under its Three Strikes provisions, whereas Washington had sentenced 85 in the slightly longer effective span of its new legislation (Clark, Austin, and Henry 1997, p. 3). The ratio of the state populations of California and Washington was six to one; the ratio of sentences under Three Strikes was 307 to 1, or *50* times the population difference of the two states (U.S. Department of Commerce 1994). If the two-strike sentences in California are not counted, the ratio of those in California to Three Strikes sentences in Washington would shrink to 33 to 1, still more than five times the population difference between the two states.

It is difficult to overstate the dominance of the California volume of Three Strikes cases. These sentences are 99.7% of the total Three Strikes sentences in Washington and California, and Washington is one of the most active of the Three Strikes states. A compilation by the Campaign for an Effective Crime Policy (1998) reports on sentences under Three Strikes laws in 22 states and the federal government. Figure 2.2 provides a visual summary of the different patterns of sentencing under legislation with the same name.

The first lesson of figure 2.2 is the enormous variation in sentencing noted among American states which adopted Three Strikes laws. A small state like Nevada reports 50 times as many special sentences as large states like North Carolina and Pennsylvania. Clearly, the Three Strikes label is not a good predictor of sentencing policy changes in the states that passed such a law. Second, most states that passed Three Strikes laws make very little use of them, and the new laws have minimal impact on punishment policies. Fourteen of the 23 states in the survey had generated fewer than 10 sentences under the terms of their laws by late 1998. When contrasting the operational and symbolic impact of criminal laws, the primary significance of most Three Strikes laws is symbolic. The third aspect so dominates the figure that it is difficult to see the other comparisons— the contrast between California and everywhere else. The federal criminal justice system has generated 35 sentences under its Three Strikes law nationwide, whereas California has handed down more than a thousand times as many. California had more than 40,000 sentences under its law when none of the other jurisdictions had yet accumulated 1,000.

This range of reports permits some guesses about the dominance of California's version of Three Strikes in the general picture. The low-end estimate would assume that, in the aggregate, the other Three Strikes jurisdictions in the United States duplicate the Washington level of sentences. Even if the other 24 jurisdictions with some form of Three Strikes laws sentence, on the average, at the levels found in the state of Washington, the state of California alone would still be generating 92% of all sentences under Three Strikes ($25 \times .00325 = .081$ of the total case volume). If numbers from the Campaign for an Effective Crime Policy (1998) are the current ratio, California alone is 94% of all Three Strikes sentences, and allowing for an additional three states would reduce the dominant share of California to 93% of the total.

To the extent that the size of a punishment policy change is a prediction of such effects as deterrence or incapacitation, the California Three Strikes law and only that law should be the subject of detailed evaluation. It towers above all other examples by so great a margin that inclusion with less broad recidivism statues in the same category is misleading.

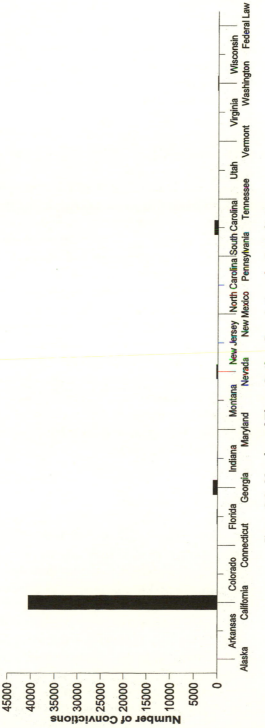

Figure 2.2. Number of Three Strikes Convictions by Jurisdiction.
Source: Campaign for an Effective Crime Policy, 1998, table 1.

We mention here a point we will emphasize in Chapter 11. The huge difference between the impact of Three Strikes in California and in settings like the federal criminal justice system are in large part a function of the intentions of the drafters. Whereas the phrase and cachet of "Three strikes and you're out" is an outside-the-beltway phenomenon, the actual drafting of the federal bill that passed Congress was a professional activity carried out by those with a personal stake in minimizing the coverage of the law. But the California law was drafted with the opposite intent: It was designed to produce maximum impact on both prison sentences and time served. In an odd sense, the marketing of both the California and the federal styles of Three Strikes laws was designed to create false impressions, but they were misleading in sharply contrasting ways. The federal statute and parallel efforts in many states were designed to look like more substantial changes than they were destined to become. The California version was designed—with a title that emphasized Three Strikes but provided mandatory sanctions after one qualifying prior conviction—to appear less ambitious than it actually was. Every strategic decision in the California scheme was a conscious effort to maximize the law's impact on the length of prison sentences and time served in California. This is indeed the only common thread that links (1) the reductions in good time, (2) the minimum terms for the second strike triggered by the offense, (3) the choice of any felony for a second- and third-strike trigger, and (4) the indeterminate 25-year-to-life mandatory third-strike sentence.

The Scale of Other Innovations

This chapter's introductory claim is not merely that California's version of Three Strikes is the biggest of all such laws but also that what was launched in March 1994 in Sacramento was intended to be the biggest penal experiment of any kind in modern American history. What can be the justification for this broader claim?

There have certainly been long-range trends in criminal justice behavior that dwarf even California's Three Strikes in both scale and impact. The expansion in the use of probation in the early years of this century and the five-fold increase in prison populations between 1972 and 1997 are two examples of American criminal justice megatrends of transcendent importance. But these were long-range trends, not abrupt policy changes, and the policies were not launched by legislation designed to make large changes. In the case of the increases in incarceration after 1975, the absence of any significant or widespread changes in law was actually one of the remarkable characteristics of the imprisonment boom (Zimring and Hawkins 1994, p. 87).

But what of the big changes that were launched by legislation in recent decades, the determinate sentencing legislation in California in 1977, for example, or the sentencing commissions in various states in the early 1980s. What of the epic Federal Criminal Code passed by the U.S. Congress in 1984, at that time the largest bill ever introduced in Congress? And what of the Federal Sentencing Guidelines promulgated under the authority of that code in 1987? These were all important structural changes in how criminal sentencing policies are made and executed, but all of these reforms were engineered to emphasize continuity in criminal sentencing rather than radical change. For example, the determinate sentencing law in California took as the basis for calculating the new determinate sentences the average time served under the indeterminate sentencing regimes that preceded it (Messinger and Johnson 1977). This was a deliberate method of keeping criminal punishment nearly equal to previous levels (Zimring 1983 chap. 3).

The deliberate engineering of continuity was also an important part of the initial design of the Federal Sentencing Guidelines of 1987. The starting point for most of these guidelines was the average time served to release by different classes of federal offenders under the rubrics of discretionary judicial sentencing and federal parole guidelines. The pioneering state guideline systems, such as those in Minnesota, also based initial sentencing guidelines on sentencing and parole release behavior under previous sentencing systems. This strategy created sentencing systems that were referred to as empirically based. There were points of departure from such empirically based standards (see Tonry 1996), but the initial logic of these guidelines was to engineer a smooth, if not seamless, transition from discretionary to guideline sentencing. When it came to the nitty-gritty of criminal sentencing, the slogan of empirically based guidelines seems to have been "Do not make waves."

What makes California's Three Strikes stand apart is its deliberately confrontational and destabilizing intention. The law was drafted with the explicit ambition of creating large and abrupt changes in punishment practice for broad categories of offenders. The search for comparable initiatives would have to include the legislative creation of juvenile courts after 1899 (see Schlossman 1977) and the attempt in New

York to generate criminal jurisdiction for juvenile offenders charged with serious felonies in 1978 (see Singer 1996). Perhaps the closest parallel to California's Three Strikes is the Rockefeller drug laws, a mandatory minimum-penalty regime that was initiated in New York in the 1970s (see Japha 1976), although the number of additional sentences generated by those reforms is a very small fraction of the impact of California's Three Strikes.

The breadth of the Three Strikes legislation and its revolutionary intent make it an important case study of the attempt to use changes in the criminal law as a method of engineering drastic changes in the performance of a criminal justice system. When the architects of penal reform start out to make a big change in "business as usual" in a criminal court, how large is that change likely to be? What systemic constituencies and inertial tendencies in the criminal justice system moderate or subvert attempts at radical change? What latent, as well as manifest, changes in the business of the criminal court will efforts at radical change carry in their wake? If our characterization of the extremity of the Three Strikes reform is correct, assessing the impact of this new law in California becomes an important study of the use of substantive criminal law to attempt to alter the fundamental policy of the criminal justice system.

Three Strikes and the Structure of California's Criminal Justice System

A brief explanation of the distribution of authority in California's criminal justice system is a necessary preliminary in understanding the strategy behind the design of Three Strikes and its likely impact on felony charges and sentencing. Before 1977 the power to determine whether felons could be sent to prison, and for how long, was shared by three institutions of government: prosecutors, judges, and parole boards (Zimring 1983). First, prosecutors had the unreviewable authority to select the individual charges to be brought against criminal defendants. If the prosecutor did not press charges, the criminal case did not go forward. If the prosecutor reduced the charges against a particular defendant, either unilaterally or in exchange for an agreement to plead guilty, such a reduction was neither reviewable nor reversible by other criminal justice agencies. Second, judges had the power to review and accept guilty pleas; the authority to select one from a typically wide variety of penalties for a convicted offender; and the legal responsibility to preside over trials, either alone or with a jury that was responsible for finding facts and following judicial instructions about the law. Third, the parole authority had the responsibility for determining the actual time that imprisoned offenders would serve. In this system, the parole authority had considerable power to determine the time actually served in prison by individual offenders and a substantial influence in the aggregate over the average length of time served in prison for classes of offenses and offenders.

California's determinate sentencing reforms, passed by the legislature in 1976, removed the parole board's authority to determine the actual time served for an imprisoned offender. The law also channeled the judicial power to select prison sentences so that conviction for a particular offense would typically result in a choice between prison and nonprison sanctions, selecting for those offenders to be imprisoned one of three determinate prison terms that would determine the length of the actual prison stay when discounted by good-time adjustments. The determinate sentencing reforms all but eliminated the parole authority's power to postpone the determination of release dates until long after the imposition of the sentence (Messinger and Johnson 1977). Some of the power formerly held by parole authorities was redistributed to sentencing judges. Most of the rest of the power, however, reverted to prosecutors (Zimring 1976, 1983).

The Three Strikes legislation was a frontal assault on the power of correctional authorities to reduce Three Strikes sentences through good-time allowances and, more important, on the discretionary power of judges to avoid imprisonment or reduce the terms of imprisonment to be served by members of the two classes of felons targeted in the legislation. Good-time credits were limited in Three Strikes cases to 20% of the formal prison term (Vitiello 1997). Imprisonment was made mandatory in both second- and third-strike cases, and the minimum mandatory term in the latter was set at 25 years. Wherever possible, the Three Strikes structure removed judicial discretion to avoid imprisonment or to select imprisonment terms.[1]

The mandatory language of the Three Strikes legislation might seem to be an attempt to control prosecutorial, as well as judicial, discretion.[2] But this is by no means clear even as an intention of

[1] This was true also in Proposition 184, which was almost identically passed by the legislature as the Jones Bill of 1994 (see Vitiello 1997).

[2] The law requires prosecutors to allege and prove all strike convictions of which they are aware.

those who drafted Three Strikes, and there is certainly no effective review of prosecutorial discretion provided in the Three Strikes legislation. There are two plausible explanations for this absence. First, those who drafted Three Strikes almost certainly regarded judges as the natural enemies of harsh sentences but may have regarded prosecutorial authorities as friendly to their punitive intentions. Second, it is much easier to provide for enforceable mandatory punishments to be administered by judges. Prosecutors can monitor the behavior of judges. If prosecutors wish to appeal judicial deviations from mandatory Three Strikes provisions, appellate courts can provide a meaningful review. But if the prosecutors wish not to bring charges under the Three Strikes laws, who is there to force them to do so? As a matter of Realpolitik, it is much easier to legislatively restrain judicial discretion than prosecutorial discretion.

Relative Versus Absolute Power

Because prosecutorial discretion remained unchanged under the Three Strikes initiative, one might conclude that the initiative had no substantial impact on the power relations between prosecutors and other agents in the criminal justice system. This would be an erroneous conclusion, however, one that misses the important distinction between absolute and relative levels of discretionary power.

When prosecutors' powers are undisturbed but judicial and correctional powers are sharply curtailed, the relative influence of the prosecutor is enhanced. Under a system of both prosecutorial and judicial discretion, the district attorney can decide what charges to file and what charges to drop; but judges will also have a substantial influence on the determination of what punishments are meted out to individual offenders. The prosecutor has an important influence in these cases, but his or hers is not the last word. As soon as mandatory provisions like those in Three Strikes remove judicial power to choose among possible penalties, the prosecutor's decision in the early stages of the system move much closer to being the last word in determining the punishment of a particular offender.

In the case of Three Strikes, the consequences of conviction for a third- or second-strike offense are automatic. Thus the prosecutor's power to choose whether or not to press the charge is very close to the last word in determining the defendant's punishment. The particular powers that prosecutors are exercising are nothing new to their office, but the impact of their discretionary power on case out-comes is much more substantial because the checks and balances of judicial and correctional discretion have been removed.

In this respect, the Three Strikes initiative is part of a process of enhancing the relative power of the prosecution that had been ongo-ing for two decades in California. First determinate sentencing cur-tailed the power of a centralized parole authority to determine the actual length of prison sentences. With parole power removed, the relative powers of judges and prosecutors were increased, and the power to determine prison sentences was pushed back from the parole stage and into the sentencing and plea-bargaining process that occurs earlier in the path of a criminal case. Then the mandatory standards for minimum punishment and for the calculation of strikes to be used in aggravation of a defendant's current charge attempted to remove discretion from the sentencing stages of a criminal trial, in-stead concentrating discretionary authority in the prosecutor's office and in the earliest stages of the case process.

This reallocation of relative power under Three Strikes has an im-portant implication in evaluating the impact of the new law on the ad-ministration of criminal justice. The earliest stages of case selection and prosecution are also the least visible part of decision making in the criminal justice system. The decision whether to label a case a sec-ond or third strike, like the overwhelming majority of decisions by prosecutors, is made behind closed doors. The impact of the Three Strikes laws has thus been to concentrate discretionary power in low-visibility prosecutorial decision making, which need not be docu-mented in the ordinary records produced by criminal processing.

Thus any comprehensive evaluation of the effect of the new legisla-tion must be capable of detecting low-visibility decision making near the very beginning of the criminal process. That is, it becomes neces-sary for the evaluative researcher to become something of a detective. The specific nature of the undercover operation necessary to measure the impact of Three Strikes is the subject of the next chapter.

Conclusion

Three Strikes legislation in the federal system and most American states was designed to have maximum symbolic impact while not making major changes in case outcomes. The Washington initiative that launched Three Strikes had somewhat larger practical ambitions but was limited in its impact to defendants with three serious felony convictions.

The California Three Strikes initiative was designed to use the Three Strikes label and logic to require long, mandatory prison terms for criminal defendants with one prior designated felony conviction and any current felony offense. Its two major innovations are the use of mandatory sentences after a single predicate felony and second- and third-strike sanctions following any subsequent felony conviction. But the restrictions on early release and the inclusion of residential burglary as a strike offense interacted with the primary expansions to generate a statutory scheme of unprecedented scope. These compound expansions were not accidental; the only consistent penal theory in the law is expanded mandatory terms of imprisonment. Notwithstanding the broad political support that Three Strikes attracted, this was a revolutionary assault on penal practices in the nation's largest state.

The research design described in the next chapter addresses three significant questions:

1. How large was the contribution of this legislation's two target groups of offenders to crime in California?
2. How much of a difference did the passage of Three Strikes make in the punishment assigned to the targeted recidivists?
3. Did Three Strikes reduce the crime rate in California, and if so, by how much?

Part II

THE STUDY

THREE

Building a Research Design

L ittle was known about the dimensions of recidivist violent crime or the likely impact of the new Three Strikes legislation in 1994 when the law was enacted and then validated by a citizens' initiative, but that is quite common at the front end of the legislative process. Quantitative estimates of the impact of the new law were almost literally beside the point, a very low priority in a process devoted to the symbolic denunciation of violent recidivists. Somewhat more surprising was the continuing ignorance about the role of the recidivist in California's crime and about the impact of the Three Strikes legislation five years after it became law. This chapter outlines the persistent gaps in knowledge about the effects of the 1994 legislation that we encountered and describes the study that we designed to address them.

We begin by showing why aggregate statistical profiles of identified Three Strikes cases and defendants cannot provide reliable estimates of either the size of the problem that the law addresses or the impact of the law on the rate and character of recidivist crime. This discussion demonstrates the need for evaluation of the Three Strikes initiative in a full historical and operational context. We then set out the dimensions of the research design we adopted and address the problem of small numbers of targeted Three Strikes cases, which is a necessary byproduct of beginning the research by collecting data on representative samples of felony arrests in large California cities. We then provide a statistical profile of the felony arrest samples that were drawn.

Journey into the Unknown

Just before Governor Wilson selected Reynolds's version of Three Strikes as California law, five different definitions of criminal recidivism were being discussed in the legislature (Zimring 1996). Each was a nonstandard set of categories that had been invented for the purposes of the newly proposed sentence enhancements. At the time that the legislation was considered, no reliable estimates were available of how many criminal defendants would fall into any of the proposed categories, let alone any notion of the types of sentences being administered to members of each category in preenhancement California practice. Finally there was no reliable estimate of the statistical importance of any of these categories to the volume or seriousness of crime in California.

Five years after the legislation, it was still not known what proportion of California criminals fit the Three Strikes criteria, what punishments were likely to be imposed on various categories of eligible defendants, and how the punishments assigned after the legal change compared to punishments that would have been expected without it. Furthermore, there were still no reliable estimates of the importance of the two classes of offenders singled out for special treatment by the law in relation to the state's crime and violence. And none of these important issues can be resolved by consulting the aggregate statistics on the performance of the system under the new legislation.

Available criminal justice statistics are an insufficient basis for evaluating the impact of Three Strikes legislation for two reasons. The first deficiency is the absence of any reliable data on how the cases singled out for special treatment under the new legislation used to be handled and so presumably would have been treated in its absence. To assess the impact of the reform on the sanctions for recidivist criminals requires a before-and-after comparison. If all we know are the case counts and sanctions under the Three Strikes law, there is no "before" sample to establish how much of the punishment now administered represents a change in California's penal policy.

The second major deficiency is the near certainty that the new legislation may have had substantial effects on defendants who are not officially identified as Three Strikes cases. In any particular county, the percentage of cases eligible for Three Strikes treatment that do receive it can vary between 100% to a very small fraction of 100%. Different types of cases (e.g., burglars versus robbers, or second strikes versus third strikes) may result in a very different proportional inclusion of offenders in the formal Three Strikes category. Moreover, the existence of formal Three Strikes processing as a possibility may have profound effects on the plea bargaining and punishment of potentially eligible cases that are diverted from formal processing as such.

Under these circumstances, it would be disastrously wrong to as-

sess the impact of the new legislation by examining only formally labeled Three Strikes sanctions and prosecutions. And as soon as one
decides that the broader and nonliteral impacts of the legislation
need to be assessed, the official statistics on Three Strikes implementation become a transparently inadequate foundation for evaluative research. The only way to take a reliable measurement of the impact of the new legislation is to construct a wide and representative
sample of criminal cases both before and after the change. Just how
widely the net must be cast and how large must be the sample
of criminal cases will depend on the concerns of the research. For
this reason, it is necessary to discuss in detail the dimensions of
priority issues to be investigated before justifying the specific research methodology selected to address these questions.

Critical Issues

The important questions to be addressed are organized under three
headings: the role of the identified recidivist populations in the magnitude of California crime, the magnitude of the change in punishment attributable to the new legislation, and the presence or absence
of additional crime deterrence from the legislation. Each of these
questions has multiple dimensions that influence the type of research design required to address them.

The 1994 legislation identified two new classes of criminal recidivists: a second-strike group with one prior conviction of a violent or
denominated serious offense and a third-strike group with two or
more special-category convictions. Our first priority is to find out
how much of California's crime problem is attributable to persons
who meet the criteria for Three Strikes treatment. No such estimate
of the contribution of either group to California's crime rate was
available before this research, and the correct estimate of the share of
crime produced by targets of Three Strikes requires very broad sampling.

It is first necessary to obtain a representative sample of offenders
from all felony arrests. At the same time, however, it is also important to know what the contribution of the Three Strikes risk group is
to very serious crime in California, and this may require a different
sampling strategy than a representative sampling of all felony arrests.
Homicide arrests, for example, are less than 1% of all felony arrests
in California, so that even a very large sample of felony arrests will

produce an extremely small number of homicide arrests. Unless a general arrest sample is vast beyond all consideration of scarce resources, a separate group of homicide cases must be added to the research design. The significance of these two different forms of statistics may make it necessary for researchers to collect two separate samples of criminal arrests.

The second research issue—measuring the impact of the new legislation on the punishment of those eligible for special sanctions—can only be accurately addressed by a sampling design that identifies accused felons who are eligible for Three Strikes sanctions, whether or not they are in fact selected for such punishment. It is necessary to identify a representative sample of cases that meet the statutory criteria and then to discover how often and under what circumstances this eligibility is translated into prosecution and punishment. To document the extent to which the 1994 legislation changed the punishment of eligible defendants requires large and representative samples of potentially eligible criminal suspects both before and after the 1994 legislation went into effect.

Accurate accounting of the wide variety of penal outcomes that discretionary actions can produce thus requires samples of arrests and prosecutions after Three Strikes that are much broader than prosecuted second- and third-strike cases; and an accurate estimate of the punishments to be expected from the system in the absence of the Three Strikes law requires similarly representative arrest samples from a period before the law was passed. The "before" sample must include all those offenders who would appear to qualify for Three Strikes treatment, and the "after" sample must be just as broad. Comparing the punishment received by all who appeared eligible for second- and third-strike treatment before the law with the actual punishment only of those who were in fact prosecuted is a particularly flagrant form of mismeasurement.

The third research priority—measuring the marginal, general deterrent effect of the new legislation—requires not a single before-and-after comparison of California crime but two quite distinct and complementary assessments of changes before and after the new legislation became effective. The traditional method of trying to measure the additional deterrent effect of a new set of penalties is an analysis of aggregate offense levels in a community both before and after the new legislation goes into effect. This is a relatively weak research design, however, because it cannot control for all of the changes that might affect crime rates over time. Properly cautious interrupted time series analysis would require a distinct and sharp downward slope in the crime rate proximate to the new penal regime before concluding that crime reductions were a result of increased deterrence.

The provisions of the Three Strikes legislation in California allow for a much more specific and much stronger research design, which takes advantage of the limited scope of the new penalties. The sharp escalation in threatened punishment in the 1994 legislation applies only to persons previously convicted of particular serious offenses. If this new legislation frightens these targeted recidivists, the proportion of persons arrested who qualify for the enhanced punishments should be smaller than the proportion of such offenders prior to the new legislation. The new disincentives provided in Three Strikes legislation apply directly only to the law's two targeted groups. This allows for a much more specific before-and-after research design to see whether the specific targets of the legislation are responsible for a drop in the crime rate. Because persons without qualifying criminal records face no new penalties under Three Strikes, the 1994 legislation in effect had a control group whose behavior over time can be compared to the two targeted recidivist populations.

The Three-city Research Design

Aggregate arrest and crime rate data are available by month for both California as a whole and for California cities. These data provide important information on trends in crime in general and in specific individual offenses. Arrest data are also available in the aggregate by both age and sex. All of this information is necessary to address the issues outlined in the previous section. But these aggregate data cannot tell us much about the role of recidivists in California's crime or about the impact of Three Strikes on the propensity of its special target audience to be rearrested.

The sine qua non for our research design was detailed information on a sample of individuals arrested for serious offenses in California before and after Three Strikes became law in March 1994. The first crucial decision was to determine the target population for the research and the point at which it should be identified. The target population we selected was all adult felony defendants, and our sample was all persons arrested rather than only those bound over for trial or convicted of felonies.

The exclusion of nonfelony arrests in the population analyzed can be justified because the Three Strikes law confers no importance on misdemeanor arrests or records. More controversial is the decision to sample from the total universe of felony arrests rather than to restrict examination of the legal impact to particular serious felonies. The disadvantage of sampling all felonies is that the sample will be dominated by offenses of lesser seriousness; a majority of reported index felonies in the state of California are nonaggravated theft (Federal Bureau of Investigation 1996). Even a large sample of felony arrests generates relatively small numbers of serious offenses like homicides and forcible rapes.

Sampling from the universe of felony arrests is a costly but necessary strategy because of the substantive terms of the statute. Although only a restricted number of serious felonies qualifies as a strike against a criminal defendant, any felony conviction after a first strike doubles the sentence and any felony conviction after a second strike requires a 25-year-to-life sentence. Since California law also provides that any theft offense committed after a prior theft that involved a felony conviction is itself a felony, the potential impact of the Three Strikes law on the penal treatment of nonviolent offenses is substantial. Indeed, the most dramatic increases in penalty threatened by the new statute are for the least serious felonies, where the 25-year-to-life minimum would be the biggest jump from prior practice. Excluding any category of felony from the analysis might miss substantial opportunities for Three Strikes punishment and, presumably, deterrence.

The before-and-after study we designed draws its sample of cases at the point of arrest because that is the earliest recorded event that can be used to construct a sample. Relying instead on criminal convictions would be dangerous because the existence of Three Strikes provisions might affect conviction rates for some classes of offenders. We consider the sample of charges drawn in this study to be a profile of all offenses committed by adults in the jurisdictions we studied. We were not trying to obtain a representative sample of criminal offenders but rather a representative sample of offenders weighted for their differing rates of contribution to the crime rate.

The basic before-and-after samples we drew came from three different large cities in California: San Diego, Los Angeles, and San Francisco. In each locale, we requested from the State Department of Justice a random sample of approximately 480 felony arrests in April 1993, the year before Three Strikes, and random samples of 330 arrests each for April 1994 and April 1995. April was the first month when the 1994 legislation was in force for the entire month. These arrest records contain the defendant's name, age, race, gender, arrest date, and instant offense. The 1994 and 1995 samples were both after the effective date of Three Strikes, and we anticipated that these two later samples could be combined into a single post-law sample for analysis unless there was statistical evidence of important changes over time between 1994 and 1995.

The three locales were selected because of their size and prosecutorial reputations. Los Angeles is by far the largest criminological entity in the state of California; omitting it in any analysis of criminal policy impact would be ludicrous. San Diego is the second largest city in the state and is by reputation one of the prosecutorial offices most enthusiastic about enforcement of the Three Strikes law. By contrast, San Francisco is, of the large California cities, a locale with a prosecutorial reputation most inconsistent with an emphasis on strict enforcement of mandatory penal legislation.

There is ample evidence that different levels of citizens' support for Three Strikes provided a different political environment for prosecutors in the three cities studied. Table 3.1 shows the percentage of voters in each of the three counties who favored the Three Strikes initiative in the election of 1994. San Diego led all metropolitan areas in voter support with 76% approval; support in Los Angeles County was 73% of votes cast, close to the statewide average of 72%; San Francisco voters opposed Proposition 184, with only 43% of the votes in favor. To what extent these differences in support were a cause or an effect of different attitudes toward the law by the district attorneys is not known; however, the wide range of support in the these jurisdictions is an important indication that prosecutorial policies might differ in these cities.

Table 3.1. Voting Support for Three Strikes, Sample City Counties

	Percent in Favor of Proposition 184
San Diego	76
Los Angeles	73
San Francisco	43
Statewide	72

Source: California Secretary of State, Supplement to the Statement of Vote, November 8, 1994 General Election.

Criminal Record Retrieval

Once names and personal identification were obtained from arrest records, the next step was to request official criminal record data from the California State Bureau of Criminal Statistics for the arrested individuals. We provided the bureau with the names, dates of birth, and arrest dates of the individuals we had selected. Even with adequate identification, however, accurate conviction histories were unavailable for a substantial number of cases. Table 3.2 provides information on the number of criminal records requested for each of the units, the number of criminal histories supplied, and the percentage of requests that resulted in apparently complete criminal records.

The average for obtaining the data is not low, ranging from 97.5% to 82.7% and clustering around 90%. On the other hand, we do not know what lacunae in the California criminal justice system are responsible for the nonmatched criminal records, and we therefore do not know whether or in what direction the unmatched records might introduce a bias into our results.

We used the criminal history records received to construct the criminal history of each of the arrestees sampled. We were particularly interested in the number of felony and strike convictions for each one. However, two elements missing from the official data produce a downward bias in the estimates of the prevalence of one-strike and two-strike criminal records in this study. First, the centralized records that we obtained do not include records of juvenile

Table 3.2. Three-city Arrest Samples

	San Diego	Los Angeles	San Francisco	Total
Prelaw	468/480	423/480	461/480	1352/1440
1993	(97.5)	(88.1)	(96.0)	(93.9)
Postlaw	316/330	319/330	312/330	947/990
1994	(95.8)	(96.7)	(94.5)	(95.7)
1995	311/330	317/330	273/330	901/990
	(94.2)	(96.1)	(82.7)	(91.0)
Total	1095/1140	1059/1140	1046/1140	3200/3420
	(96.1)	(92.9)	(91.8)	(93.6)

Number of records received/number of record requested (percentage).

adjudications. According to the terms of the Three Strikes legislation, delinquency adjudications can qualify as strikes for subsequent adult sentencing if it is proved that of the juvenile offenses
meet the statutory criteria of a strike. Second, out-of-state felony
convictions can count as strikes in California sentencing but are
not documented in the criminal histories obtained for the study. We
cannot estimate the potential undercount here except to note that
all the distinctive Three Strikes sentences found in the sample
were supported by offenses noted in the criminal records available
to us.

The three "before" samples, taken from San Diego, Los Angeles,
and San Francisco, can be analyzed separately, as well as combined
into a stratified sample of prosecutorial policy in large cities prior
to the effective date of Three Strikes. Similarly, the two different
post–Three Strikes samples in each city were designed so that the
data included could be analyzed as six, three, and even one stratified
sample of post–Three Strikes arrests. No attempt was made to weigh
any of the cities by population or to construct a sample of arrests that
made any claim to statistical representation of the state's population
or the state's crime. What we have is big-city crime from three big
cities.

Thus, the three individual city samples are each representative of
felony crime arrestees in each city, but the aggregate totals used in
our analysis are nonrepresentative of the state as a whole in two respects: No area other than large cities is represented in the sample,
and the cities are not combined in a way that takes account of very
different city populations. However, where the individual city profiles show similar patterns in the three subpopulations, the aggregate
totals can be taken as typical of urban crime in California.

The Supplemental Homicide Sample

To investigate whether the persons arrested for homicide have criminal records, with a different probability of second- and third-strike
qualification, we drew a random sample of 50 adult homicide arrests
from Los Angeles and San Francisco and all 45 adults arrested for
homicide in San Diego in 1993. Criminal records for these 145 persons were requested, and 144 records were obtained. The results of
this analysis are discussed in chapter 4. These defendants were not
integrated into the main samples.

Conclusion

The nature of California's Three Strikes law dictated the terms of our research design. Because the penalties apply to *all* felonies committed by the targeted groups, a comprehensive evaluation must sample all felony arrests. The city police departments generate arrests, so the best unit of analysis for arrest data is at the city level. We drew samples from Los Angeles, San Francisco, and San Diego, large cites that we believed might differ in their implementation of Three Strikes. The main before-and-after design involved 1352 arrest defendants from 1993 and 1848 arrest defendants from 1994 and 1995, a total of 3200 urban felony arrests followed up to the criminal record of the suspect. In addition to this main sample, we requested from the state 145 homicide arrest records. The 144 records we received formed the basis of a supplemental homicide sample.

Because of the wide coverage of the Three Strikes law, even large samples of arrested defendants will produce relatively small numbers and proportions of persons accused of the most serious crimes. But only a broad cross section of those accused of felonies can produce reliable estimates of how much crime is committed by targets of the 1994 legislation, what kinds of crimes are committed, and how they are punished. The research design, therefore, must be just as wide as the legislation we seek to evaluate.

FOUR

The Role of Recidivists in Urban California Crime

This chapter examines the impact on crime and violence in California of recidivist felons who meet the criteria for extended prison terms under the Three Strikes law. The data we use for this exploration is the sample of 1,352 felony arrests in three cities in 1993, almost a year before California's Three Strikes became law. The objective of this analysis is to estimate the size and character of the problem that Three Strikes addressed.

The first part of the chapter examines the share of the law's two targeted groups—the second- and third-strike defendants—of felony crimes in California and the proportionate share of these two special-sanction groups of particular serious crimes. We then discuss the demographic characteristics of the two targeted groups compared to the demographics of persons arrested for felony crimes in California with no outstanding strikes against them. The offenders we study were arrested long before Three Strikes became California law and a potential influence on criminal offenders. We are thus measuring in this chapter not the effect of the Three Strikes law, but the size and character of the problem the statute was intended to address and how the Three Strikes target groups compare to the general population that commits serious and violent offenses in California. Our preliminary analysis did not reveal any substantial differences in the three separate city samples for 1993.

Arrests as a Measure of Crime

The strategy of our research design is to use the distribution of felony arrest rates among different classes of offenders as a estimate of the share of the crime rate that each group is responsible for committing. Thus if persons with a single strike were 10% of all felony arrests, we estimate that they are responsible for 10% of all felonies committed, even though most reported crimes do not result in an arrest. The

41

strategy is the same as using a large sample of people who have won the state lottery to estimate the population of people who buy lottery tickets. The lottery study will not produce an accurate sample of all the people who ever bought even one lottery ticket because the people who bought 1,000 tickets will be much more likely to win the prize than those who purchased only 1 or 2 tickets. But it is a very good sample of lottery dollar volume. In the same way, the arrest sample is a better profile of the contribution of each group to total crime volume than of the share of one-strike and two-strike records in the total population of persons who ever committed a crime because the multiple offenders are much more likely to be arrested.

But a group's share of arrests will only suggest a parallel share of total crimes if no major biases are operating to select which crimes lead to arrests. Even though the odds of winning the lottery are one in millions, we know that a large sample of winners is representative of tickets purchased because each ticket faces the same statistical odds of winning. The key question in this research design is whether the odds of arrest are similar for offenders with one or two strikes in their criminal records and for other offenders. Although there are reasons to believe that one- and two-strike offenders may have had different arrest risks than others in the past because of the selection biases in assembling the category, there is no reason to believe that the arrest risk per 100 crimes committed was any different for this category during the period in which we collected arrest samples.

What separates the one- and two-strike groups from others arrested during 1993, 1994, and 1995 is the length and type of the arrest record they had accumulated in earlier periods. For those earlier periods, what is called a selection bias operates: Because only persons apprehended are eligible for the one- and two-strike groups, the risk of getting arrested if a crime was committed was probably higher for them than for other offenders. If a higher-than-average arrest risk carried over to a later period, these groups would have a higher share of arrests than of crimes. To return to our introductory example, if they made up 10% of all arrests, they would be responsible for less than 10% of all crimes.

However, no differential selection bias is operating in 1993, 1994, and 1995. All members of the groups were selected because they were arrested in the period. If the arrest-to-offense ratios of strike and nonstrike offenders is the same during the period, the share of each group in the arrest pool is representative of the share of crime attributable to that class of offender. Since the one-strike and two-strike

defendants were not selected on the basis of differential arrest or offense performance during the test periods, there is no indication in
any prior studies of any bias in the use of arrests as an estimate of
crime share (see Chaiken and Chaiken 1982; Greenwood and Turner
1987). Since these groups were selected not for their high offense
rates but for their high conviction rates, any operative bias would reduce the proportion of crime attributable to each group from the estimates we provide.

Recidivism, Three Strikes, and Crime

The first question we address is this: What percentage of felony
crime in California is committed by the specially targeted groups in
the Three Strikes legislation? The sample of adult felony arrests collected in three California cities in 1993 provide a start for this estimate as shown in figure 4.1.

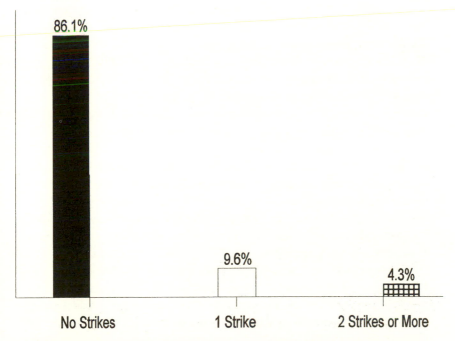

Figure 4.1. Distribution of Felony Arrest Defendants by Criminal History,
1993 Sample, Three Cities (Adults).
Source: Bureau of Criminal Statistics, Criminal Records of Felony Arrest
Samples.

The figure indicates that 9.6% of all persons arrested for felonies in California as adults in 1993 had criminal records with one previous strike conviction, making them eligible for mandatory double imprisonment under the Three Strikes statute; 4.3% have two strike records, making them eligible for the 25-year-to-life sentences, which are the most severe penal classification in the statute. The contrast between felony records generally and the pattern of designated strikes was pronounced in the 1993 sample, particularly for two or more convictions. Whereas only 9.6% of the felony arrest sample had only one prior strike, 17.4% had only one prior felony conviction. The ratio was just under two to one. Whereas only 4.3% of the arrest sample had two or more prior strikes, 27.4% had at least two prior felony convictions. The ratio of total multiple convictions to strike multiple convictions was over six to one.

To adjust these data to account for crimes committed by juveniles, we need to address the fact that our sample did not include juvenile arrests. We began by computing the proportion of felony arrests attributable to juveniles in California in 1993 (25%) and then adjusting the estimates of crime share in figure 4.1 downward by multiplying them by .75 (1.00–.25) (U.S. Dept. of Justice 1994). This adjustment results in an overestimate of the percentage of crimes attributable to juveniles (see Reiss 1986; Zimring 1981), but the magnitude of the overestimation in the California context is unknown. As modified, one-strike defendants are estimated to be responsible for 7.2% of all California felonies, whereas the two-strike group is estimated to be responsible for an additional 3.2% of California felony crimes in the year before the law was passed.

Figure 4.2 extends this analysis to the seven index felonies. The bar for each crime category shows what percentage of all persons arrested for the crime had a one-strike (black) or two-strike (white) prior criminal record. For the seven index crimes, the estimated shares attributable to persons who would be eligible for second- and third-strike treatment ranges form 7.1% (rape) to 17.1% (robbery). Of the three crimes with the highest concentration of strike offenders, two (homicide and robbery) are violent whereas the third (burglary) is not. Conversely, of the three crimes with the lowest concentration of strike offenders, two (rape and assault) are violent whereas one (auto theft) is not. For almost all crime categories, the defendants eligible for a second strike are responsible for much more crime than those eligible for a third strike—the overall ratio is more than two to one, and the concentration for crimes of violence is more than three

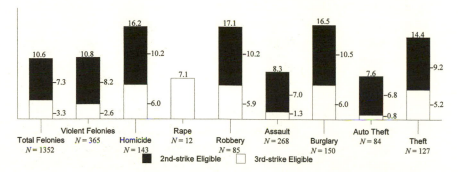

Figure 4.2. Estimated Crime Share by Offense Type (Adults Only).
Source: Homicide (supplementary sample); all other offenses, Three-city
sample, 1993.

to one. The proportion of individual offenses committed by defendants eligible for Three Strikes ranges from 0.8% to 7.1%.

The small percentage of felony crimes committed by one- and
two-strike recidivists in the three major cities that we studied is both
good news and bad news. The good news is that the percentage of all
felony defendants eligible for extended imprisonment is also rather
small, and the percentage of persons with criminal records eligible
for the 25-year-to-life sentence is very small. From the standpoint of
the resource drain on the prison system and the state treasury, the
smaller the proportion of California felony arrests that qualify for aggravated treatment under Three Strikes, the smaller the economic
resources required. The bad news is that the maximum amount of
crime prevention that can be expected from an intervention program
targeted at the two classes of recidivists established by the statute is
also rather small. If all the people arrested for felonies who met the
criteria for California's third-strike eligibility were to disappear from
the earth without a trace, the felony crime rate in the cities we studied would go down by between 3% and 4%. If all the people arrested
for felonies in 1993 who met the criteria for second-strike eligibility
were also to disappear, this double exodus would avoid 10.6% of
felony crimes.

The actual crime savings attributable to special treatment of
second- and third-strike cases will inevitably be less than the maximum possible impact, meaning that the potential savings from third-
strike enhancement is much less than 3%. It is also worth noting that
the share of the one-strike group of felony crimes is more than twice

as substantial as the impact of the two- or three-strikes group, so the largest potential crime control in the Three Strikes schema is associated with the class of defendants with the smallest punishment enhancement.[1]

Recidivism and California Violence

The modest overlap between recidivists eligible for aggravated treatment under Three Strikes and total felony crimes in California might be considered the byproduct of the statute's selectivity. In this reading, the target of the statute's special sanction is not crime in general but rather the most serious forms of criminality. Thus, the real test of the strategic success of the Three Strikes classification system is the overlap between the targeted category and especially serious crimes in California.

Figure 4.3 is an attempt to estimate the potential impact of the Three Strikes classification on violent crimes in the samples from the three cities. The graph shows the proportion of all persons arrested

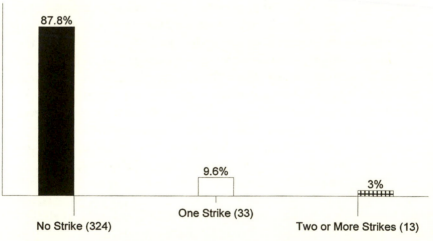

Figure 4.3. Criminal Records of Adults Arrested for Violent Felonies. Source: Three-city sample, 1993.

[1] Although many more defendants have one strike than have two or more, many more have two or more felony convictions (27.4%) than have one (17.4%).

for felony crimes of violence (homicide, rape, assault, and robbery) in the three sample cities during the sample period before Three Strikes was passed. When the 1993 arrest sample is restricted to current violent offenses, the proportion of offenders eligible for aggravated sentences under the statutory criteria goes *down* slightly rather than up. Nearly 88% of all defendants arrested for violent felonies in the three cities have no strikes in their official criminal records; 9.6% have one strike; 3% have two or more previous strikes and thus qualify for the most aggravated mandatory sentence. If violent felonies are an appropriate category of aggravated crime, the statistics reported in figure 4.3 seem perverse. One out of 33 adult violent offenders qualifies for the Three Strikes maximum, compared to 1 out of 23 for felony defendants generally. By contrast, the proportion of felons eligible for a second strike remains unchanged when arrests for violent felonies are compared with felony arrests in general. Is violence inappropriate as a measure of severity, or are the Three Strikes classifications simply wrongheaded?

Table 4.1 breaks down the four categories of violent felony arrests in our sample according to the defendant's current specific charge. The first finding worthy of comment is the very small number of homicide and rape arrests in the sample. The three-city random sample of felony arrests produced a total of 5 homicide cases and 12 rapes in a total of over 1,300 arrests. Well over 90% of the felony arrests for violence were for assault and robbery. This is typical of violent crime patterns. The second striking finding is the contrast between the Three Strikes profile of assault defendants and the profile of defendants currently charged with robbery. About one-fifth of the robbery defendants have criminal convictions in their prior history that generate eligibility for Three Strikes enhancement; the figure

Table 4.1. Criminal Record Profile by Current Offense Arrest, Violent Offenses

Strikes	Homicide	Rape	Robbery	Assault
2 or more	20	8.3	7.1	1.5
1	—	—	14.1	8.6
0	80	91.7	78.8	89.9
	100%	100%	100%	100%
N	(5)	(12)	(85)	(268)

Source: Three-city sample, 1993.

for those arrested for felony assault is 10%. Furthermore, the low percentage of Three Strikes overlap in the assault category combines with the very high volume of assault cases to pull the aggregate violent felony average below the total felony average when Three Strikes coverage is compared.

The Three Strikes statute contributes to this result by excluding most felony assaults and batteries and assigning strike designation to all robberies and first-degree residential burglaries. Whether these distinctions make any sense depends on judgments about the relative danger from assault defendants, as well as judgments about the appropriate seriousness of various grades of robbery, burglary, and assault. For example, the rate of injuries and deaths attributable to assault is probably higher than the death rate from robbery and rape (see Zimring and Hawkins 1997, chap. 4), yet robbery and rape are strikes, whereas assault is not. There is no record of the justification for this peculiar classification in the statute in the legislative history of Three Strikes. One reason why the classification system was neither discussed in detail nor justified is that no questions were asked about its scope, the rationale for particular inclusions and exclusions, and the likely overlap between the categories in the statute and the crime problem in California; Mike Reynolds's version of Three Strikes passed without significant change or discussion (Zimring 1996).

Three Strikes Targets as Criminal Groups

We have used data from the 1993 sample to assess what proportion of various types of crime were committed by persons targeted for special punishment in California's Three Strikes law. We now address a different issue: the likelihood that persons eligible for Three Strikes had committed serious and dangerous crimes on the occasion of their current arrest. The groups eligible for Three Strikes might account for a small fraction of all California's serious crimes simply because their total numbers are small. If it turns out that persons eligible for second- and third-strike treatment are much more likely than other criminal defendants to commit quite serious crimes, they might still be attractive candidates for larger doses of imprisonment both because their crimes are more serious and because current arrest for a more serious charge gives evidence of greater-than-average dangerousness. Since the California statute provides for second- and third-strike enhancement for any felony charge, any clustering of eligible defendants in particular current-offense categories would not occur as a result of statutory restrictions on punishment enhancement to especially serious felonies. Most of the current crop of states' three-strike laws do restrict the enhancement to current convictions for listed aggravated offenses;[2] so California is an exception in this regard.

Table 4.2 shows the impact of this all-inclusive approach on the distribution of current offenses that would call for mandatory double and 25-year-to-life terms.

The left column shows the distribution of the current criminal charges of arrestees with no previous strikes. The next column shows the offense profile for the arrestees with one previous strike, the group targeted for double the prison terms mandated for their current offense. The rightmost column reports the profile for the third-strike group. There are some differences in the offense profiles of the three groups, which we will presently discuss; but we first note that the overall offense profiles of the second- and third-strike defendants are quite similar to that of the no-strike group. When we look only at their current charges, offenders singled out for aggravated punish-

Table 4.2. Current Charge by Three Strikes Eligibility (Adults Only)

Violent Offenses	No Strikes $N = 1164$	1 Strike $N = 130$	2 or More Strikes $N = 58$
Homicide and rape	1.2	—	3.4
Robbery	5.8	9.2	10.3
Assault	20.7	17.7	6.9
Total violent	27.7	26.9	20.6
Burglary	9.8	17.7	22.4
Other thefts	15.4	17.7	15.5
Drugs[a]	24.4	18.4	18.9
Other	22.7	19.3	22.6

[a]Excludes marijuana offenses.

Source: Three-city sample, 1993.

[2]Only Louisiana, with a four strike system, combines a life term with eligibility generated by a terminal conviction for any felony. Traditional habitual-felon laws, by contrast, typically do not discriminate by type of felony. Compare Morris (1951) with Clark, Austin and Hewey(1997).

ment under Three Strikes look more like a representative sample of persons arrested for felonies than like an especially dangerous group of criminal recidivists, and some of the differences that do emerge are rather surprising.

On the one hand, the one- and two-strike defendants have been arrested for burglary approximately twice as often as defendants with no strikes and arrested for other theft offenses at the same rate as the no-strikes group. On the other hand, both the no-strike and one-strike groups contain a larger proportion of violent offenders than the group singled out for the statute's most serious mandatory punishments. Violent offenses are disproportionately concentrated in the no-strikes group because of the significant presence of felony assault charges. Offenses of violence constitute a relatively small group of current arrests in the Three Strikes profile; burglary charges are a larger proportion of the crimes committed by the Three Strikes group than are all the offenses of violence combined, and drug offenses occur nearly as often.

From the standpoint of penal proportionality, the data in table 4.2 show that the two- and three-strike defendants mesh with the provisions of the Three Strikes statute in a very problematic fashion. In the sample of more than 1,300 cases, burglary or drug offenses are twice as likely to be the precipitating charge for a mandatory 25-year-to-life sentence as are all of the violent offenses in the California penal code combined. More than 75% of Three Strikes defendants in this sample would face a 25-year minimum sentence for a current nonviolent offense.

To the extent that the current charge data in table 4.2 speak directly to questions of the special need for protection from the two targeted groups, there is no evidence to suggest that these groups are especially dangerous. However, the offense profiles of the targeted groups are not so decisive on this issue as they are on the issue of penal desert. Although the current charge does not distinguish either targeted group as particularly dangerous, perhaps other characteristics, such as the frequency of criminal activity, might do so.

In one sense, the fabulous heterogeneity of the current charges that would trigger Three Strikes provisions is a poetically just outcome for a statute that denies the relevance of the seriousness of the current charge in determining the appropriate punishment of defendants with more than two previous strikes. But there are two things we do not know about the reactions of those who designed or voted for Three Strikes to the data in table 4.2. First, we do not know whether the people who drafted the statute would be at all surprised by the current charge distributions of the two targeted groups. Second, we do not know whether they would be pleased or disappointed. It is difficult to measure the data of table 4.2 against the formal justification for the different levels of statutory treatment because *no* explicit penal theory accompanied the Three Strikes proposal into the arena of public debate.

The Extent of Criminal Histories

The specially targeted groups in the Three Strikes system may not commit different types of offenses than the general offending population, but they certainly do commit a larger number of felonies. Table 4.3 compares the distribution of felony convictions in the 1993 sample for offenders arrested with no strikes, one previous strike and two or more strikes.

The big difference between the no-strike defendants and the specially targeted groups is that almost two-thirds of the former have no prior felony convictions. By definition, the minimum number of prior felonies for the one-strike group should be one and the minimum number of prior felony convictions for the two-strike group should be two. As the table shows, the criminal histories of one-strike defendants are distributed very differently than the those of the two-strike defendants. One out of three of the former have only the one-strike conviction, 55% have two or fewer felony convictions,

Table 4.3. Felony Conviction by Three Strikes Status

	No Strikes	One Strike	Two or More Strikes
No felony record	64.1		
1 felony	16.5	33.1	
2 felonies	9.9	21.5	15.5
3 felonies	4.8	19.2	20.7
4 felonies	2.8	9.2	17.2
5 felonies	1.1	7.7	15.5
6+ felonies	0.8	9.3	31.1
	100%	100%	100%
N	(1164)	(130)	(58)

Source: Three-city sample, 1993.

and 75% have three or fewer felony convictions. By contrast, for the group with two or more strikes, only 15.5% have the minimum number of felony convictions that would qualify for Three Strikes treatment and just over a third have three or fewer convictions. Also, a large number of defendants in this most serious category, what a statistician would call a "positive skew." Thirty-one percent have six or more felony convictions, or four more than required for entry into the category. Only 17% of the one-strike group have as many as four more convictions than are needed for inclusion in that category.

All these comparisons may overstate the degree to which one- or two-strike qualifiers are more active than average criminals, however, because the former are older than the latter in our sample and criminal activity generally drops off with age. We correct for this potentially confounding element by computing a rate of felony convictions per year of criminal justice exposure since the age of 18. The mean rate of felony convictions per year for the no-strike group is .077. For the one-strike group, the mean rate of felony conviction per year of adult exposure is 0.24, more than three times as high as the zero group. The mean rate for the group with two or more strikes is 0.33 per year.

Whereas the contrast between the targeted groups and the no-strikes group is substantial, the frequency of criminal conviction and, by implication, of the historical number of criminal acts per year that can be attributed to these defendants is not very large. The group qualifying for third-strike treatment has been held responsible for less than one felony for every three years of prior adult exposure; and most of the criminal charges against them were run-of-the-mill theft, drug, and burglary offenses.

One important test of the Three Strikes legal categories as a way to identify previously active criminals is to compare the mean rate of historical criminal offenses per year for persons with one-strike offenses against the same measure of criminal activity for persons with one felony conviction of any kind, and to compare the group with two or more strikes with the criminal history of persons with two or more convictions for any felony. The question this comparison addresses is whether a history that includes a strike offense is a good differential predictor of an active criminal history. The mean rate of felonies for one-strike defendants in their prior adult history is 0.24 per year, whereas the mean conviction rate for offenders with a single prior felony conviction is 0.13. The one-strike designation is associated with a substantially higher criminal history. For criminal defendants with two or more strikes the mean history of felony offenses is 0.33 per year, and it is 0.30 for defendants with two or more felony priors of any kind. So the third-strike category does not differentially predict high rates of offenses any better than would a system that singles out all persons with two felony convictions.

Two different strategies are intermixed in the Three Strikes statute: a "dangerous-offender" approach, which reserves serious sanctions for particularly dangerous criminals, and an "habitual-offender" approach, which emphasizes the number of felony offenses rather than their seriousness. What our data demonstrate is that if the provisions in the Three Strikes law were applied literally to our 1993 sample, the results would more closely resemble the habitual-offender than the dangerous-offender paradigm. But even as a habitual-offender strategy, the Three Strikes category would not perform any better in identifying high-rate offenders than would a system triggered by three felony convictions of any kind.

One final caveat needs to be attached to our discussion of the historical criminal activity of the 1993 sample. Statistical models that identify past criminal activity are not the equivalent of predictions of future offenses, particularly when a group has to have been defined as criminally active in order to be included in the analysis (Zimring and Hawkins 1995, chap. 5). The rate of offenses for such a preselected group will probably be lower than its rate during the period that was the basis for inclusion because one cannot assume that 100% of the sample will commit a crime in any future period.

The Supplementary Homicide Sample

Homicide, the most serious offense, is a low-rate event that will not be a visible presence in representative samples of felony arrests. The 1352 felony arrests in the main sample contained only 5 homicide arrests, obviously not enough to permit investigation into whether homicide suspects include important concentrations of defendants targeted for the special sanctions. We therefore constructed a supplementary sample of approximately 50 arrests in 1993[3] for homicide from each of the three cities we were studying in the main sample.

---

[3] Only 44 adults were arrested for homicide in San Diego in 1993.

Using this sample, we obtained a total of 144 criminal records from the Department of Justice files. When used as a single aggregation, this is a stratified sample of homicide suspects from Los Angeles, San Francisco, and San Diego because arrest records were drawn in approximately equal numbers from each city.

Our attempt to determine how much of California homicide is committed by the target groups involves the same two steps used in the main felony arrest sample. Step one is to find out what percentage of adult homicide arrestees had criminal records that made them eligible for aggravated sentencing under the Three Strikes criteria. These are the data reported in figure 4.4. The pattern found for adult homicide arrests is similar to that for all felonies. More than four out of five homicide suspects have no strikes against them at the time of arrest, about one defendant in eight has one strike, and 7% have two or more strikes. Single-strike defendants outnumber those with two or more strikes by approximately 70%, a ratio lower than the two to one found in the main felony sample. But the difference between the two distributions is not statistically significant at .05, so it is not prudent to suppose that the ratio for this group differs from that found among persons arrested for other felonies.

The second step is to reduce the percentages in figure 4.4 to ac-

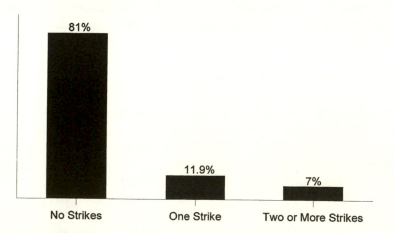

Figure 4.4. Distribution of Adult Homicide Arrest Subjects in Three Cities by Criminal Record at Time of Arrest: Los Angeles, San Francisco, and San Diego, 1993.
Source: Supplementary homicide sample, Three-city sample, 1993.

count for the proportion of homicide arrests that involve juveniles. In the 1993 California data, this percentage was 26, so the percentages in the previous figure should be multiplied by 0.74 to produce a provisional estimate of the impact of the two target groups on homicide. With this adjustment, 5.2% of all homicide arrests involve suspects with two or more strikes on their criminal records, and 8.8% of homicide arrests involve suspects with one strike against them. Thus, the odds that a homicide suspect would qualify for Three Strikes classification was 1 in 20 in 1993 and 1 in 11 that the suspect would have a one-strike record.

The Demographics of Three Strikes Eligibility

How do the two groups that the legislature targeted compare with other felony defendants in standard demographic characteristics? Figure 4.5 begins to address this question by comparing the gender distribution of defendants with no strikes, one prior strike, and two or more strikes. Sixteen percent of the persons arrested for felonies who do not have any conviction for statutory strikes in their criminal records and about 5% of both second and third strike groups are women. So the drop in female participation is sharp but occurs nearly completely in the transition from no strike to one.

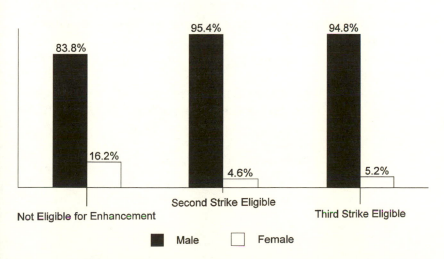

Figure 4.5. Three Strike Status by Gender, Persons Arrested for Felonies. Source: Three-city sample, 1993.

Table 4.4 provides information on the median and mean age at arrest for the adults arrested for felonies in the three-city sample during 1993. The median age at a felony arrest for our adult sample was 29, indicating that about half of the arrested sample was younger than 29 and half was older. The mean age at arrest for adult felons was 30 years, a full year higher than the median. The mean is higher than the median because it is computed by dividing the number of defendants into the total years of age of everyone in the sample. Since no one can be younger than 18 but some accused felons can be 50 or 60 years of age, there is what statisticians call a "positive skew" to the mean age value.

Each of the targeted groups in the Three Strikes law is older than the adult felony sample average. The median age for defendants with one strike against them is 32, three years older than the general median. The median age for the two-strikes group is 33, or four years older than the general average. This tendency toward older suspects in the specially targeted group is easy to explain. Offenders with strikes tend to be older because they had to have had time to accumulate adult felony records. Unless the fact of a strike record is associated with longer persistence in criminal careers, older felons are also further along in their adult criminal careers and closer to the end (see Blumstein et al. 1986). On the average, the defendant with two or more strikes has an almost 40% longer criminal adult career behind him (estimated at 16.6 years) than does the no-strikes felony defendant. All other things being equal, this means that the 25-year-to-life mandatory prison sentence will prevent fewer crimes among the third-strike group than the same sentence would in the general population of felons because the group eligible for it is somewhat older.

Figure 4.6 divides the sample into three racial and/or ethnic categories, determined by taking the three predominant designations

Table 4.4. Median and Mean Age at Arrest by Strike Status

	Median	Mean
No strikes	29	30.0
One strike	32	33.0
Two strikes and above	33	34.6
Total	29	30.5

Source: Three-city sample, 1993.

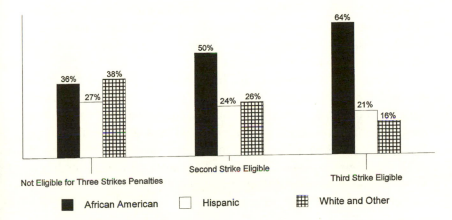

Figure 4.6. Demographic Distribution of Defendants in Three California Cities. Source: Three-city sample, 1993.

(white, Hispanic, and African American) and then combining all of the smaller ethnic groups with the whites. The concentration of minorities increases at each step into Three Stikes statutory coverage. African-American defendants are 36% of the no-strike group and 50% of the second-strike group. Both concentrations are much larger than the African-American share of the populations of the three cities, and there is a significant increase in African-American defendants in the second-strike group. Also, from second strike to third strike, the proportion of African-American defendants jumps again, from one-half to about two-thirds of the total sample. This expansion of the African-American proportion is accompanied by a sharp reduction in the white and other group, which constitutes more than one-third of criminal defendants generally but only 16% of the group targeted for 25-year-to-life mandatory minimum sentences.

A number of categorical strategies in the Three Strikes statute are associated with the differential racial concentration in the targeted groups. First, the focus on robbery defendants increases the percentage of African Americans to be expected in the sample because robbery arrests and convictions are particularly concentrated among that group (Zimring and Hawkins 1997, chap. 5). Second, the fact that residential burglary is included as a strike offense reduces the concentration of African-American offenders from the figure that would be produced in an all-robbery category because burglary arrest rates are more evenly spread across urban ethnic groups (Zimring and

Hawkins 1997, fig. 5.1). Third, the failure to include assaults and battery in the strike categories increases the racial and ethnic concentration because a larger proportion of assault defendants are white (Zimring and Hawkins 1997, fig. 5.1).

This analysis of demographics has two principal uses. First, the profiles of those eligible for Three Strikes treatment can be compared with the profiles of those who actually receive that treatment to test for discriminatory effects of prosecutorial and judicial discretion. Second, the detailed information on the demographic distribution of different offense categories can show how particular elements in the Three Strikes statute are linked to particular impacts in the distribution of defendants by age, race, and sex.

Conclusions

The objective of this analysis was to locate the groups targeted by the California Three Strikes legislation in the larger context of crime in California. How much crime was the third-strike eligible group responsible for? How much crime was committed by people who would be eligible for second-strike mandatory penalties? How serious are the crimes of these specially targeted groups when compared to the general run of people arrested for felonies in California? How extensive are the criminal histories of second- and third-strike offenders? Because the existence of the Three Strikes statute might have already reduced the role of these two targeted groups, the proper method of measuring the magnitude of recidivist criminality addressed by the statute is to analyze its impact on crime prior to the effective date of the statute. The analysis in this chapter is based on data from a stratified sample of felony arrests in the cities of San Diego, Los Angeles, and San Francisco. The names of over 1400 April 1993 felony arrestees were submitted to the California State Department of Justice in order to obtain the defendants' criminal records. A total of 1352 criminal histories were obtained, constituting more than 90% of the names submitted.

These arrestees were intended to be a not unrepresentative sample of felony arrests and of felony crime in the big cities of California. Only by sampling that broadly could we accurately determine the proportionate importance of second- and third-strike offenders in California crime. Using the metaphor in chapter 1, the felony arrest samples were the haystack, and the individuals arrested who already had one or two previous strike convictions were the two sets of needles we were trying to find.

The estimated proportion of felony crimes attributable to the second- and third-strike defendants was 7.3% for the second strike and an additional 3.3% for the third. Thus, just over 10% of felony crimes were committed by the two targeted groups, and two-thirds of that total was committed by second-strike rather than third-strike defendants. In the year before "Three strikes and you're out" became California law, about 1 felony in 30 was committed by a defendant eligible for third-strike status on the basis of an adult criminal record.

There is no pronounced tendency for the market share attributable to the second- and third-strike defendants to increase with the severity of the felony charge. The two target groups account for a disproportionately large share of robbery and burglary arrests but a substantially smaller fraction of felony assaults in California. When the focus shifts to the current offense that makes the second- and third-strike defendant eligible for mandatory punishment, there are very few pronounced concentrations by type or seriousness of offense. About the same proportion of one-strike and no-strike defendants have been currently arrested for violent offenses, whereas fewer defendants with two or more strikes have current arrests for a crime of violence. This apparently perverse differential is largely the result of much larger concentrations of assault in the group of felony defendants with no strikes on their criminal records.

Criminal defendants eligible for second- and third-strike treatment have a larger number of previous felony convictions than persons with no strikes. When a comparison is made between the criminal records of persons with one or two strikes at the time of the 1993 arrest and those of persons with one or two felony convictions of any kind, the verdict is mixed: One-strike defendants have a substantially higher rate of felony convictions per years of adult exposure than do defendants with one prior felony conviction of any kind (0.24 per year of exposure versus 0.13 per year), but the group with two or more strike convictions has about the same frequency of felony convictions in their criminal histories as defendants with two or more convictions for any felony.

The demographic profile of the specially targeted groups shows that females are substantially underrepresented in both the one- and two-strike record groups and that persons arrested with one- and two-strike records are, on the average, three and four years older, respectively, than felony defendants without strikes. The race and ethnicity breakdown of the second-strike offenders shows a somewhat higher proportion of African-American defendants than does the no-strike profile, and the group eligible for Three Strikes mandatory sentences has a still larger concentration of African-American offenders (64% versus 36%) and a much smaller concentration of white and other offenders (16% versus 38%) than the population of persons arrested for felonies in the sample without strikes on their record.

Almost all of the patterns observed in these data should be regarded as peculiar to the California statute. All of the features that increase the coverage of the California statute over those in other states dilute the degree to which those groups eligible for aggravated treatment will differ from the general population of felony defendants. So although the California statute is one of the most extreme of its kind, the offenders it singles out for special treatment are probably far closer to typical felons than the targeted population of other Three Strikes laws.

The two most remarkable characteristics of Three Strikes in California are its small magnitude when compared to serious crime in California and the non-selective character of the defendants it targets when compared to others arrested for felony crimes. Both categories of targeted groups together account for slightly more than 10% of both felonies or violent felonies in California. And more than two-thirds of the Three Strikes crime coverage is a result of the so-called second-strike group. The third-strike multiple offenders targeted account for just over 3% of California's crime. So any nontrivial preventive effects from the law must depend on its less famous provisions for mandatory double imprisonment, added to 80% (versus 50%) of the time served whenever a single strike is on a defendant's record. The potential crime-reducing impact of the third-strike provisions is tiny.

Although the two targeted categories account for about 10% of California's crime rate, that does not mean that the defendants targeted for this special treatment are selected because of their personal dangerousness or the severity of their current offense—quite the opposite. The only crime characteristic that sets the second- and third-strike group apart from other big-city felony defendants is the existence of one or two strike offenses on their prior records. The offense charged at the current arrest is less likely to be a crime of violence for a third-strike defendant than for a defendant with no strikes at all. The intensity of the prior criminal career of the defendant who is facing a third-strike charge is no greater than that of a defendant with two previous nonstrike felonies.

Just as the categories of offenses lumped together in the Three Strikes statute are best regarded as miscellaneous in character, the criminal defendants who meet the criteria turn out to be a mix of the dangerous and nondangerous, the violent and the nonviolent. It would not be fair to characterize the 3.3% of adult felony defendants who meet the criteria for 25-year-to-life sentences as a totally representative cross section of California criminals. They are older than the norm and have been more active. But when the relatively small differences between the Three Strikes group and other criminal defendants are scrutinized in the light of the very large differences in punishment, the justification for the exceptional penal category is by no means obvious.

There is more than a little irony in finding a targeted group to be simultaneously a small and a nonselective sample of criminal defendants. Also, it is important to underscore the fact that the offenders described in this chapter are those who would seem to be qualified for Three Strikes prosecution rather than a group that has already been prosecuted and assigned this punishment. It is the statute's standards themselves that are non-selective. What remains to be seen is whether those who wield administrative power will use discretion to further narrow the group selected for Three Strikes treatment and try to make the defendants targeted in practice a more selective group of demonstrated high-risk offenders. Any attempt to make the Three Strikes statute selective in practice, however, will reduce the group that receives special punishments. It will also violate the clear purpose of the legislation.

The Impact of Three Strikes on Criminal Punishment

This chapter presents data on the impact of the Three Strikes law on punishments in felony cases. The analysis proceeds under three headings. The first uses sample data and statewide prison statistics to present estimates of the level of enforcement of the new law's second-strike and third-strike provisions. The second part presents the data on punishment before and after the law from our three-city sample. The third part concentrates on the different patterns found in each of the three cities.

Contrasting Levels of Enforcement

Detailed information is available from the California Department of Corrections on the volume of prisoners sentenced under the second-strike and third-strike provisions of the Three Strikes statute. This section combines the detailed statistics on prison admissions with the study's estimates of Three Strikes eligibility to produce rough estimates of the degree to which the two main provisions of the law are being enforced. The assumptions we make to produce these estimates are heroic ones. But the contrast between the levels of second-strike and third-strike enforcement is obvious and not dependent on the quality of distributional assumptions made in constructing specific estimates.

Figure 5.1 is a summary of our estimate of second-strike and third-strike enforcement. During 1995, the California Department of Corrections reported 10,024 admissions for second-strike offenses. One way to estimate the number of cases that were eligible for second-strike treatment is to multiply the fraction of felony convictions that involved persons eligible for such treatment in our three-city sample (9.6%) by the number of felony convictions in fiscal 1994–1995 in California (162,906), which produces an estimated volume of 15,639 second-strike offenses. The actual number was 10,024, or 64% of the

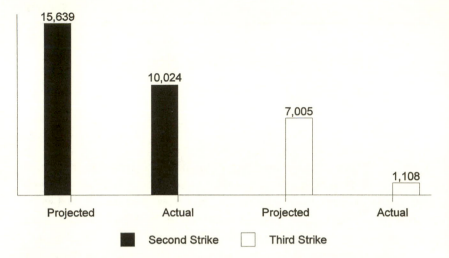

Figure 5.1. Projected Three Strikes Totals, 1994 Arrests and 1995 Admissions.
Source: California Department of Corrections; Three-city sample, 1993.

estimated eligible cases. The parallel analysis for third-strike cases produces a much lower estimate. Taking 4.3% of 162,906 produces an estimate of 7,005 potential third-strike convictions. The actual number was 1,108, or just under 16% of the total eligible.

The estimates in figure 5.1 are very rough and also higher than some other plausible assumptions would produce. We compare 1994 arrests with 1995 commitments to account for a prosecution time lag. We assume that the percentage of second- and third-strike offenders is the same statewide as in our three big cities. These assumptions produce a large margin for error but no clear bias in our estimates. The bias comes from counting only cases that result in felony convictions, whereas many cases in the 1993 sample were diverted by parole violation procedures or reduced to misdemeanors through plea bargaining even though a felony conviction could have been obtained if the prosecutor had enthusiastically sought one. The estimates of enforcement in figure 5.1 could be overestimated by as much as double because of this decision. So the best way to think of the estimates is to see them as the top of a range: second-strike enforcement in the range of 30% to 60%, and third-strike enforcement in the range of 8% to 16%.

Second- Versus Third-Strike Enforcement:
A Ratio Approach

As the previous analysis demonstrates, it is difficult to construct a precise estimate of the extent to which the provisions of the law for aggravating the punishment of two-strike defendants are being literally enforced. It is, however, much easier to show that enforcement of the second-strike provisions has been far more vigorous than enforcement of the banner headline, "Three strikes and you're out," provision. In the 1994 and 1995 sample of felony arrests in three cities, the ratio of cases that met the criteria for second-strike prosecution to cases that met the criteria for third-strike prosecution was 9.3% to 3.5% of adult arrests—a ratio of 2.66 to 1. During the first three years of Three Strikes exposure, fully 90% of all prison commitments under the terms of the statute were for the less serious second-strike status—a ratio of 9:1. If these two ratios are compared, it appears that the percentage of two-strike offenses that is prosecuted and punished as such is more than three times as high as the percentage of three-strike cases that is so prosecuted and punished. This is an inference that follows from the size of the case attrition that would be necessary to convert a 2.66 ratio of eligible cases into a 9.0 ratio of actually punished cases. On this basis, we can estimate that the enforcement rate of second-strike cases is about 3.4 times higher than the rate for three-strike cases. What we do not know is the precise enforcement rate for either class of case.

The differential drop in third-strike from second-strike cases is the probable explanation for an inconsistency between the findings reported in our study of eligible cases and the findings of the California Department of Corrections on cases actually punished. The department reported that less than one-fourth of second-strike admissions to prison were for what it called "violent or serious offenses," whereas approximately one-third of third-strikers were admitted to prison for such offenses. This is graphically illustrated in figure 5.2.

The mysterious part of this comparison relates to the current-charge pattern we found in our 1993 study, when more of the defendants eligible for second-strike treatment were currently charged with a violent crime than were defendants eligible for third-strike treatment (26.9% and 20.6%, respectively). Adding in burglary makes the two groups equal in proportion. The only reason for this

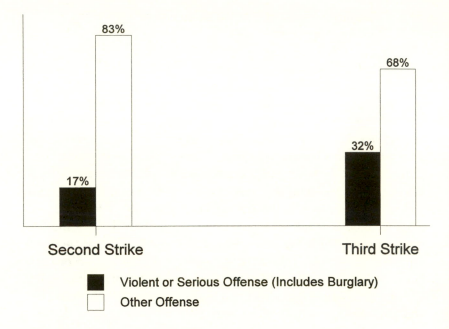

Figure 5.2. Current Offense for 1994 Three Strikes Commitments.
Source: Legislative Analyst's Office. 1995.

difference would be the much more selective use of the third-strike charge by many prosecutors.

Impacts of the Three Strikes Law on Punishment

The samples of felony arrests described in earlier chapters provide an important but limited opportunity to test the impact of the new law on actual punishments administered to the special targets of the legislation. The significant advantage of this sample of cases over the aggregate statistics available on Three Strikes in California is that official statistics can only describe cases that have been officially labeled and punished under the Three Strikes law. It is possible, by using California Department of Corrections data, to determine the number of defendants committed to prison under each provision of the law and to outline some of the characteristics of the offenses and offenders associated with the second- and third-strike cases in the official statistics. What is missing from this account is any sense of what proportion of those eligible for aggravated sentencing actually received it and how the offenders who did not were treated. Our analysis of 1,848 felony arrests in 1994–1995 provides a context for comparing the profile of eligible criminal defendants to those actually prosecuted and convicted, and it also allows us to test the effect of the new law on the punishment of those who did not receive official second- and third-strike sentences but may nonetheless have been affected by the existence of the new legal framework. Do defendants eligible for Three Strikes plead guilty instead to other charges and accept larger punishment to avoid the new penalties? These are issues that can only be addressed by following a sample of persons who could have been targeted for Three Strikes treatment, whether or not they actually were.

There are, however, three significant limitations to the use of the data in this way: small numbers, the incomplete and nonlongitudinal documentation in the criminal records we used, and the possibility that not all data that should have been entered in the Bureau of Criminal Statistics were in fact entered. Each limitation deserves separate commentary. The problem of small numbers arises because of the need to capture representative samples of all felony arrests, and it is compounded by the fact that not all felony arrests lead to punishment opportunities and sentencing decisions. Criminal conviction, the official sine qua non for punishment, is by no means a high probability after a felony arrest. The breadth of the sample is an important limit on the number of felony arrests that meet the second- and third-strike criteria. In the 1994 and 1995 samples, a total of 171 cases would have been eligible for second-strike punishment if the defendant had been convicted of a felony on the current charge, and an additional 64 arrests would have met the criteria for third-strike sentencing if a felony conviction had resulted.

But these relatively modest subsamples shrink again because of the many dispositions other than felony conviction that can follow an arrest on a felony charge. A generation ago, President Johnson's Commission on Crime produced a now famous graphic representation of all the stages and contingencies that can occur after arrest; the diagram was universally referred to as the "leaky pipe."

Among the more common ways in which a felony arrest can fall short of a conviction in California are the following: The charge is dismissed by a felony-screening unit in the district attorney's office;

the charge is reduced to a misdemeanor either on the prosecutor's initiative or as part of a plea-bargaining agreement; a defendant who had been on probation or parole is returned to the California prison system briefly instead of being prosecuted for a new felony charge; the charge is dismissed or reduced to a misdemeanor by a judicial officer either at a preliminary hearing or at trial; the defendant is acquitted by a judge or jury of all felony charges.

The existence of the Three Strikes penalties and awareness of them by prosecutors, defendants, and judges might very plausibly influence a number of these dispositions, so a broad arrest sample is the only legitimate frame for a before-and-after analysis of the impact of Three Strikes on outcomes. But collecting cases this broadly leads to significant shrinkage in the number that qualifies for any punishment decision whatsoever. Only about two-thirds of the second-strike arrests resulted in any punishment, and about one-third of these were misdemeanor adjudications or other results not involving the Three Strikes law. Only about 62% of third-strike arrests resulted in a sentencing decision, and that included a slightly higher proportion of misdemeanor punishments. So about one-third of all the second- and third-strike eligible arrests resulted in felony convictions that could have triggered the applicable consequences. Thus the analysis of punishment outcomes concerns 72 strike cases that resulted in felony convictions, including just 23 third strike cases with felony convictions. This volume is too small to serve as the foundation for confident system-wide projections.

On the other hand, we believe that much of this reduction is the result of self-conscious avoidance of formal Three Strikes consequences and that, therefore, studying trends in these phenomena is crucial to understanding the impact of the new law on felony convictions. So the case mortality rate that is a natural result of our study's wide sample strategy is the price that must be paid, even if the result is a small sample of actual punishment decisions for analysis.

The second problem in using criminal histories is that these records frequently do not contain documentation of dropped charges and never document such phenomena as plea agreements, which may be the motivation for charge reductions and guilty pleas. The best way to study punishment decisions in an environment like Three Strikes would be a longitudinal study of the progress of sample cases through the court system. Even if the official criminal record can be regarded as the next best source, the gap between best and next best is significant.

The third problem was brought to our attention in 1996 and influenced both the conduct and timing of our study. During the manpower shortages at the California Department of Justice occasioned by the budget cuts in the early 1990s, there was a backlog in data entry of approximately 18 months. To minimize this problem, we retrieved all information from the system in the summer of 1998, about three years after the last criminal record used for the study. To test for the possibility of delayed entry as an influence on record availability, we examined the no-entry case percentages in the 1994 and 1995 samples and found no difference that was consistent with delays or missing data. We cannot dismiss the existence of missing data, but we have observed no differential time bias associated with these gaps. It is thus feasible to use the data set to search for trends over time.

Some Data

Table 5.1 launches the analysis of punishment data by reporting sentencing patterns for defendants arrested in our three-city sample who did not have prior strike convictions on their adult criminal records and thus apparently did not qualify for Three Strikes enhancement. These data on no-strike defendants provide some background measure of trends over time in the severity of criminal sentences in California that is independent of the Three Strikes law. In this sense, the defendants portrayed in table 5.1 are a control group, which can be compared with the punishment records of the targeted groups in the legislation.

Table 5.1. Percentage of Arrests Leading to Imprisonment and Average Prison Sentence of No-strike Defendants

	1993	1994	1995
Percentage arrests leading to incarceration	22.5%	21.1%	23.3%
Median imprisonment sentence	9.0 months	9.0 months	9.0 months
Mean imprisonment sentence	16.8 months	20.0 months	17.3 months
N	(1,172)	(822)	(791)

Source: Three-city sample.

Three separate measures of penal severity are reported in the table. The first measure is the proportion of felony arrests of defendants without strikes that resulted in a prison or jail sentence. That percentage drops from 22.5% in 1993 to 21.1% in 1994 and rises to 23.3% in 1995. This percentage starts low and stays low. The second measure is the median sentence for those offenders sentenced to prison or jail time following a felony conviction. By arranging all the convicted felons from the shortest to the longest term of incarceration and reporting the term of the defendant exactly halfway up the distribution, the median tells us the location and distribution of punishment around which most of the defendants in the class are clustered. The median sentence starts low and stays low, remaining at 9.0 months throughout the period studied.

The third measure is the mean prison sentence reported in the criminal records. A mean sentence is computed by adding all the terms of imprisonment that all the defendants are sentenced to and dividing that total by the number of defendants. The particular value of the mean as a measure of average is that it accurately conveys the gross amount of imprisonment of the group as a whole. Since some members may be sentenced to very long terms of imprisonment, the mean prison sentence will be larger than the median, where there is a positive skew to the distribution of criminal sentences. For example, the mean prior sentence for this group in 1993 was 16.8 months, nearly 90% higher than the reported median of 9 months. The mean prison sentence increases somewhat, growing to 20 months in 1994 and falling back to 17.3 months in 1995. These figures represent sentence trends not attributable to Three Strikes's impact on potentially eligible defendants. The overall impression is one of stability in the punitive treatment of nontargeted offenders over the period 1993–1995.

Table 5.2 provides before-and-after information on defendants arrested for felonies with adult criminal records including a conviction for a single-strike offense. These are the offenders who by the terms of the new legislation should all be sentenced to imprisonment, with a minimum nominal term of incarceration twice that of the norm for their current offenses. (The actual time served will increase even more because the maximum amount of good-time credit for early release will be reduced.) We cannot compute the proportion of actual second-strike sentences for all the defendants in our three-city sample in the same way that we can for three-strike defendants. Because there was no pronounced trend in prison sentencing be-

Table 5.2. Trends in Punishment for Second-strike Defendants, Before and After Three Strikes Law

	Pre–Three Strikes 1993	Post–Three Strikes (1994 and 1995)
Percentage of arrests leading to incarceration	30.7%	35.1%
Median imprisonment term	24 months	32 months
Mean imprisonment term	30.2 months	56.9 months
N	(130)	(171)

Source: Three-city sample, 1993.

tween 1994 and 1995 and in order to increase the size of each cell reported, we combined the 1994 and 1995 information into a single post–Three Strikes category.

One important finding of the table is that defendants with a single-strike conviction were treated with substantially greater penal severity than were defendants without a previous strike conviction even before the statute was in effect. The 30.7% of all arrests that led to incarceration after felony conviction for this group is nearly 40% percent higher than the incarceration percentage of the no-strikes group. Furthermore, both the median and mean term of imprisonment for the defendants arrested with a previous strike are about twice as long as the parallel figures for the no-strikes group before the statute was on the books.

There is also evidence that Three Strikes increases both the severity of punishment assigned to the target group and the differential between the penal treatment of no-strike and one-strike defendants. The before-and-after Three Strikes comparison shows a 14% increase in the arrests leading to incarceration after a felony conviction and an increase in median and mean prison terms. This is a group of criminal defendants who were always singled out for stern punishment, but the passage of Three Strikes has exaggerated this difference in penal treatment. Most of the punishment differences between one-strike and no-strike defendants antedate "Three strikes and you're out" in California, but the new statute expanded the already substantial difference in sentencing. Restrictions on good-time credits no doubt added to this increment.

Table 5.3 gives the before-and-after picture for persons arrested for felonies with two or more adult strike convictions, a target group for

Table 5.3. Trends in Punishment for Third-strike Defendants, Before and After Three Strikes Law

	Pre–Three Strikes 1993	Post–Three Strikes (1994 and 1995)
Percentage of arrests leading to incarceration	37.9%	36%
Median imprisonment term	24 months	72 months
Mean imprisonment term	28.2 months	123 months
N	(58)	(64)

Source: Three-city sample, 1993.

the 1994 law's most extreme mandatory sentences. The punishment of Three Strikes candidates was much higher than for run-of-the-mill felony offenders before the new law came into existence. Over one-third of all prelaw arrests led to imprisonment after a felony conviction, about 70% more than the fraction found in the 1993 no-strikes group, and the median and mean prison terms were both substantially greater for third-strike-eligible defendants in the prelaw period than for felons in general. The comparison between second- and third-strike defendants in the prelaw period presents a more complicated picture. The percentage of arrests that led to felony incarceration was higher for the three-strike cases in 1993 (37.9% and 30.7%, respectively), but the median prison term for the third-strike defendants (24 months) was the same as the median for the two-strike candidates. Also, the mean prison term in 1993 for the three-strike group was actually shorter than that for the two-strike group (28.2 months and 30.2 months, respectively). Why?

The higher mean sentence for second-strike offenders was probably linked to the different mix of offenses for current arrests in our 1993 second- and third-strike samples. The proportion of current charges that involved violence was substantially higher in the second-strike group. The most plausible explanation of the higher mean in the second-strike sample, therefore, is that the severity of the current offense was a major factor in long prison terms; moreover, because the 1993 second sample had more serious offenses than the third sample, it will also have a longer average sentence.

But the relatively modest mean or median third-strike sentences carry two further implications. First, whereas the criminal records associated with Three Strikes eligibility were good predictors of an increased likelihood of incarceration in the pre–Three Strikes era, there was no pronounced tendency on the part of judges or prosecutors to impose or to seek long incapacitative sentences for these offenders. The systemic tendency before Three Strikes became law was to lock the offender up but very rarely to throw away the key. There is no positive skew in the 1993 three-strike sentences, which means that few, if any, extremely long prison terms were imposed on this group.

The second implication of this pre–Three Strikes sentencing pattern is that the gap between prelaw sentences and postlaw, systemwide mandatory minimums was the greatest for the third-strike defendant. The median nominal sentence for this group prior to Three Strikes was less than one-twelfth the mandatory minimum sentence under the new legislation, and the minimum sentencing provisions in the new law widened the gap to about 20 years of time served under the new law, from 1 year of time actually served under the previous practice. When judged against the previous performance of the criminal justice system, the Three Strikes minimums are far and away the most revolutionary of the new law's objectives.

Judging by the small number of cases that flowed through our sample, we find that the impact of the new legislation is mixed. The percentage of arrests that led to incarceration in third-strikes cases actually declined from 37.9 to 36. Meanwhile the median prison term increased 200% from 24 to 72 months, and the mean imprisonment sentence increased more than fourfold, from 28.2 to 123 months.

The dramatic increase of the median prison term demonstrates both that the new law had a dramatic impact on prison sentences for the third-strike group and that many of the increased prison terms were not formally connected to the new Three Strikes minimums. The new minimum prison term for those convicted of felonies and eligible for a third strike was more than four times as great as the median prison term handed out in the first two years after Three Strikes became law. So the principal mechanism for increasing the punishment of defendants eligible for Three Strikes could not have been the sentencing provisions in the Three Strikes law. (Indeed only 6 of the 64 defendants with third-strike records who were arrested for felonies received the Three Strikes minimum punishment in our sample.)

The escalation in punishment may have been unofficial, but it was also substantial. Median prison terms for this group were more than twice as great as the increase in median prison terms that we found among the second-strike defendants. Furthermore, the mean prison term handed out to eligible defendants grew faster than the median, and most of the differential growth was the product of a very few, very long, official Three Strikes sentences. Only six 300-month minimum sentences account for over 60% of the total prison months of the 20 eligible defendants sentenced to prison. And reduction of credit for good time means that an even greater percentage of the total months served by the group of 20 will be served by the 6 who were officially sentenced in conformity with the new law's provisions. The systemic effect of the new Three Strikes provisions was to increase the aggregate punishment of this category of offenders and to create a substantial positive skew in the distribution of punishments where none had previously existed. Based on these data, the third-strike provisions in the new California law appear to be a classic case of mandatory minimum provisions in the formal law, producing an increased disparity of sentences in actual practice.

The mysterious stability in the fraction of Three Strikes arrestees eventually incarcerated is credibly explained by an analysis of individual cases. After Three Strikes came into force, a total of 7, out of 58 eligible defendants, were returned to prison as parole violators rather than being prosecuted for a new felony. This method of case disposition imprisons the defendant for a short time but does not result in a new felony conviction. Only one such return to prison on parole was noted in the pre–Three Strikes sample. Therefore, including parole violations would increase the percentage of incarceration in the postlaw sample to nearly 50%, considerably higher than the prelaw rate with the lone parole violator added. The effect of adding parole violations to the estimates of sentence length is to reduce the median sentence and to reduce the mean sentence, but by less. The short sentences for parole violations increase the gap between the mean and median probably beyond two to one. Unfortunately we have no data on the precise length of these terms for our sample cases.

Trends in the Individual Sample Cities

The previous section analyzed the three different before-and-after samples gathered from Los Angeles, San Diego, and San Francisco in a single aggregation. In this section, we will study the trends separately in the three sample cities before and after Three Strikes became law. The advantage of this change is that it provides an opportunity to test the variety of different responses to Three Strikes that may have been averaged out in the larger aggregation. The disadvantage is the smaller number of cases of each kind that is available for analysis at the individual city level.

Table 5.4 begins our city-level inquiry by providing outcome and sentencing data for cases involving defendants who do not qualify for second- or third-strike treatment. We will analyze this class of cases to see whether there are background trends in patterns of sentences over time in the communities under study that might be operating independently of the Three Strikes law.

The pattern revealed by the table does not suggest a pronounced trend in either Los Angeles or San Francisco. Los Angeles imprisoned 18.4% of its no-strike defendants in 1993 and 22.2% in 1994 and 1995. The median term of incarceration dropped from 16 months to 12, and the mean punishment dropped from 27.3 to 20.3 months. The pattern in San Francisco shows one important trend—a decline in the percentage of incarceration from 19.7 to 15.6, or nearly 80% of the 1993 rate. The median incarceration term also declined whereas the mean rate increased dramatically—indicating the imposition of a few long sentences.

The city closest to a pronounced trend over time even for cases unconnected with Three Strikes is San Diego. Whereas the percent-

Table 5.4. Time Trends for No-strike Felony Arrests

	Before	After
Los Angeles	N = 66	N = 125
Percentage of arrests leading to incarceration	18.4	22.2
Median incarceration months	16	12
Mean incarceration months	27.3	20.3
San Diego	N = 117	N = 154
Percentage of arrests leading to incarceration	28.9	28.6
Median incarceration months	6	9.0
Mean incarceration months	13.7	17.4
San Francisco	N = 80	N = 80
Percentage of arrests leading to incarceration	19.7	15.6
Median incarceration months	10.5	8.1
Mean incarceration months	12.7	18.2

Source: Three-city sample, 1993.

age of cases in this category that led to incarceration went down very slightly, the sentences actually increased. So this evidence of the no-strike sentencing alerts us to a change in the direction of increased toughness across the board by the district attorney in San Diego; any increased punishment for the two targeted groups in the Three Strikes legislation might be regarded as a combination of legislative change and prosecutorial proclivities to actively seek increased punishment.

Specific Offenses

The next step is to separately analyze punishment trends in four different classes of offenses: robbery, burglary, theft, and narcotics offenses excluding marijuana. All the robbery charges are strikes in California. First-degree burglary is a strike offense, although lesser grades of burglary are not . We group all forms of burglary charges together, however, because there is frequent use of reduced charging as a dispositional device for burglary offenders. One of the more sensitive ways to study punishment trends for residential burglars is to examine the sentences meted out to all classes of burglary offenders.

The remaining classes of criminal offense, theft and drug offenses, are the most frequent felony charges. To the extent that other charge categories count as strikes in California and may have distinctive patterns of change over time, the theft and drug categories can serve as two control groups. Table 5.5 is the most detailed (and for many people, the most unreadable) tabular breakdown in this study. For each of the four offense groups we compare pre–Three Strikes and post–Three Strikes sentencing for defendants with no previous strike in their criminal records, for defendants with one prior strike conviction who qualify for second-strike treatment for any subsequent felony conviction, and for third-strike defendants. To further complicate matters, we report four measures of sentence severity: the percentage of all arrested defendants in a class who are sentenced to prison, the proportion of all arrested defendants in a class who are sentenced to jail, the median sentence of incarceration, and the mean sentence of incarceration. This produces a proliferation of subdivisions in the table that is the natural enemy of easy reading.

The first pattern of importance is the general significance of a criminal record, including one or more strike offenses, in the punishment of all four classes of offenders before Three Strikes became law.

Table 5.5. Punishment Patterns Before and After Three Strikes, Four Offenses

	Robbery		Burglary		Drugs		Theft	
	Before $N=21$	After $N=29$	Before $N=47$	After $N=53$	Before $N=103$	After $N=170$	Before $N=32$	After $N=50$
No Strikes								
Percent sent to prison	14.9	23.9	8.8	15.2	9.2	7.2	10.5	6.7
Percent sent to jail	4.5	7.0	18.4	20.5	23.3	21.6	14.3	16.0
Median incarceration	24.0	24.0	8.0	12.0	8.0	6.0	12.0	10.5
Mean incarceration	47.5	33.1	11.3	15.0	13.9	12.9	13.1	12.8
One Strike								
Percent sent to prison	50.0	62.5	26.1	28.6	20.8	42.2	21.4	33.3
Percent sent to jail	—	12.5	8.7	7.1	8.3	6.7	7.1	8.3
Median incarceration	42.0	66.0	24.0	44.0	24.0	32.0	36.0	32.0
Mean incarceration	68.0	72.4	27.0	88.0	24.1	43.3	23.0	28.2
Two Strikes								
Percent sent to prison	33.3	20.0	53.8	66.7	36.4	20.0	12.5	75.0
Percent sent to jail	—	—	7.7	22.2	—	6.7	12.5	—
Median incarceration	48.0	—	24.0	72.0	48.0	54.0	12.4	32.0
Mean incarceration	48.0	120.0	27.5	139.2	45.0	45.4	12.4	83.3

Source: Three-city sample, 1993.

Whether the offense was drugs or theft, burglary or robbery, both the chances of imprisonment and the average sentence escalated long before Three Strikes went into effect. In 1993 the proportion of burglary arrestees who faced a prison sentence rose from 8.8% (no strikes) to 26.1% (one strike) to 53.8% (two strikes). For drug offenders, the imprisonment percentage more than doubled between no strike and one strike and increased again between one strike and two strikes. For theft defendants, the imprisonment rate increased by a factor of more than two when no-strike defendants were compared with defendants who had one-strike records. The proportion of robbery offenders imprisoned was more than three times as great for the one-strike group as for the no-strike group. And the average term of incarceration increased substantially with the existence of a strike record in all four crime categories.

A conviction record that included a serious offense was thus a significant predictor of lengthy incarceration in pre–Three Strikes California, regardless of the crime. But the very longest sentences in the pre–Three Strikes sample were reserved for robbery offenders with one and two previous strike offenses. The median length of the prison term was nearly twice as long for this one-strike group as for any other one-strike group and almost as long as any two-strike group.

Two time trends are worthy of special mention in the offense-specific, before-and-after analysis. The first relates to the sentencing pattern for burglary charges among offenders with no previous strikes on their records. The punishment for this group is technically unaffected by any provision in the Three Strikes law. Yet both the chances of imprisonment and the span of incarceration increased for this group after the law went into effect. The percentage of no-strikes burglars sent to prison nearly doubled after the new legislation, the median incarceration term increased by 50% and the mean term went up 33%.

The pattern for no-strike defendants accused of theft, robbery and drug charges is flat. The percentage of theft defendants with no strikes sentenced to prison decreased, whereas the percentage sent to jail increased. For drug crimes, both the proportion sent to prison and the proportion sent to jail dropped slightly. The average length of incarceration was also modestly down. The modest downward trends for theft and drug charges were too slight to suggest any Three Strikes impact on defendants in this class of cases. Finally, the proportion of robbers sent to prison and jail increased, although the average sentence decreased.

The contrast between no-strike drug and theft cases and no-strike burglary and robbery cases does suggest a Three Strikes spillover impact of modest importance. It does seem that prosecutors and judges were putting somewhat more penal emphasis on the classes of offense that lead to Three Strikes upgrading, even when the defendant's criminal record puts the case beyond the reach of the new statute.

The second time trend concerns the impact of a prior record, including a strike, on chances of imprisonment and term lengths. The presence or absence of a criminal record that included a strike charge was always an important predictor of going to prison and staying there for a rather long time. But the influence of a prior strike record seems to be more substantial after the effective date of Three Strikes than before. There is no uniform pattern in the before-and-after comparison when specific offenses and prior record combinations are examined, but there is a tendency toward higher probabilities of incarceration and longer incarceration terms, particularly when the mean level of a sentence rather than the median is measured. Mean incarceration levels jump for burglary in both second- and third-strike cases, for theft in the third-strike cases, and for drugs in the second-strike but not the third-strike category.

To some extent the uneven pattern in the table may be a function of small cell size and random fluctuation. But this uneven pattern is also an indication that the mechanism that accomplished change in sentencing policy after Three Strikes may have been something other than the terms of the law. Discretionary decisions made one at a time are the primary currency of change in case prosecution under Three Strikes. Completely unanticipated changes, such as increasing penal severity in no-strike burglary cases, make it very difficult to draw direct connections between changes over time in the processing of felony arrests and the effect of Three Strikes legislation. The nonliteral impacts of Three Strikes are spread over a wide variety of different categories. The literal impacts turn up less frequently and occur only with cases that qualify for second- and third-strike treatment under the new California statute. But the extremely long sentences mandated for third strikes mean that the literal impacts of the law, when they occur, will have a substantial influence on the allocation of penal resources.

For this reason, the stratified sampling technique that we used in the study had an unfortunate effect on the distribution of cases that we picked up for 1994 and 1995. Five of the six third-strike sentences came from San Diego, a city where the rate of Three Strikes prosecution per 1,000 felony arrests was quite high. Because our Los Angeles sample was the same size as the samples collected from San Diego and San Francisco, we had a much smaller proportion of Los Angeles's much larger felony case flow in our study. Los Angeles was responsible for more than 40% of all Three Strikes imprisonments statewide during the first three years that the law was in effect, and there is strong circumstantial evidence that Three Strikes prosecutions in Los Angeles are far more frequently for offenses of violence than Three Strikes imprisonments in San Diego.

Second-strike Cases

Table 5.6 provides information on incarceration propensities and average sentences under the new California law for second-strike arrestees. Los Angeles and San Diego had similar policies in these cases before Three Strikes and similar responses to the new legislation after its passage. Los Angeles incarcerated 29.6% of the second-strike defendants before the new law, with a median incarceration sentence of 16 months. The San Diego pattern before the legal change was quite similar (40.8% and 24 months). The incarceration tendency in Los Angeles went up 13 percentage points after the new law took effect, and the median prison term increased nearly threefold, to 44 months. For San Diego, the percentage increase in incarceration was smaller than Los Angeles, and the increase in the median prison term was more modest (33%). For both cities, however, the percentage increase in incarceration from a rather high base was smaller than the increases in sentence length. Evidently the increased penalty provisions had more direct and indirect effect than did the mandatory imprisonment features of the law, in part because incarceration rates for this class of cases were already quite high in both cities.

Policies for second-strike cases were very different in San Francisco both before and after the effective date of the new legislation. The percentage of arrests leading to incarceration was significantly lower than in Los Angeles and San Diego before the Three Strikes law came into effect and actually decreased in the two years after. The incarceration rate for these arrests was one-half of the Los Angeles and San Diego rates before the change in law and approximately one-third afterward. Similarly, the median and mean incarceration terms remained unchanged in San Francisco after Three Strikes went into effect, whereas both Los Angeles and San Diego experienced in-

Table 5.6. Incarceration Rates in Second-strike Cases

	Before	After
Los Angeles	$N = 14$	$N = 23$
Percentage of arrests leading to incarceration	29.6	42.6
Median incarceration months	16.0	44.0
Mean incarceration months	36.9	76.4
San Diego	$N = 20$	$N = 30$
Percentage of arrests leading to incarceration	40.8	42.8
Median incarceration months	24.0	32.0
Mean incarceration months	28.2	49.5
San Francisco	$N = 7$	$N = 7$
Percentage of arrests leading to incarceration	18.9	14.9
Median incarceration months	24.0	24.0
Mean incarceration months	23.9	24.1

Source: Three-city sample, 1993.

creases. But the key statistic for San Francisco is an incarceration percentage of 14.9 after the law took effect.

Based on the evidence in table 5.6, the impact of second-strike enhancement was modest in Los Angeles and San Diego and was focused on increasing the incarceration terms of those who were already being locked up before the law took effect. The impact of the second-strike provisions in San Francisco was difficult to find, as the median and mean sentence lengths decreased and the percentage of second-strike defendants who were sentenced to incarceration at all dropped as well.

Third-strike Cases

The small number of cases in which the defendant was eligible for third-strike treatment is reported in table 5.7. The numbers are very small, and any conclusion about substantive patterns in these three cities should be qualified by the minuscule size of the sample. The three cities in our study produce three distinctly different reactions to the third-strike provisions in the new California law. In Los Angeles the incarceration percentage starts high and goes even higher, whereas the expansion in the length of terms is relatively modest. The median term of incarceration increases from 36 to 54 months,

Table 5.7. Incarceration Rates in Third-strike Cases

	Before	After
Los Angeles	$N = 20$	$N = 19$
Percentage of arrests leading to incarceration	40.0	52.7
Median incarceration months	36.0	54.0
Mean incarceration months	38.0	74.2
San Diego	$N = 15$	$N = 22$
Percentage of arrests leading to incarceration	40.0	36.4
Median incarceration months	24.0	186.0
Mean incarceration months	25.7	175.0
San Francisco	$N = 23$	$N = 23$
Percentage of arrests leading to incarceration	34.7	21.7
Median incarceration months	24.0	72.0
Mean incarceration months	20.3	137.0

Source: Three-city sample, 1993.

and the mean rate increases from 38 to 74 months. An increase of about 50% in median imprisonment might seem large but not in comparison to the size of the Three Strikes minimum sentence. The median and mean terms of imprisonment in Los Angeles after the effective date of Three Strikes were about one-sixth and one-quarter, respectively, of the mandatory minimum specified in the legislation. There is, in fact, only one 25-year-to-life term in our Los Angeles sample of felony arrests.

The pattern in San Diego is a contrast with that of Los Angeles in two respects. The rate of incarceration starts high, as it does in Los Angeles, and stays high, but it drops from the prelaw level of 40%. Given the extremely small number of cases, this decline is probably not significant. However, the increase in prison terms in San Diego is extraordinary—almost eight times in the median and much more than that in time served because the new law substantially reduced the available sentence reduction for good time. The chief distinction between San Diego and Los Angeles is that San Diego drastically increased all of its incarceration for this class of offenses and also made use of the 25-year-to-life sentences mandated by the statute. Los Angeles, by contrast, increased prison terms for the group but did not use the Three Strikes minimum as a standard of reference. The result of this difference in policy can best be shown by comparing each city's Three Strikes sentences with the terms provided for second-strike offenders. The median second-strike incarceration in Los Angeles was 44 months, or over 80% of the median third-strike incarceration term in Los Angeles. The median second-strike sentence in San Diego was 32 months, or less than one-fifth of the median third-strike term.

The San Francisco response to the new law, as measured by incarceration percentages, is perverse, with the percentage of arrests of third-strike cases that are sentenced to incarceration falling by more than a third—the precise opposite of the statutory intention. In fact both that precipitous decline and the increase in median and mean sentences are artifacts of the new mode of diversion used by the San Francisco prosecutor's office in third-strike cases. The San Francisco response was to have the accused third-strike felon briefly returned to prison on a parole violation and to decline to prosecute on the arrest charge. The inclusion of the parole violation in San Francisco would push the incarceration percentage back up to the prelaw range and would also reduce time served very substantially from the median and mean levels reported after the law. Our best guess about the effect of the new legislation on the amount of punishment delivered to third-strike offenders is that little net change occurred.

Conclusion

Even though the two segments of California's Three Strikes law use the same formula of mandatory minimum sentences, their actual impact is a study in contrasts. Statewide, it appears that each offender who qualified for a second-strike sentence was about three and one-half times as likely to get one as was a defendant who qualified for a third strike to actually receive that punishment. Thus second-strike penalties are nine times as frequent in California as third-strike penalties, even though our study found that second-strike offenders outnumber third-strike offenders only by 2.66 to 1. The second-strike penalty increases were less drastic departures from prior practice, and prosecutors were much more likely to pursue them.

The data from our three-city sample shows that before Three Strikes, defendants with long criminal records had a much higher chance of going to prison and getting a longer prison sentence than less experienced offenders. Still, the 1994 law consistently increased both the chances of incarceration and the length of incarceration for offenders who were eligible for second-strike treatment. For third-strike offenders, there was no consistent trend toward increased chances of a new term of incarceration, but the average sentence length for those who were confined under new sentences went up very substantially.

Both the certainty and severity of incarceration increased for the second-strike group. For third-strike offenders, the average length of incarceration went up but the certainty of incarceration did not increase. As might be expected, this meant that the gap in punishments assigned to lucky and unlucky third-strike defendants was very wide. The same criminal record and current crime could result in a short stay in a parole return center or a 25-year-to-life prison term.

Three Strikes as Crime Control

This chapter concerns the issue that has captured the most public attention in the years since the law took effect: the extent to which this new law and its enforcement has reduced crime in California since March 1994. We first outline the claims made by California law enforcement about the effectiveness of Three Strikes. We then provide the most detailed statistics available on crime trends in California cities before and after the effective date of Three Strikes and discuss the ambiguities of these trends as evidence of the new law's impact. We define and contrast two potential sources of Three Strikes crime prevention—incapacitation and deterrence—and address the likely timing of the impacts from these two different mechanisms. The following discussion reviews the data about the contribution of second- and third- strike offenders to crime in California in order to show the maximum levels of crime prevention possible by reducing the criminal activity of the targeted recidivist groups after 1993. Finally, we exploit the fact that the new law changes penalties for only two identifiable subgroups in the offender population to estimate the extent of its impact. We compare the proportion of crimes in the three cities attributable to the targeted groups before and after the new law went into effect. The theory of this test is that the main Three Strikes effects should be a reduction in the share of crime attributed to third- and second-strike defendants.

The results of these new tests place a low upper limit on the short-term crime prevention apparently attributable to the Three Strikes law. Only the third-strike group shows any reduction in the proportion of felony crimes after the change in law. If this chapter's method of estimating crime reduction is appropriate, the true level of short-term crime reduction in California because of lower activity among the target groups is somewhere between 0% and 2% of all felonies.

The Official Story

In 1998, the California attorney general's office released a report entitled "'Three Strikes and You're Out'—Its Impact on the California

Criminal Justice System After Four Years." This report is typical in tone of other claims by California's governor and attorney general but more detailed in its supporting documentation (see Lundgren 1997; Wilson 1997b). The introductory paragraphs of this analysis are reproduced below:

> In 1994, RAND Corporation predicted a 22% to 34% drop in California's crime rate over 25 years as a result of "Three Strikes" [Footnote 7]. RAND was correct in predicting that California's crime rate would drop.
>
> However it did not take 25 years for California's crime rate to drop more than 22%. It took just four years. Since the passage of "Three Strikes," in fact, the violent crime rate in California has dropped 26.9% with a 30.8% drop in the six major crime categories [Footnote 8].
>
> California has experienced its largest overall drop in crime over any four-year period in history with double digit drops in every major crime category between 1994 and 1997. The result of this drop in crime means that California now has its lowest murder rate since 1970 and its lowest overall crime rate in 30 years.

"Three Strikes" Era Drop in California's Crime Rate (1994–1997)

Homicide	dropped 40.2%
Rape	dropped 17.1%
Robbery	dropped 38.7%
Assault	dropped 19.2%
Burglary	dropped 32.1%
Motor Vehicle Theft	dropped 33.2%

The apparent implication of this language is that the totality of change in California crime after 1993 is attributable to the impact of Three Strikes. The report supports this conclusion by comparing the crime rates in six offense categories from 1990–1993 with the rates from 1994–1997.

The logic of the comparison is evidently that the 1990–1993 crime trends are a control estimate, an indication of what might have been expected in California after 1994 in the absence of the new law. This is never explicitly argued, and some declines in nationwide crime levels during the later period are acknowledged elsewhere in the report. But using the two four-year periods as a before-and-after comparison is the central statistical emphasis in the report. The "'Three Strikes' Era Drop in California Crime Rate" is presumed to be caused by the threat and actuality of more severe punishments under Three Strikes. And the report used the total drop in the crime rate to claim a $5 to $15 billion saving by adding up the total estimated reduced cost of all of California's decline in crime.

As an interpretation of crime statistics, this official story jumps to firm conclusions on the basis of pretty ambiguous figures. Packaging crime statistics in two aggregate time categories that are four years in length obscures rather than clarifies the question of when crime rates changed in California. This is particularly troublesome when any number of other factors could be affecting crime rates in the state, because the particular timing of increases and decreases in reported crime can indicate how closely trends in other presumed influences on crime rates vary in relation to the actual rates of crime.

Monthly Crime Trends and Three Strikes

The first step toward estimating the independent effect of the new legislation is to obtain detailed data on the particular timing of crime trends in California to see whether the effective date of the new law is closely connected to a disjunction in crime trends. California cities report the frequencies of crimes reported to them on a monthly basis. We compiled data on crime volume by month for the 10 largest California cities before and after Three Strikes. Reliable figures for 36 months before and after the March 1994 legal change were available for 9 of the top 10 cities. Oakland could not report crime volume at all during 1995 because of a reporting system difficulty, so it was deleted from the entire time series, leaving 9 cities for analysis. We aggregated the crime volume each month for the 9 cities throughout the period. The solid line in figure 6.1 reports the level of all index crimes for January 1990 as 100 and then reports each monthly volume after that date in proportion to the initial total. It has been seasonally adjusted.[1] The dotted line shows a trend slope for the four index crimes of violence

---

[1] We used a standard technique to compute the seasonally adjusted value for each month. We added to each month's crime rate value the difference between the annual average (calculated over the entire period) and the average value for that month (also calculated over the entire period). For example, the seasonally adjusted January 1990 value was arrived at by adding to the crime rate for that date the amount by which average January crime rates fell below the average crime rate for the entire period. See Pindyck and Rubinfeld (1991, pp. 432–435).

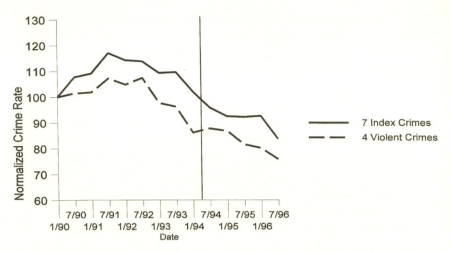

Figure 6.1. Index and Violent Crime Rates, Nine California Cities, 1990–1996.
Source: California Department of Justice, Criminal Justice Statistics Center, 1997.

aggregated to 100 in January 1990 and also seasonally adjusted. The objective here is to create a common scale for trends over time for different types of crimes. Both series have been seasonally adjusted to smooth out recurrent fluctuations due to seasonal variations. The vertical line in the chart separates February from March 1994, to separate pre– from post–Three Strikes crime reports.

The temporal patterns are similar for both violent crimes and crimes in general. Offense levels increase until October 1991 and then start to drop prior to the passage of Three Strikes. The monthly trends show two reasons to doubt that the 1994 legislation is the major cause of a reversal of direction in crime trends. First, the break comes too early, long before the passage of Three Strikes was considered likely. Second, the downward slope does not increase after the new law takes effect. The drop in crime levels is just as abrupt before the effective date of the legislation as at any time after the new law took effect. So the effective date is not a marker for either a beginning or an intensification of a decline in the crime rate.

On the other hand, most of the crime reduction in California has occurred since the new law came into effect, and there is no guarantee that the decline that started in the early 1990s would have persisted in the pattern observed without the effect of the new legislation. So the lack of a tight fit between the start of California's crime decline and the "Three Strikes Era" is neither a proof nor a decisive rejection of a Three Strikes theory of the decline. Nor will resorting to crime trends in other jurisdictions resolve the considerable ambiguities generated by the detailed temporal patterns of California crime. General crime trends during the period after 1993 were lower in most of the United States, but different places experienced different levels of decline at different times. For example, should Los Angeles (as the nation's second-largest city) be compared with population-leading New York's (New York crime drop was larger) or with the number-three Chicago (Los Angeles wins handily)? Figures 6.2 and 6.3 show the trends in all three cities over the 1990s.

Because the selection of appropriate areas of comparison to represent what would have been the temporal trend for a California without Three Strikes is necessarily arbitrary, no area is a reliable surrogate for the counterfactual condition of California without legal change.

For many types of shifts in penal law, changes in aggregate levels of crime over time are the strongest available indications of the effects of legal change. Were Three Strikes a legal change of this type, the temporal trends just considered would yield indeterminate results. The large declines in crime that occurred after March 1994

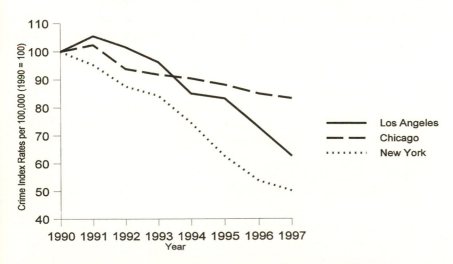

Figure 6.2. Crime Index Trends per 100,000 for Los Angeles, New York, and Chicago, 1990–1997 (1990 rates = 100).
Source: Federal Bureau of Investigation, 1990–1997.

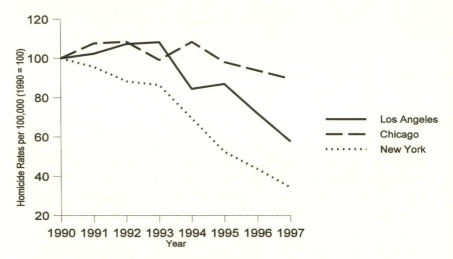

Figure 6.3. Homicide Trends per 100,000 for Los Angeles, New York, and Chicago, 1990–1997 (1990 rates = 100).
Source: Federal Bureau of Investigation. 1990–1997.

would be powerful evidence for those who wished to believe in the law's efficiency whereas the problematic timing of the decrease would be a license for nonbelievers to dismiss the claims.

Our approach is to exploit the peculiar structure of California's Three Strikes to test whether the target groups account for a large share of the post–Three Strikes decline in crime. After contrasting the two preventive mechanisms that might be triggered by the new legislation, we will attempt to determine whether its special targets are major contributors to lower crime rates in California cities. If so, the Three Strikes law is a strong candidate as a major cause of the crime drop. If not, the declines over time probably have other causes.

Two Methods of Crime Prevention

A legal change that increases the terms of imprisonment threatened and imposed on offenders can reduce the number of offenses committed through deterrence and incapacitation. If the threat of additional punishment persuades some potential offenders to forgo criminal opportunities they would otherwise have pursued, the new threat has a marginal, general deterrent effect and can reduce the crime rate regardless of whether or not additional punishments are actually administered (Zimring and Hawkins 1973). Prevention by incapacitation refers to crimes avoided because the persons who would commit them are physically restrained from doing so. Incapacitation thus requires the actual imposition of physical restraint and not merely its threat (Zimring and Hawkins 1995).

The initial emphasis of the Three Strikes advocates was on the use of protracted imprisonment to avoid the eventual recidivism of repeat felony felons who would otherwise have been punished and released from California's prisons. The long terms of imprisonment were believed to be necessary because the recidivist offenders were incorrigible, thus not good candidates for persuasion by deterrent threats (Green 1995; Podger 1993). With that focus, the added impact of imprisonment would likely be eventual rather than immediate and more concerned with incapacitation than deterrence.

However, the focus of attention shifted after 1995 from long-term to immediate effects and from incapacitation to deterrence because the crime rate in California stayed in a pattern of sustained decline in the first years after the new law came into effect. For advocates of Three Strikes as incapacitation, the immediate decline in crime in the mid-1990s was both tempting and mysterious. The temptation was to claim that the decline was caused by the new legislation. But the mystery was why a program that was dedicated to long-term incapacitation should have any high-magnitude short-term effects. The provisional answer was to claim that the threat of Three Strikes prosecution was a significant deterrent to recidivist crimes by people who had been threatened by the new, extended mandatory penalties. This is a claim examined in some detail in the course of this chapter.

Incapacitation

The strategic intention of the Three Strikes legislation was to make prison sentences longer and to make them mandatory when defendants with qualifying, prior criminal records were convicted of new offenses. There are three ways in which this kind of program can increase the number of offenses avoided because the persons who would have committed them are behind bars. First, to the extent that protracted imprisonment increases the gross amount of imprisonment in the state of California, it can also increase the number of offenses avoided by incapacitation; even if there is nothing about the particular population subject to the new penalties that makes them either more active than other offenders or more likely to commit serious crimes, crime will be reduced simply because there are fewer offenders on the streets. Second, even if the protracted punishment of recidivists merely shifts imprisonment from one group of offenders to another, if members of the new target group are likely to be more criminally active than the previous target group the gross amount of crime prevented by the same level of imprisonment will increase. Third, selective extensions of mandatory prison sentences can make the community safer by preventing more serious crimes. Even if the expected level of criminal activity for second- and third-strike offenders is not any higher than for other felons, if their offenses were more violent or destructive than the offenses of other criminals the avoidance of the same volume of crime would produce greater crime prevention. We will be referring to incapacitation benefits that come from expanding the scale of imprisonment as *increased incapacitation impact*. We will refer to benefits that come from the incarceration of higher volume or more violent offenders *as increased incapacitation efficiency.*

Because the sine que non of incapacitation is the physical restraint of potential offenders, trends in levels of incarceration should be reliable indicators of the levels of incapacitation that a policy can deliver. Figure 6.4 is a profile of trends in the imprisonment of adult offenders in California.

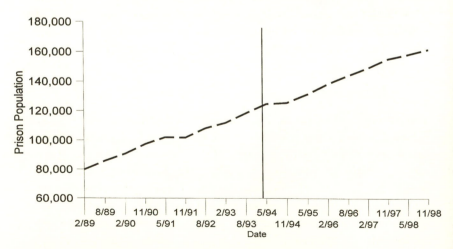

Figure 6.4. Trends in California Imprisonment, 1989–1998.
Source: California Department of Corrections, 1999.

These trends are inconsistent both with a major Three Strikes incapacitation impact in 1994 and 1995 and with incapacitation trends as a major explanation of the shift in 1993. Figure 6.4 undermines incapacitation as a trend-setting force in either 1993 or 1994 because of the relatively even pace at which prisoners were added in California corrections. There was no discontinuous shift in incarceration trends that tracked the change in crime trends. Table 6.1 shows year-to-year increases in both jail and prison incarceration by percentage and gross volume. These yearly data are superior to the prison-only quarterly information in figure 6.4 because the best measure of the incapacitation potential of a criminal justice system is the broadest measure of secure confinement.

Table 6.1 reports both the net number of prisoners added to California prisons and jails each year (which should be the best measure of the gross amount of incapacitation from new imprisonment) and the percentage change in imprisonment (which should indicate the trend). In 1994, there were 11,217 additional prisoners, a total only slightly above the average in the 1990s of 9,200. The 5.9% increase in 1994 is within a tenth of a percentage point of the median increase for the 1990s. Furthermore, both the numerical and percentage changes in imprisonment after 1993 do not indicate a break in pattern that should produce additional incapacitation to explain declining crime in 1994 and 1995. Whereas the increase in imprisonment was substantial after Three Strikes, it was business as usual for California imprisonment. The new law did not have the kind of discrete impact on

Table 6.1. Changes in the Volume and Percentage of Incarceration, California, 1990–1997

	Total Incarceration Change	Total Percentage Change
1990	10,253	6.4
1991	1,924	1.1
1992	10,137	5.8
1993	5,030	2.7
1994	11,217	5.9
1995	12,452	6.2
1996	8,966	4.2
1997	13,623	6.2

Source: California Department of Corrections, 1999 (prison data); California Board of Corrections (jail data).

secure confinement that would be consistent with significant change in crime prevention through incapacitation.

These patterns of imprisonment rule out increased incapacitation impact as an explanation for large declines of crime in the early 1990s. But what of the possibility that the shift in who goes to prison may have increased the efficiency of new imprisonments in California by preventing more serious crimes or by confining a larger number of high-rate offenders?

The findings reported in chapter 5 readily dispose of both of these hypotheses. The odds of imprisonment for second-and third-strike defendants went up only modestly, and these defendants were not more likely to be committing the most serious offenses in the arrest samples. Even if this group had continued to offend at historic levels, their changed incarceration over 1994 and 1995 would have had a tiny impact on total crime volume and no effect on the mix of serious offenses avoided. There is no credible case to be made for dramatic qualitative improvements in the rate of imprisonment from the advent of Three Strikes in 1994 and 1995.

General Deterrence

General deterrence became the reason for attributing the decline in crime to Three Strikes by a process of elimination. Since there were no large and immediate changes in the rates of incarceration to generate crime reductions, any prevention attributable to Three Strikes must be the result of the threat of punishment, which is persuading potential offenders not to commit crimes.

Why should the Three Strikes legislation make potential offenders more fearful of penalties if their crimes result in apprehension? The answer to this question depends critically on a potential offender's criminal record. For persons with qualifying one- and two-strike records, the imprisonment sanctions announced by the statute have at least tripled and have become mandatory. The literal impact of the newly threatened punishment is confined, however, to this discrete segment of the population of potential criminals. For potential criminals who do not have any strikes on their criminal records, the rules of punishment did not change in California when the new law was passed. If the deterrent effect of this new law has been driving down crime since March 1994, the proportion of all crime committed by persons vulnerable to the new punishments—that is, with one and two strikes—should go down, whereas persons not eligible for the law's provisions should not be affected by it.

The segmented structure of the new threat can be used to assess the plausibility of a deterrence explanation for the drop in crime volume. What is necessary is to generate reliable estimates of the share of crime attributable to persons liable to enhanced penalties under Three Strikes. To the extent that this measure declines after the law takes effect, it seems plausible that the specific threats of the new legislation are providing crime prevention through marginal general deterrence (Zimring and Hawkins 1973).

How Much Deterrence Is Possible?

The data reported in chapter 4 on the character of California crime in 1993 place important limits on the extent to which Three Strikes penalty enhancements could reduce the aggregate offense volume after that date. Chapter 4 found that 13.9% of all the adults arrested in the three-city sample were eligible for either second- or third-strike penalties. When the volume of juvenile arrests was considered, the estimate of crime committed by groups subject to enhanced penalties under the new law was 10.6%, distributed between second- and third-strike eligibility as shown in figure 6.5.

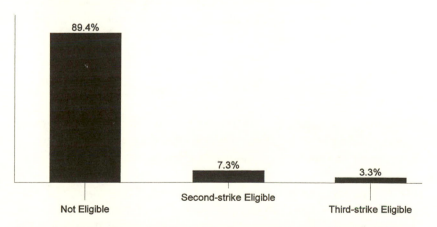

Figure 6.5. Felony Arrests Affected by Increased Penalty Threat of Three Strikes, Arrest Samples (Adult and Juvenile).
Source: Three-city sample, 1993.

Three conclusions can be derived from figure 6.5. First, even if the new penalties eliminated all offenses by eligible recidivists, only 10.6% of all California crime in 1993 could be prevented in this way. The perfect Three Strikes law would prevent 1 crime in 10, or about one-third of the 30% reduction that then Attorney General Lundgren was hoping to attribute to Three Strikes.

Second, being eligible for second-strike crime is a much more important source of potential deterrence than for third-strike crime. More than two-thirds of the offenses that are the potential target for the new legislation are in the second-strike category. By itself the third-strike share of offenses is about 3.3%, just over one-tenth of the decline that is attributed to the new legislation in the attorney general's report, and a 3% crime decline would be quite hard to differentiate from chance variation in California's crime rate. Yet 3% third-strike crime reduction could only come from assuming perfect deterrent efficacy from the top group of chronic offenders. It thus seems that the only hope for a noticeable dent in crime from the deterrent force of the new penalty threats would come from the second-strike target group.

Third, any research methodology that hopes to measure in this data environment deterrent impacts that are greater than chance variations must disaggregate the subsets of crime that are specially targeted by Three Strikes. So, the maximum amount of crime directly subject to the special deterrent threats of the new law is 10.6%, most of which is in the second-strike group, and the deterrence impact on these small segments of the crime population can be measured only by disaggregated research designs. These related conclusions lead us to the disaggregated analysis in the next section.

Disaggregation in Search of Deterrence

If the new punishment threats operated as an additional deterrent on potential offenders, the contribution of those offenders liable to the new penalties should decrease much more than that of other criminals. The research design we employed gathered data in three cities before and after the new law went into effect. There were two samples of "after" arrests for each city—one from 1994 and one from 1995. Because there was no significant difference in the pattern between the 1994 and 1995 samples, we combined the two years into a single "after" sample for each city. This produced three individual city-level before-and-after comparisons, as shown in table 6.2.

Table 6.2. Share of Crime Attributed to Targeted Groups Before and After
Three Strikes

	Second Strike		Third Strike	
	Before $N = 130$	After $N = 171$	Before $N = 58$	After $N = 64$
Los Angeles	10.4	8.5	4.7	3.0
San Diego	10.5	11.2	3.2	3.5
San Francisco	8.0	8.0	5.0	3.9

Source: Three-city samples, 1993.

A statistical analysis of the data in table 6.2 produced two important results. First, none of the three cities in our study experienced a
decline in either the total crime share of all targeted groups or the
total crime share of either single targeted group that was statistically
significant at <.05. There was in fact no general decline in the
second-strike share of crime. However, a decline in the third-strike
share was observed in Los Angeles and San Francisco, but it was
below conventional tests of statistical significance in any individual
city. Second, there was no statistically significant difference among
the three cities. This finding justified combining the three data sets
into a single before-and-after contrast to maximize its statistical
power. That is, combining the three cities was part of an effort to
search through the data to find the strongest possible case for deterrence. The result of this combination is reported in figure 6.6.

Estimates of Crime Prevention

We now report on some estimates of crime prevention that are based
on three measures: (1) probability tests on the data in figure 6.6, (2)
literal projections, and (3) computation of the minimum size of a
crime decrease that would be statistically significant if observed.

The share of adult arrests attributable to specially threatened
groups under Three Strikes was 12.8% after the law was in effect and
13.9% in pre–Three Strikes arrest samples. This difference is not statistically significant. So a prudent response to the data in Figure 6-6
is to conclude that no differential decrease in the crime share of the
targeted group took place and to reject the hypothesis that Three
Strikes generated an additional deterrent force that resulted in crime
prevention.

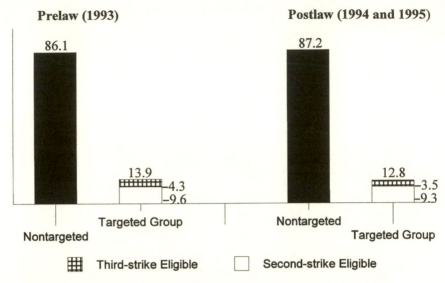

Figure 6.6. Percent Distribution of Adult Felony Arrest Suspects by
Three Strike Eligibility of Defendants.
Source: Three-city sample, 1993.

When the combined three-city sample is divided between third-strike and all other defendants, however, the statistical significance tests we used produced a mixed result. The two-tailed chi-square result for this comparison was not significant past <.05, although it was very close. However, because only a reduction in the proportion of third-strike defendants would provide a case for deterrence, it makes more sense to utilize a one-sided test for statistical significance. A one-sided Fisher exact test revealed that the decline in the proportion of third-strike defendants among the arrestees would occur by chance less than 4 times in 100. This test measures statistical significance by ignoring the chance of unusual events in the tail, which would suggest an increase inconsistent with a deterrent effect. We think that the exact test is the more appropriate test of deterrent shrinkage in the specially targeted group. The comparison of the third-strike defendants to all others is therefore evidence of trace amounts of a general deterrent effect, perhaps 1% or 2%. But the failure to find a significant drop in the share of crime attributable to both targeted groups qualifies the possibility of deterrence considerably.

An alternative analysis would assume that the 1.1% (13.9% before and 12.8% after) decline in targeted group arrests was a real rather than a chance variation. Under these circumstances, the estimated crime prevention due to Three Strikes would be derived by multiplying the reduction in adult arrests of the targeted group, 1.1%, by the percentage of crime estimated to be committed by adults, 0.76%. The provisional estimate of crime reduction by this method is just over eight-tenths of 1% in the first two years of Three Strikes.

One last perspective would ask how large a reduction in the crime rate would have to have been observed before our before-and-after comparison would conclude that the reduction was statistically significant at <.05. If we had observed a 2% decline in the share of arrests by the targeted groups, that result would have met conventional tests of significance for both the statistical tests we employed. We are here calculating the "power" of the test to provide some indication of how large a crime reduction the methodology would not miss.

The Fisher's exact test and the two-tailed chi-square approach would yield significant results if the share of adult arrests attributable to second- and third-strike defendants had decreased as much as 2.4% in the postlaw sample, and the Fisher's test would be significant with a 2% reduction in the share of adult felony arrests. The 2.4% significance threshold would translate to a reduction of crimes of about 1.84%, and the Fisher test would detect what would amount to a 1.5% reduction in total felony crimes. So the sample size of this study would have confirmed an observed effect of the new law as modest as a 2% crime reduction, but no effect that large occurred.

Looking for Spillover Deterrence

Whereas the targeting of repeat offenders was widely publicized, the specific offenses that were the basis for strike classification were not well advertised and were probably not widely known. It is likely, therefore, that some persons not targeted by the law, but with felony convictions on their records, might think themselves the repeat offenders so targeted and might feel at special risk. To see if the new law reduced the involvement of repeat felons in California, figure 6.7 compares the proportion of persons arrested with one and two or more total felony convictions before and after the law became effective. The persons with genuine strike records are retained in the sample of felony records.

As chapter 4 reported, the proportion of defendants with single

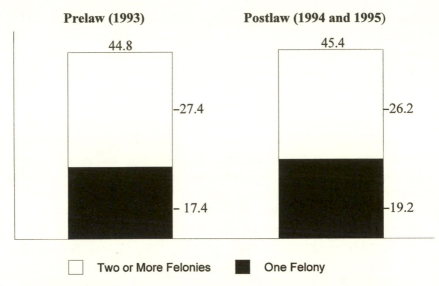

Figure 6.7. Felony Arrests by Prior Criminal Record, Before and After Three Strikes.
Source: Three-city sample, 1993.

and multiple felony convictions is much larger than the true one-strike and two-strike categories in the arrest samples. But there is no significant difference between the former proportion after and before the law went into effect.

It is, of course, possible for other groups to believe that the California law applied to them because of a juvenile court record or police contacts or a mistaken idea that the new law increases punishments for nonrecidivists. What is fanciful, however, is imagining that groups without any larger direct vulnerabilities should be deterred as much as or more than the repeat offenders, who had become the targets of long, new mandatory sentences. The notion that a legal threat's effectiveness would be inversely proportional to its applicability is missing from the literature on deterrence (Zimring and Hawkins 1973). It is one thing to acknowledge that the deterrent effects of a law like Three Strikes may not be limited to those that are its evident targets. But to argue that significant deterrence is taking place in nontargeted populations when no significant reaction can be measured in the targeted groups would break new ground in deterrence theory. Without any visible special decline in the criminality of Three Strikes targets, it does not seem likely that this new law is the moving force behind the general decline in crime.

Conclusion: Testing Two Theories of California's Crime Decline

The significance of these comparisons is best understood in the original context of the research design. The research strategy was created to arbitrate between two theories about the decline in California crime that began in late 1991 and continued after Three Strikes had become law. One theory was that the new statute played a major role after early 1994. If that were true, we reasoned that the groups that were special targets of the new law should show larger drops in criminal participation than other groups. If the crime decline was not caused by Three Strikes, we would expect to see the decline spread evenly among targeted and nontargeted groups. The results displayed in figure 6.6 show that the lower crime rates in 1994 and 1995 are evenly spread among targeted and nontargeted populations. This result suggests that the decline in crime observed after the effective date of the Three Strikes law was not the result of the statute.

Limits of the Study's Findings

Although the study's design is powerful, it is limited by the assumptions of the research strategy and the time constraints of the comparisons employed. The first problem we have already discussed: The emphasis on targeted groups does not exhaust the possibility of marginal general deterrence. Some potential offenders who were not covered might have thought they had strikes and might have been deterred by mistake. Perhaps persons with second-degree burglary convictions or robbery arrests without convictions might have believed that the new law targeted them, although the data in figure 6.7 argue against a significant level of spillover deterrence in nontargeted populations. It might also be possible that some potential offenders might have taken Three Strikes as evidence that "crime doesn't pay," even though they knew that they were not at further immediate risk. How such a general impression could be causally linked to Three Strikes and why the law's sentiment rather than the hazards it promises should generate general deterrent effects is not obvious, however, and cannot be measured in this study.

What is obvious and important as a limit on the conclusions of this study is that the impact of the law was analyzed only in the short term. The design would have detected both general deterrence and incapacitation, but there was very little extra penal confinement to produce incapacitation during that two-year period. Ten years into Three-Strikes, as third-strike sentences retain in prison many offenders who would previously have been released, some further marginal incapacitation will no doubt result. How much crime this will prevent depends on the number of crimes the third-strikers would have committed in the community during their 40s and 50s. But the data we gathered on the first two years of Three Strikes cannot address these eventual effects. Yet the short-term impact of "Three strikes and you're out" in California is far removed from the claims made on its behalf. There is no reason to believe that the deterrent impact over the first four years would be any greater than over the first two years.

The major suggestion of this analysis is that the new penalty threats and new penalties actually imposed were not an important influence on crime in California in the mid-1990s. The state of California experienced substantial declines in crime rates over the period 1991–1998. Our findings suggest that most of these declines had nothing to do with Three Strikes.

Some Other Studies

How do the findings reported in this chapter compare with other studies of the law's effects? It turns out that there have been no studies that attempt to measure its general deterrence. But a brief review of published reports on crime and Three Strikes is helpful if only to document the absence of impact studies in the literature. Published reports on Three Strikes fall into three categories: First, commentators are debating whether its effects can be inferred from general crime trends. The attorney general's report, already discussed, is the most prominent example of affirmative claims of this kind. A vigorous critique of those claims was published by Linda Beres and Thomas Griffith in 1998 (Beres and Griffith 1998).

The second group of often-cited studies of Three Strikes are projections of its costs and benefits. Because these analyses were constructed prior to implementation, they depend on assumptions about the extent of enforcement and its impact on crime rates. One set of assumptions, prepared by the California Department of Corrections in 1994, projected levels of Three Strikes sentencing. A second set of projections, prepared by the Rand Corporation, was a compound guess about levels of Three Strikes sentences and the likely incapacitative effects of the extra imprisonment generated by the new regime (Greenwood et al. 1994). The levels of enforcement and additional incarceration projected by the Rand report never occurred, so the crime reductions estimated would not be expected by the authors of the study even in the 25-year time span of the report (p. 14). But reports like that of the attorney general quote the estimate of crime reduction out of context. In fact, the Rand study could make no measurement of either deterrent or incapacitative effects of the proposed law.

One after-the-fact study by Michael Males, Dan Macallair, and Khaled Taqi-Eddin (1999) did attempt to measure both incapacitation and deterrence by constructing a correlation at the county level between Three Strikes sentencing and the relative fluctuation in crime rates. Failing to find a correlation between a county's relative enforcement of Three Strikes and its relative crime variation, the authors argue that Three Strikes has no measurable impact. The negative findings of that study are consistent with the conclusion reached in this chapter about incapacitation. On the issue of general deterrence, however, the county-level cross-sectional comparison cannot measure the general deterrent impact of the new law because that might be a constant across all the counties they studied. The cross-sectional study suggests that no increment of general or special deterrence gives an advantages to counties with higher than average levels of Three Strikes enforcement.

Males and his associates (1999) also note that declines in arrests are concentrated in younger age groups with low Three Strikes sentencing rates, a result inconsistent with the law's deterrence as a major factor in declining crime. But the impact of the new legal threat on potential offenders could not be addressed with that research design. There is certainly no inconsistency in the negative finding of Males et al. and the small but significant Three Strikes reduction we uncover.

What a search of the literature reveals is a series of arguments about the deterrent impact of this California legislation but no prior study that could test its impact on its target audiences.

A Summary: Theory Versus Practice in General Deterrence

When measured against the claims made for Three Strikes, the findings of this study are abundantly clear. But this does not mean that the statute was responsible for no general deterrence on potential offenders in the three cities we studied. Instead, a careful review of the results suggests a clear contrast between the second-strike and third-strike responses to the 1994 legislation that is consistent with prior deterrence theory and of interest in assessing the behavioral impact of punishment threats.

There is no hint in our results of any decline in the second-strike group's share of felony crime in California. This group is twice as large as the third-strike cohort, but even if its relative size had been eight times as great, there would have been no basis for projecting any decline that larger numbers could make more significant.

The third-strike group, by contrast, was not an important part of California's crime decline for the most part because of its tiny share of crime in 1993. Our three-city study projected that this group declined from 4.3% to 3.5% of adult felony arrests, a total of 0.8% of adult felonies and 0.6% of California felonies. Yet this decline is also a 19% drop in the share of crime attributable to this specially targeted group. If it is plausible to separate the third-strike group from the second-strike group, the before-and-after third-strike results are not likely to have occurred by chance. And if this group had been responsible for 33% of California crime instead of 3.3%, a 19% reduction in this population's arrest share would amount to a 6% reduction in total crime.

There are two good reasons why the third-strike targets deserve the separate analysis that suggests some deterrent effect. First, the escalation in threatened punishment was much larger for this group than for the second-strike group. Second, the publicity surrounding the third-strike provisions was much greater than for the second-strike provisions. This law, after all, was not captioned "Two strikes and you're out," and the second-strike provisions may not have been as widely known to eligible offenders, as well as to the general public. So a separate analysis of the effects on the third-strike group is not an arbitrary statistical procedure.

There are three indications that any decrease detected in the third-strike share of crime is accountable to general deterrence rather than to increased incapacitation. As seen in chapter 5, there was no increase in the percentage of third-strike defendants that were incarcerated. Furthermore, the drop in the third-strike share was as great just after the new law came into effect as one year later, and it was larger in San Francisco, with little enforcement, than in San Diego, with high enforcement (see table 6.2). These patterns make deterrent impacts the more plausible interpretation of any significant declines in 1994 and 1995.

What aspect of our findings is considered of greatest importance depends on whether practical impact or theory is a higher priority. The most obvious practical finding of this study is the tiny maximum impact of the new law on crime in California. For the third-strike group, however, our results are also consistent with behavioral impacts that would be significant in other contexts. The results are weak evidence of a detectible, marginal deterrence on the primary targets of the legislation.

Part III

IMPACTS

The Jurisprudence of Imprisonment in California

This chapter will examine the theory and practice of Three Strikes in the broader context of sentencing throughout the criminal justice system in California. Chapter 1 discussed the mix of theories in the Three Strikes legislation but did not compare its approaches to the animating principles of sentencing in non–Three Strikes cases. This chapter will compare the new law's approaches with the principles of sentencing in other criminal cases and will analyze how the different approaches interact. Chapter 5 addressed the impact of the new law on aggregate measures of criminal punishment; that is, did punishments increase? This chapter will show how the new law influenced the distribution of punishments among crimes and criminals, particularly the most serious punishments imposed. The central task of this analysis is to examine the principles and practices of Three Strikes as they interact with other provisions that govern criminal sentencing.

The first part of the chapter traces the modern history of sentencing reform in California, particularly the replacement of indeterminate sentencing with determinate sentences in 1976. A second part profiles the mix of theories that now applies to different classes of felony offenders in the current statutory pattern. The third part uses data from our study to assess the impact of the new law on proportionality of punishment and on sentencing disparity in cases in which long prison terms are imposed.

Cycles of Reform in Criminal Sentencing

A brief history of criminal sentencing in California is a necessary introduction to the business of this chapter for two reasons. First, the current legal framework of sentencing is a composite of the indeterminate sentencing system that dominated law and practice in California until 1976 and the determinate sentencing system created in the mid-1970s that, for the most part, displaced it. To understand both the principles of sentencing that operate outside of Three Strikes and the terms of imprisonment that those principles produce requires a tutorial in the evolution of sentencing law. Some background in the intellectual history of determinate sentencing is also necessary to understand the offense-based emphasis of the dominant system in California that Three Strikes was designed to override.

Although California is only one of 50 states, debates surrounding its principles of punishment have played a prominent role in the intellectual and political history of criminal sentencing in the United States. The indeterminate sentencing scheme that governed imprisonment in California for the decades before 1976 was the iconic example of a rehabilitative philosophy that governed the terms of imprisonment in adult criminal sentencing, and the attack on that system in California was the major battle over sentencing reform in the United States during the 1970s (Zimring 1983). In the older California regime, when imprisonment was a part of the criminal sanction, formal sentencing authority was divided between superior court judges and the California Adult Authority. Except where mandatory minimum penalties required imprisonment, the sentencing judge could choose between imprisonment and a sentence less than imprisonment. If imprisonment was selected, the judge would specify a minimum term and the law would provide a maximum term, typically greatly in excess of the minimum. The archetypal indeterminate sentence was not less than one year nor more than life, and the power to choose the actual term that an individual would serve resided with the adult authority.

The structure of indeterminate sentencing was such that both the sentencing judge and the adult authority had wide discretion, to be exercised individually on a case-by-case basis. The final authority for setting a term of imprisonment to be actually served resided in the adult authority, and the release date was set only after the offender had served a significant sentence of imprisonment. The formal rationale for setting release dates late in the prison term was the ability this gave the adult authority to take account of behavior in prison when considering the advisability of release. It was thought that conduct in prison was relevant to the progress of the inmate in rehabilitation programs and that in-prison behavior reflected the dangerousness of the offender if released to the community.

A long list of complaints had accumulated about indeterminate sentencing in California by the mid-1970s. It was alleged that parole

boards lacked the capacity to accurately assess progress toward rehabilitation and to predict dangerousness on an individual basis (Morris 1974). Adult authority decisions were seen as arbitrary exercises
of power that were neither scientific nor morally coherent. The elas-
ticity of indeterminate sentences was offensive to hard-liners because prison terms could be drastically reduced. The wide range of
the sentencing system was problematic for liberals because periods
in confinement could be arbitrarily extended for long periods by the
refusal of parole. After a critical summary of the operation of indeterminate sentencing, the study group that prepared *Struggle for Justice*
in 1971 concluded:

> The suffering caused by indeterminacy and the hypocrisy of
> the newer systems may be different from that experienced in
> earlier, more openly punitive systems, but it is not necessarily
> any less severe, nor has the suffering really been alleviated by
> the introduction of various comforts, such as television and
> recreation programs. Those who were concerned about remov-
> ing earlier forms of suffering have shown a curious insensi-
> tivity to the newer forms. The middle-class person who
> blanches at the thought of the cat-'o-nine-tails apparently ac-
> cepts without undue feelings of guilt the cat-and-mouse game
> whereby the prisoner never knows whether the sentence is
> three years or ten and discipline is maintained by the threat of
> more time. (p. 46)

The most popular criticism of indeterminate sentencing in the
1970s was of the tendency for parole power to produce disparity in
sentences (see Fogel 1975; Messinger and Johnson 1977). The model
case of sentencing disparity at that time was imagining two individuals who were convicted of exactly the same offense but ended
up serving very different terms of imprisonment as a result of substantially different in-prison behavior. The power to choose widely
different parole release dates, one case at a time, was rightly seen as
pregnant with the potential to treat like cases in unlike ways.

There is an implication in this 1970s conception of disparity that
deserves special emphasis. Whereas the system of indeterminate sentencing pays extensive attention to the nature of the individual offender in determining the appropriate term of imprisonment, the
1970s view demands more emphasis on the nature of the offense.
Any criticism of sentencing disparity requires a conception of the
moral currency of deserved punishment because cases cannot be
judged similar until such criteria have been agreed upon. In the

1970s, what makes "like cases alike" is for the most part the serious-ness of the offense and the harm suffered by the victims. This is in-formation that the legal system has at the time of the criminal trial; and if it should dominate the calculus of sentencing, no delay in coming to a conclusion about the appropriate length of a prison term is necessary.

The emphasis on the offense in the determination of just prison terms is explicit in the criticisms of the period, and the shift of em-phasis from offender to offense is palpably obvious in contemporary reformist literature (see Fogel 1975; Von Hirsch 1976). The authors of *Struggle for Justice* (1971) sum up their strong preference for unifor-mity of punishment in these terms: "A necessary corollary of our principle of punishing for the act is that specific punishment be as-signed to the act. All persons found guilty of the same criminal act under the same circumstances are dealt with uniformly" (p. 148). Al-though some allowance is permitted for more substantial punish-ments of repeat offenders and modest good-behavior reductions, the preferred alternative to the injustices of indeterminacy was unifor-mity in punishment for those who were to be imprisoned.

The Negative Architecture of Determinate Sentencing

The radical restructuring of criminal sentencing passed by the Cali-fornia legislature in 1976 was designed only to negate the perceived injustices of indeterminate sentencing and parole board power. There was no pressure either to increase or to decrease the aggregate amount of imprisonment in California, so the new determinate sen-tencing terms in the legislation were derived by reference to the aver-age sentence served during the last years of that regime. What the new sentencing structure did seek to change was the disparity in time served. The preamble to the reform legislation was forthright in announcing its purposes and priorities. In its singular emphasis it is one of the most noteworthy passages in all of penal legislation:

(A) (1) The Legislature finds and declares that the purpose of imprisonment for crime is punishment. This purpose is best served by terms proportionate to the seriousness of the offense with provision for uniformity in the sentences of offenders committing the same offense under similar circumstances. The Legislature further finds and declares that the elimination of disparity and the provision of uniformity of sentences can best be achieved by determinate sentences fixed by statute in proportion to the seriousness of the offense as determined by the Legislature to be imposed by the trial court with specified discretion.

The reactive nature of the new legislation is evident in the first sentence of the statement: a declaration that "the purpose of imprisonment for crime is punishment." As the topic sentence for major penal reform this statement would be extraordinarily opaque except for its context. Why was such a legislative finding necessary? The answer is: that it is an explicit rejection of the use of imprisonment to rehabilitate criminal offenders, a major theoretical justification of indeterminate sentencing. The second sentence in section 1170 sets forth an explicit theory of the justification of imprisonment by asserting that punitive purposes are best served "by terms proportionate to the seriousness of the offense with provision for uniformity in the sentences of offenders committing the same offense under similar circumstances." The last sentence in the paragraph adds the eradication of sentencing disparity as a major goal of the new law, and it asserts that it can best be eliminated by allowing the seriousness of the offense to dominate the selection of a prison term.

This statement of purposes and the system that was designed to meet its goals are a moving testimony to the power and limits of negative thinking in law reform. No new positive theory of crimes seriousness was advanced in the determinate sentencing legislation. Indeed, the average terms that had been selected by the hated parole authority were to determine the specific sentencing range for each offense. What preoccupied the framers was not the correct sentence for robbery versus the correct sentence for burglary in the new California system, but rather to make sure that all of those offenders sent to prison for burglary received similar terms of imprisonment. The mechanism for achieving this objective was a presumptive "middle term" for each offense and one greater and one lesser term that could be selected in appropriate circumstances; but the gap between the base term and its variations was deliberately much smaller than the range of sentences that had been served by persons convicted of the same offense under the previous indeterminate system. This was a negative theory of justice in the sense that the removal of one form of disparity was the preoccupying if not exclusive basis for the change.

Because the objective of the determinate system was the undoing of indeterminacy it should not be difficult to find sharp contrasts in the priorities and principles between the two regimes. Rehabilitation is a priority in indeterminate sentencing and is totally excluded from determinate regimes. Equality of punishment for crimes of equal seriousness is a major emphasis in the new system but not in the old. However, the contrast in emphasis between the two regimes goes deeper than that: Indeterminate sentencing was an *offender-based* jurisprudence, with emphasis on the behavior and prospects of the individual offender. Commission of a serious offense is a necessary precondition of imprisonment; but the nature of the offense need not determine the term of imprisonment to be served. The jurisprudence of determinate sentencing is explicitly *offense-based,* so that the specific term of imprisonment should be dominated not by who the offender is but rather by what he or she has done. And major adjustments to terms of imprisonment based on the character of the individual offender are to be regarded with suspicion by a penal code that fixes sentences "in proportion to the seriousness of the offense."

This shift in emphasis downgrades the importance not only of amenability to rehabilitation but also of predictions of dangerousness. If the central justification for the prison term is the seriousness of the offense, the importance of differential predictions of the future conduct of individuals convicted of crime is correspondingly diminished. Thus the shift from offender to offense in the mid-1970s was an important step away from personal dangerousness as a significant influence on the appropriate length of penal confinement.

The sharp contrast between the offender-based structure of the old system and the offense-based structure of the new was blurred somewhat by the amendments to the latter that enhanced prison terms for certain classes of recidivists; however, the offense-based structure of the California Penal Code still remains, nearly a quarter century after the birth of the determinate system.

Whatever their defects, wide gaps between the minimum and maximum prison terms in indeterminate schemes provide an opportunity to increase periods of confinement for offenders who are considered habitual or career felons or are otherwise regarded as especially dangerous. If the parole board places great importance on criminal records, an indeterminate sentencing scheme need not formally announce especially lengthened prison terms for repeat offenders, as long as it consistently makes parole decisions that produce that effect. Whatever the virtues of a determinate sentencing system, the narrowing of the difference between the minimum and maximum prison terms for the same offense means that multiple recidivists need not serve much longer prison terms than first and second offenders.

The emphasis on seriousness and just deserts is thus vulnerable to the charge that it directs penal resources away from a priority on career criminals. In that sense, just as indeterminate sentences are a convenient target for the proponents of the determinate system, the priorities and impacts of determinate sentencing are a convenient target for the proponents of "Three strikes and you're out."

The Jurisprudence of Imprisonment in Current California Law

Current penal practice in California is a mixture of three distinct sentencing systems and more than three separate rationales for imprisonment. The old indeterminate sentencing system lives on only in sentencing provisions for murder and other crimes that carry high minimum prison terms and life as a maximum sentence. By so restricting indeterminate sentencing frames, the system reduces the discretionary impact of the California Board of Prison Terms. Fifteen-years-to-life as a sentence provides far less power to a parole board than one-year-to-life. So the residual of indeterminate sentences carried over in the 1976 legislation reduced the discretionary power exercised by the release authority.

The great majority of all prison sentences imposed in California are determinate sentences with no parole board power for early release but with a mandatory period of postrelease parole supervision. The offense-based sentences remain the sentencing system most often used, and the time served under determinate sentences is fixed by the single period of imprisonment selected by the sentencing judge minus the allowable reduction for good time that the inmate earns.

"Three strikes and you're out" added two distinctly different principles of criminal sentencing to the statutory pattern in place in 1994. For offenders who were prosecuted under the second-strike provisions (and these are 9 out of 10 of all sentences under the law), the statutory approach is both offense-centered and offender-centered in an unprecedented mix. It is offense-centered because the defendant's current conviction provides the starting place for calculating his or her minimum punishment. Whatever the felony of the current conviction, the minimum prison sentence must be twice the standard sentence for that crime, and the maximum deduction for good time is reduced from 50% to 20% of the sentence. This means that an offender with one strike who is convicted of theft must serve about three times as much time as would be selected for a theft conviction with no strikes. But the actual minimum term for a current theft conviction under the second-strike rules will be much lower than the same offender's minimum sentence if robbery had been the current crime. Offense seriousness plays an important role in determining the base level of incarceration, but the defendant's status triples that base term and makes it mandatory.

For offenders who qualify for third-strike treatment, the sentencing philosophy in California is almost completely offender-based. No matter what the crime, the appropriate sentence is 25-years-to-life and the minimum time served must be 20 years. The characteristics of the individual rather than the crime dominate the statutorily prescribed penal sentence even more in third-strike cases than in the indeterminate sentences of the period before 1977. For third-strike cases, the terms of the statute remove both the judges' power to avoid prison and sharply curtail the parole boards' ability to secure early release. There is thus less worry about sentencing disparity because all time served under these provisions will be clustered between 240 months as a minimum and the remaining life of the offender. But if one were to favor an offense-based theory of sentencing disparity, the third-strike provision creates minimum punishment vastly in excess of the prison terms allowed for felonies of minor importance outside the Three Strikes framework. And the data on actual punishment patterns (presented in chapter 5) shows that avoidance of the three-strike penalty in the great majority of cases produces large disparities between diverted and nondiverted eligible cases.

The formal justifications currently in force for imprisonment in the state of California in the year 2000 thus run the gamut from determinate sentences preoccupied with the reduction in offense-based disparity to provisions deliberately designed to produce extraordinarily wide variations between prison terms for persons convicted of the same crime. The penal code section that denounces dissimilar prison terms for offenses of equivalent seriousness now coexists with third-strike provisions that provide 25-year mandatory minimum sentences for petty theft.

To our knowledge the inconsistency in principles between the major sentencing schemes in the state has never drawn much critical attention; nor has there been any empirical inquiry into how these two diametrically opposed sentencing schemes interact to produce a distribution of punishment. Can the joint penal product of all these coexisting systems be justified on the animating principles of any of them? On any other principles?

Proportionality and Disparity in Criminal Sentencing

We will now explore how the inconsistent penal theories behind determinate sentencing and Three Strikes interact in representative samples of criminal cases. We will use the limited window provided by our sample of big-city arrests before and after Three Strikes went into effect to determine the practical impact of the new law on proportionality and disparity.

Table 7.1 provides a profile of the most severe sentences in our sample of 1,350 arrests before Three Strikes and 1,800 arrests in the same cities after the law went into effect. We compiled data on the most serious current conviction for the 10 most severe sentences in the pre–Three Strikes arrest sample and for the 14 most severe sentences identified in the Three Strikes sample. The larger number of post–Three Strikes sentences is reported so that the same proportion of the case sample is covered for the larger group of arrests.

Two significant differences emerge when the most severe punishments imposed are compared before and after Three Strikes. The first difference is that the punishments are much more severe in the post–Three Strikes sample. The shortest sentence in the "before" sample was 6 years, but almost double that in the "after" sample. If the minimum number of years in a life term is estimated at 25, the mean minimum sentence at the most serious end of the scale in this cross section of urban arrests more than triples, from just over 10 years before the new law to 33 years after, and the median sentence increases from 7 to 25 years. Even these statistics understate the difference in actual prison stays because the legislation increased the amount of time that many defendants must serve, from 50% to 80% of the minimum. Thus the effective minimum sentence for the most serious end of the prison distribution increased more than threefold.

The second powerful effect concerns the nature of the crimes that produced the most serious sentences in our three-city sample. In the felony arrests before Three Strikes, 80% of the longest sentences handed down were for violent offenses and only one nonviolent of-

Table 7.1. Severe Outcomes of Felony Arrests Before and After Three Strikes

Before Three Strikes		After Three Strikes	
Term	Offense	Term	Offense
20-years-to-life	Murder	Life	Murder
21 years	Robbery	Life	Rape
16 years	Burglary	61 years	Rape
11 years	Firearm assault (with prior felony conviction)	28-years-to-life	Murder
7 years	Robbery	25-years-to-life	Burglary[a]
7 years	Robbery	25-years-to-life	Burglary[a]
7 years	Assault with a deadly weapon	25-years-to-life	Receiving stolen property[a]
6 years	Drug possession for sale	25-years-to-life	Motor vehicle theft[a]
6 years	Robbery	25-years-to-life	Grand theft[a]
6 years	Battery with great bodily harm	25-years-to-life	Burglary[a]
		15-years-to-life	Murder
		12 years	Robbery
		11 years	Robbery
		11 years	Voluntary manslaughter

[a] Three strikes.

Source: Three-city sample, criminal sentencing data, 1993.

fense produced a nominal prison sentence greater than 7 years. In the most serious sentences after Three Strikes, just under half of the longest prison terms were imposed for nonviolent crimes, and a majority of the sentences of more than 15 years were for property crimes that produced the 25-years-to-life sanction that had been selected for the third-strike category. Only two murder and two rape convictions produced nominal minimum sentences that were longer than the sentences handed down for grand theft, car theft, burglary, and receiving stolen property under the mandate of Three Strikes. And these sentences were significantly longer than the terms for murder, voluntary manslaughter, and robbery, which round out the group of the most severe sentences imposed after Three Strikes.

The problem with sandwiching burglars and car thieves in the middle of a distribution of murderers and robbers is the issue of proportionality in punishment, particularly in a state where section 1170 of the penal code provides that its purposes are "best served by terms proportionate to the seriousness of the offense with provision for uniformity in the sentence of an offender committing the same offense under similar circumstances."

Disparity

If the contrast between third-strike sentences for burglars and murderers raises problems of penal proportionality, so does the contrast between sentences for theft and burglary under Three Strikes and the usual punishment for these crimes. The California determinate sentencing preamble states that disparity can best be eliminated "by determinate sentences fixed by statute in proportion to the seriousness of the offense." But the trajectory of the third-strike sentencing provisions is in exactly the opposite direction. No matter how modest the base term of imprisonment in the determinate sentencing scheme, the minimum punishment under Three Strikes is 25 years, and 80% of that minimum must be served.

Our preliminary study of the administration of the Three Strikes law suggests two distinct kinds of disparity problems. The first is the distinction between third-strike thieves and thieves with different types of criminal record. Third-strike penalties, which are much higher than the standard terms of imprisonment for the same offense, are inconsistent with the ethic of antidisparity as expressed in the 1976 legislation, even though the longer and more serious criminal record of the third-strike offender might justify some difference in punishment. The second kind of disparity is the extreme difference in punishment between third-strike felons who are sentenced under the terms of the law and the great majority of those eligible for third-strike sanctions who are not so prosecuted.

Table 7.2 begins our analysis of sentence disparity by contrasting the "middle term" of the determinate sentence for each of six offenses with the minimum punishment that the sentencing judge must impose if the convicted offender already has two strikes. The rightmost column in the table shows the ratio between the standard and Three Strikes minimum sentences for each crime, which is understated because the adjustment of allowable good time is not estimated.

The gap between the standard and the Three Strikes minimum

Table 7.2. Presumptive Sentence and Third-strike Sentence, Selected Felonies

	Middle Term	Three-strike Minimum	Ratio
Rape	6 years	25 years	4:1
Robbery, first degree	4 years	25 years	6:1
Robbery, second degree	3 years	25 years	8:1
Burglary, first degree	4 years	25 years	6:1
Burglary, second degree	1 year[a]	25 years	25:1
Grand theft	2 years	25 years	13:1

[a]Can be charged either as a felony or a misdemeanor.

Source: California Penal Code §1170(a)(1).

sentence is quite substantial for all of the listed offenses, but the law provides much larger escalation of sanctions for less serious felonies than for the more serious crimes. The rape offender who qualifies for a third strike will receive a minimum sentence just over four times the middle term he would have received without any qualifying criminal record. For first-degree robbery the ratio is 6:1; for grand theft the third-strike severity is 12.5 times the base penalty; for second degree burglary, the third strike increases the minimum sentence by a factor of 25.

There are three problems with the pattern of punishment outlined in table 7.2. The first problem for a penal code that is supposed to be focused on the seriousness of the criminal act is that the offender's criminal record increases the minimum punishment by such a high multiple. Conviction after an arrest for grand theft results in imprisonment rather infrequently in our sample, occurring in 24 out of 182 cases, or 13.2%, in 1993. When nonconviction cases are excluded, the ratio of imprisonment increases to just under 1 in 4. But Three Strikes not only requires imprisonment for such an offense but also multiplies the minimum sentence by a factor of more than 12; it also increases the gap between no-strike and third-strike prison time to about 20 to 1. A second-degree burglar with no prior convictions will serve a 1-year sentence; but a third-strike second-degree burglar will serve about 30 times as long in the California prison system. Since these two widely different sentences are based on the commission of similar crimes, the magnitude of the escalation for recidivism is a clear disparity problem in a jurisdiction where the basic jurisprudence is "act-based."

The second distinct problem raised by the table is the nonproportional or indeed antiproportional impact of third-strike penalties. As long as the base penalty for a particular act does not exceed one-third of the Three Strikes minimum, the third-strike classification adopts a "one size fits all" theory of sentence severity in which crimes of greatly differing seriousness and social harm produce identical 25-year-to-life sentences. The presumptive middle term for a rape charge in California, which is 6 years, is six times as long as the middle term for second-degree burglary and twice as long as the middle term reserved for second-degree robbery. The Three Strikes minimum for any of these crimes can be regarded as nonproportional because the seriousness of the particular crime has no bearing on the severity of the sentence.

A characterization of the third-strike pattern as nonproportional may be too charitable, however, because in one respect the *escalation* in punishment that is imposed because of the offender's prior criminal record is inversely proportional to the seriousness of the current offense. A rapist with two prior strikes will suffer a penalty four times as great as the ordinary penalty for rape as a result of his criminal record under the 1994 legislation, whereas a second-degree burglar will suffer a penalty 25 times as great because of the nature of his prior criminal convictions. The less serous crimes uniformly generate the largest penalty escalations, and the most serious crimes, such as rape and robbery, multiply punishment at far lower rates. To create a "one size fits all" outcome, the third-strike provisions have to turn ordinary considerations of proportionality upside down.

The third problem with the pattern profiled in table 7.2 is the inconsistency between the assumptions of dangerousness and public priority and the escalation of punishment that is observed at the third-strike level. The most serious four of the six offenses listed in the table are classified as strikes in California and will triple the penalty if the offender commits another felony. But burglary in the second degree and grand theft are not strikes, so the 1994 legislation does not require any additional minimum punishment at the next felony conviction. The distinction between the two classes of offenses must be based on the greater harm, the closer proximity to a violent outcome, or the larger severity of the more serious strike crimes. Yet it is these least serious crimes, the ones that do not require aggravated punishment, that become the basis for the largest increments in punishment when there are two prior strikes in a criminal record. And this is not an inconsistency that comes from the interaction of Three Strikes with other provisions in California law; it is instead an internal inconsistency in the 1994 legislation.

Selective Enforcement and Disparity

We have compared the sentences of third-strike offenders guilty of various crimes with the presumptive sentences that nonstrike defendants would receive for the same offense. Although the wide gap in punishment is troublesome to an act-based jurisprudence, the same cases did not elicit different punishments. Instead, different sorts of offenders with different criminal records received substantially dissimilar penalties. Yet the way in which the statute has been enforced also produces textbook cases of sentencing disparity because the great majority of persons eligible for third-strike treatment did not get 25-years-to-life prison terms. When offenders with two-strike records are charged with the same offense and convicted of what could be felony charges, they are equal in the eyes of the law but they can receive substantially dissimilar punishment. The third-strike defendant who pleads guilty to a misdemeanor or is returned to prison as a parole violator is out in 6 months. His or her officially processed neighbor gets 25-years-to-life.

Before Three Strikes became law, the subjects in our 1993 sample who had at least two prior strike convictions and a current criminal conviction for burglary received a median sentence of 24 months. After Three Strikes became law, the median prison term for persons with two strikes who were convicted of burglary was 72 months, six times the median sentence for no-strike defendants and three times as high as the average sentence before Three Strikes. However, aggregating the penalty obscures a very large variation in criminal sentences. Two of the eight Three Strikes burglars received 300-month sentences that will produce 20 years of time served before the possibility of parole. These offenders received sentences of imprisonment more than four times as large as the 72-month median sentence, and the actual time served will be seven times that served by persons with qualifying records who escaped formal sanctioning under the new law.

The situation for those charged with theft is even more extreme. The 10 offenders convicted of theft with Three Strikes qualifying records received average prison terms of 24 months before Three Strikes, and that median term grew to 32 months in the postlaw sample for the 6 offenders who were eligible for Three Strikes. But 2 of the 6 received Three Strikes sentences of 300 months minimum and will serve at least 240 months. The other 4 thieves will serve less than one-tenth of the sentence the statute says they deserve. Moreover, the gap between the Three Strikes and non–Three Strikes penalty is again much greater for the less serious offense of theft (at 12 to 1) than for the more serious offense of burglary (just over 4 to 1). When more serious crimes like robbery and rape are the predicate crimes of third-strike sentences, the difference in punishment will be smaller. So we again confront the irony that the less serious the crime, the greater the aggravation in punishment that is caused by the defendant's criminal record in the third-strike category.

We must speculate about the punishment escalation in Three Strikes cases that involve crimes of violence because none of the six sentences in our sample was linked to a defendant convicted of a violent crime. In this respect our sample differs from the wider experience of Three Strikes in California, where 35% of all third-strike sentences followed arrests for a violent crime and an additional 10% followed weapons violations (California Department of Corrections 1999).

If both the proportionality and the disparity problems generated by Three Strikes are considered important, the law enforcement community in charge of administering the law confronts a dilemma. If sending away petty thieves and nonaggressive burglars for 20 years of secure confinement is considered a serious compromise of a system of proportional punishment, an obvious solution is to enforce the law only very selectively for serious crimes of violence or truly extensive criminal careers. But this kind of selective enforcement does more than defy the spirit and the letter of the Three Strikes law. It also produces circumstances of extreme disproportionality of punishment when the occasional burglar or pickpocket is given a prison sentence grossly in excess of the punishments administered to other defendants equally culpable in the eyes of the law.

Conclusion

The problems of principle that Three Strikes have generated for criminal punishment in California are the product of multiple causes. There is, first, the internal inconsistencies in the statute, where, for example, the seriousness of an offender's current crime has an important influence on the new term of imprisonment for a second-strike conviction but not for a third-strike conviction. There is, second, the glaring inconsistency between the principles of punishment emphasized in California's determinate sentencing scheme and the priority distinctions for the distribution of punishments in Three Strikes. The act-centered focus of determinate sentencing is as far removed from the "any felony equals 25-years-to-life" of the third-strike provisions as any two principles for criminal sentencing now existing in the Anglo-American legal world.

If the contrast in principles between determinate and Three Strikes sentencing is extreme, the policies and principles served by a sentencing system that mixes these two are an unprincipled jumble. The existence of a single strike marks the boundary between discretion and mandatory imprisonment, and the existence of a second strike provides a transition between a sentencing scheme in which the seriousness of the defendant's current crime is of great importance and one in which it is irrelevant. We know of no one who believes that the current mixture of sentences can be rationalized; but then no one feels the need to justify the joint product of determinate and Three Strikes sentences. The determinate scheme has its constituency of defenders and the Three Strikes system has its constituency, but nobody seems to feel the need to rationalize the current operation of the system as a whole. Furthermore, questions about proportionality and disparity have not played a prominent role in debates about Three Strikes in California.

The patterns in determinate sentencing might have played a role in creating a demand for a scheme of offender-based punishment that would allow substantial additional punishment for persons thought to be dangerous. Over the last generation, the current system of criminal sentencing in California seems to have resulted from a series of extreme pendular swings from offender-based to offense-based and back to offender-based sentences. But because the Three Strikes provisions apply only to a minority of California felony cases, the two systems now coexist and jointly produce a hodgepodge of penal outcomes that defy collective justification.

Has this unprincipled jumble been regarded as a major problem in California? Absolutely not. Although disproportionate results, such as a life sentence for the man who stole a slice of pizza, have received some public attention, the systemic incoherence of California's criminal sentencing has captured the attention of no important constituency in the nation's largest state. There is general interest in estimating both the costs and benefits of Three Strikes, but the absence of principle is a serious problem on no one's agenda.

EIGHT

Living with Three Strikes: Courts, Corrections, and the Political Process

The statute passed in March 1994 was both the culmination of a political process (discussed in chapter 1) and a singular chapter in the legislative, administrative, and political history of criminal justice in California. This chapter is an attempt to briefly outline some major developments in the first half decade after the new law took effect, changes that can be attributed to Three Strikes, and the reaction to it in various government and political constituencies. The major headings in this analysis are the courts, the state correctional system, and the politics of criminal justice.

This recent history of Three Strikes as a penal regime is important in its own right and also a significant indication of the extent to which radical reforms in penal law are influenced by their implementation process. For political matters, the boundary between "before" and "after" is November 1994, when California's voters adopted by initiative the Three Strikes provisions that were identical in scope and language to the legislation passed in March of that year. For operational purposes, the new regime was launched in March 1994.

The Courts

The administration of California's Three Strikes law put pressure on the state's judicial system in two ways. The new law increased the judicial resources necessary by raising the penal stakes in thousands of felony dispositions and altering the incentives available to induce guilty pleas and other waivers of procedural protection. The recipients of this type of pressure were principally the criminal trial courts in metropolitan counties. The second set of pressures was felt most acutely by the California Supreme Court, which was forced to decide a number of questions concerning the scope of a new statute that was anything but a model of clarity.

As we shall see, the case-processing pressures on courts that were created by Three Strikes were substantial, but the trial crunch fell far short of the system-paralyzing seriousness that some had projected. The pressures on the California Supreme Court were more subtle, and the record of the court in responding was mixed.

Trial Courts: The Not-quite Crisis

Those who regarded the passage of Three Strikes as a disaster for California's trial courts based their estimates on the theory that the mandatory prosecution of thousands of cases that carried very high minimum prison terms would increase the number of defendants who demanded full procedures in the processing of their criminal cases, including preliminary hearings and felony jury trials. Even though the new law would generate no new felony prosecutions in California, the shift of a significant number of felony cases from guilty pleas to full criminal trials would put overwhelming pressure on a court system that had become addicted to nontrial dispositions in more than 90% of all felony cases.

This was the basis for a series of predictions about the increasing demand for court resources under the new legislation. The official forecast in 1994 of the Los Angeles District Attorney's office was that felony jury trials would more than double between 1994 and 1995 (Feeley and Kamin 1996, p. 147). An administrator in Los Angeles projected an increase in criminal trials that would leave only half as many judges available for civil trials in that city. Other projections ranged between a doubling and a tripling of trials.

During the first years of Three Strikes, its actual impact on court resources has been substantial but far short of the paralysis that had been projected. Most criminal courts were required to allocate more of their resources to processing criminal cases, and this resulted in some reported reduction of judicial resources that could be allocated to general civil cases over the same period (California Judicial Council 1996). The additional workload reported by most of the counties with many criminal cases was between 10% and 25%, by no means an increase of paralyzing proportions.[1]

How did the trial courts avoid the disaster that would have resulted if thousands of criminal defendants had insisted on full criminal trials? Two separate diversionary processes rescued the superior

[1] Only two counties reported increases of more than 25% (California Judicial Council 1996).

courts from collapse under the new statute. First, the mandatory provisions for second-strike offenders left ample room for plea-bargaining incentives after such charges were filed. Figure 8.1 compares the median trial rates reported by superior courts for three classes of cases: no-strike filings, two-strike filings, and three-strike filings.

Although defendants insisted on trial twice as often in second-strike cases as in no-strike cases, the median trial rate for the former is a comparatively modest 9%, which is slightly more than one-fifth of the trial rate the same courts report for third-strike filings. The crucial statistic from the standpoint of the administrative health of the superior courts is that more than 90% of the second-strike cases were disposed of without trial. The large gap between second-strike and third-strike trial rates is strong evidence that there was ample room for plea bargaining in second-strike cases. One easy path to a lower sentence is to accept a plea to a felony charge that carries a smaller sentence than the initial charge. As we observed in chapter 4, the number of prison sentences for second-strike cases in California was

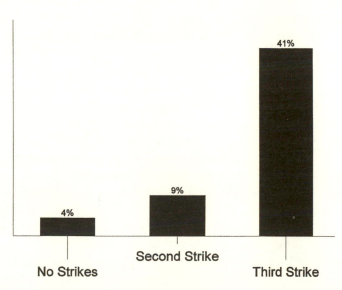

Figure 8.1. Median Trial Rate by Case Type—Survey of Superior Courts. Source: Judicial Council of California. 1996.

substantial. What saved these cases from crushing the trial court system were the incentives that kept nontrial dispositions over 90%.

But what saved the court system from being crushed by the high trial rate of three-strikes cases? A 41% trial rate would be a prescription for administrative disaster if there had been a high volume of cases in that category. The prediction that the prospect of a mandatory minimum term leaves defendants with little to lose if they fully contest the charges is not contradicted by the data for three-strike offenders. However, the system was rescued by the low volume of completed third-strike prosecutions. With a prosecution rate as low as 10%, the court system survived the pressure of third-strike trials because the new law was subverted by nonprosecution.

Appellate Review

With the exception of federal constitutional challenges, the provisions of California's Three Strikes legislation are matters of state law on which the Supreme Court of California is the final and binding authority. The substantial deference that federal courts have paid to the behavioral assumptions and penal categories in the states' habitual-criminal legislation have all but removed California's Three Strikes legislation from a plausible constitutional attack based on due process, equal protection, or cruel and unusual punishment. This in turn means that the main arena for judicial review of Three Strikes has been the California Courts of Appeal and the California Supreme Court. The latter is the ultimate authority on the new statute and has been closely observed.

Challenges to the scope and validity of the Three Strikes legislation came before the California Supreme Court less than a decade after the politics of criminal justice had reshaped and reoriented the court in a manner never previously seen in American history. In 1986, the chief justice of the California Supreme Court and two of the six associate justices were removed by a majority vote in a recall election that had been launched with the vigorous support of California's governor. The three judicial vacancies were quickly filled by appointments of judges with judicial philosophies closer to the views of "law and order" Governor George Deukmejian.

The impact of this change on court personnel was not hard to measure. Before the three removals, the court had *reversed* more than 80% of the death penalties that came before it on appeal, the second-highest rate of reversal among states with large numbers of such appeals. After the removal, the California Supreme Court presided over by Chief Justice Malcolm Lucas *affirmed* more than 80% of the death sentences, the third-lowest rate of reversals among states with high-volume death cases. (see Kamin 2000).

The political developments of the preceding decade had two probable impacts on the Supreme Court. First, most of the judges had been selected by Governor Deukmejian and his Republican successor Pete Wilson, both men who were reputed to require pro–law enforcement orientations as a necessary condition for appointment. Second, all of the judges in the California Supreme Court had acquired proximate experience with the potential political costs of judicial hostility to popular criminal justice policies like capital punishment. If ever a successful challenge to a Three Strikes law would seem to be a difficult proposition before a state supreme court, California in the 1990s seems to be the place.

The usual way in which a dispute about the Three Strikes statute came to the California Supreme Court was after the superior court judges made rulings based on competing constructions of the statute and the losing party appealed the lower court's ruling. This appeal would be heard by one of the state courts of appeal. The losing party there could petition the Supreme Court. The contested issues that reached the state's high court by this route were both numerous and various. Do findings of juvenile delinquency based on factual allegations that would constitute strikes in the criminal court count as strikes against the former juvenile in a later Three Strikes prosecution? Can two criminal convictions coming from the same course of conduct on the same day be regarded as two separate strikes in a later prosecution of the defendant under Three Strikes? Does a criminal conviction for an offense in another state that would have constituted a strike if committed in California stand as a strike in any subsequent Three Strikes sentencing? Can a superior court judge disregard a previous strike conviction of a defendant on his own motion and over the objection of a prosecutor? When the same conduct leads to two separate felony convictions covered by the Three Strikes legislation, can the judge sentence the offenses concurrently or does Three Strikes require consecutive sentences?

The usual contest in Three Strikes litigation before the California Supreme Court was at its core a competition between ordinary canons of construction in criminal statutes and "get tough" legislative intent. The defendant who is opposing a judicial construction that the statute required his pre-1994 juvenile record to count as a prior strike will argue that the penal provisions should be strictly construed and held to their clear and essential meanings. The proponent of a broad reading of Three Strikes will emphasize the unambiguous intention of the drafters to increase punishment for recidivist felons as broadly defined. When the technical meanings in the Three Strikes statute are not clear, the district attorney will emphasize the pervasively punitive intentions of the persons who drafted the language.

As might be expected, in any simple competition between canons of construction and legislative intent, the California Supreme Court was inclined to adopt a broad reading of Three Strikes to effectuate the maximum punitive result. Court decisions have turned away constructions of the statute that would have disallowed out-of-state convictions and prelaw juvenile adjudications and would have restricted multiple felony convictions arising from the same act to a single aggravating strike for the purposes of future Three Strikes liability. In these cases, the results have been predictable and the court's methodology transparent.

People v. Benson, decided by the California Supreme Court in 1998, is representative of the "law-and-order" versus "strict construction" style of argument. The defendant in *Benson* had "entered an apartment intending to assault the resident and did so, stabbing her some 20 times. For that atrocious act, he was convicted of (1) burglary for entering the apartment with the intent to assault and (2) assault with intent to commit murder" (Chin, dissent, *People v. Benson* 74 Cal. Rptr. 2d 294 at 302). The question under review was whether the burglary and assault convictions that were based on the same transaction can be considered two separate strikes, so that any further felony conviction carried a 25-years-to-life term. A closely divided Supreme Court decided that question in the affirmative.

In *People v. Davis* (1997), the Supreme Court confronted the portion of the Three Strikes statute that allows use of a juvenile court finding of delinquency as a strike if, among other conditions, "The juvenile was found to be a fit and proper subject to be dealt with under the juvenile court law" (Mosk dissent, 64 Cal Rptr. 2d 879, 884 quoting Cal. Penal Code §667 (d)(3)(c)). Because express findings of fitness occur only when juvenile court judges reject the transfer of cases to criminal court, requiring these findings would reduce the number of juvenile court adjudications later eligible for strike treatment. A four-member majority of the Court held, to the contrary, that every juvenile found delinquent by juvenile courts had been implidely found fit, and this would suffice under the terms of the Three Strikes law. The problem with that construction of subsection C was that under it the requirement would have no meaning in the context of the other provisions of the law, as the dissenting justices were quick to point out. All of the juvenile court findings that meet the other requirements of the statute would automatically also satisfy subsection C. The majority rejoinder on this issue was to point out that "the presence of some duplication in a multiprong statutory test does not automatically render it meaningless" (*Davis*, 1997, 64 Cal. Rptr. 2d 879, 883). The opinion did not, however, provide any theory for the separate purpose of the subdivision as the majority of the justices had interpreted its language.

Two times in five years, law-and-order constructions of Three Strikes failed to win judicial approval. In each of these cases, the California Supreme Court rejected an interpretation that would extend the mandatory reach of the statute at the expense of traditional judicial prerogatives. The most famous example is *People v. Superior Court (Romero)*, decided by a unanimous Supreme Court in June 1996. The issue in *Romero* was whether superior court judges retained the power to disregard a defendant's previous strikes for sentencing purposes "in the interests of justice" when the Three Strikes legislation expressly gives that power only to prosecutors. The Supreme Court relied on other statutes that conferred on judges the right of dismissal and found that the new statute itself did not compel a construction that such judicial power was removed. Missing from the opinion in *Romero* are references to the intent of either the voters or the legislature in passing Three Strikes. The majority opinion was satisfied to argue that the legislative language does not compel the conclusion that judges lack the power to discount strike offenses in the interests of justice.

The other restrictive reading of Three Strikes by the California Supreme Court involved a similar contest between traditional judicial prerogatives and mandatory punitive impact. The issue in *People v. Hendrix* (1997), whether a judge had to impose consecutive sentences on persons convicted of more than one felony, also depended on construing ambiguous language in the statute. The Supreme Court adopted a reading of the statute that left the judge free to choose between consecutive and concurrent sentencing.

Judged in its entirety, the California Supreme Court's *corpus juris* on Three Strikes gets much higher marks for practical impact and political bravery than for the quality of its judicial reasoning. Notably missing from the Court's opinions are any attempts to fashion a penal theory of the law as a whole as a test against competing interpretations of particular provisions. As daunting as the task might be, a coherent theory of what the statute is attempting to achieve would seem to be an important aspect of resolving disputes about the meaning and scope of the statutory language. There is also an evident inconsistency in interpretative style when the majority opinions of the court on Three Strikes are surveyed. A slavish search for the meaning of each word in a phrase animated the court's decision in *Benson* to allow a single transaction to count as multiple strikes. Yet an entire subsection of the provision, defining when juvenile court findings constitute strikes, was rendered a nullity in *Davis* without regret. None of the California Supreme Court's pronouncements in the first five years of Three Strikes stand as notable examples of rigorous judicial reasoning.

However, the practical impact of the Supreme Court's decision in *Romero* was substantial and far outweighed the punitive effect of the liability enhancements allowed in *Davis* and *Benson*. By allowing trial judges to disregard prior convictions as strikes in the interests of justice, the California Supreme Court gave trial judges the power to avoid 25-year-to-life sentences for minor crimes even when prosecutors were adamant in their pursuit of that result. There are substantial indications that this judicial prerogative is frequently exercised in jurisdictions like San Diego, where prosecutors for third-strike sentencing are common (Marion 2000).

The other judgments of the California Supreme Court will affect the outcomes of far fewer cases than will *Romero,* for two reasons. First, enhancements of penal liability will only be urged on trial courts in those cases in which the prosecutor chooses to push the law to its limits. In a state where as few as 1 third-strike case in 10 is punished as such (see chapter 5) there may not be so many cases that the prosecutor wishes to push to the very outer limits. Second, trial court judges who doubt the appropriateness of a juvenile court strike or of double strike liability for the same transaction can always invoke the power provided to them by *Romero* to set aside a strike "in the interests of justice." The majority opinion of the court in the *Davis* case explicitly refers to this possibility. On balance, the supreme court cut back on the mandatory extremes of the Three Strikes statute far more than it had enhanced them.

The significance of the judicial power recognized in the *Romero* case did not go unnoticed by the political friends and sponsors of Three Strikes. Bills were introduced in the legislature that purported to undo the *Romero* result, and a ballot initiative to reverse it by amending the state constitution was threatened but not pursued in earnest. Nevertheless, all seven justices on a state court that had experienced the electoral removal of three of its members only 10 years before were willing to risk the political consequences to preserve traditional judicial prerogatives. Although this was bravery infused with self-interest, it was also the first important government action to test the political power and will to punish of Three Strikes supporters.

Prisons: Estimating Eventual Impact

The government function most directly affected by the Three Strikes legislation is the state prison system. The currency of Three Strikes is mandatory sentences that are far longer than had been available or used in previous law. The first government effort to estimate the impact of the Three Strikes proposals was a population projection by the California Department of Corrections in February 1994 at the request of California's government. Projections of this kind involve two kinds of guesses. First, the observer must estimate the proportion of offenders who fit the eligibility criteria for enhanced sentences under the Three Strikes law. The second guess concerns the proportion of eligible offenders who will actually receive the sentence provided for in the legislation.

Figure 8.2 contrasts the projections of prison populations throughout the remainder of the 1990s with and without the Three Strikes provision. The 1994 projections assume a non–Three Strikes baseline of 46% growth throughout the 1990s, from 115,000 in 1993 to more than 165,000 in 1999. Adding the law produces an increase that starts in 1995 with the projection of 6,000 more inmates and quickly expands to a total prison population of 245,000 in 1999, or 80,000 prisoners more than the non–Three Strikes estimate for the same year.

It did not take long for these extraordinary projections to be contradicted by early experience with the new legislation. The total California prison population with Three Strikes had in fact stayed close to the non–Three Strikes projections in figure 8.2 throughout the late 1990s, mostly because projections assumed that 75% of all persons eligible for strike enhancements would receive them. This estimate is at least four times higher than the actual figure for third-strike cases.

In the period after Three Strikes became law, the California Department of Corrections has been gearing down its population projections. Figure 8.3 compares annual projections for the total postlaw

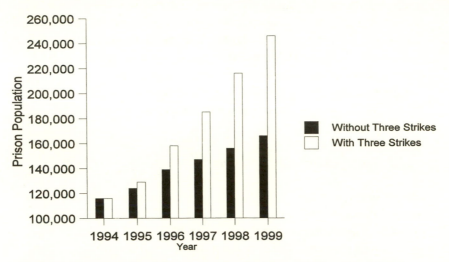

Figure 8.2. Projected California Prison Population, With and Without Three Strikes.
Source: California Department of Corrections, 1999.

prison population from the February 1994 study with subsequent projections published in the fall of 1995 and the fall of 1996. The original estimates projected that the population would increase by an additional 130,000 between 1993 and 1999 if Three Strikes became law. By the fall of 1995, the projected growth had been cut by 50,000, from 130,000 to 80,000, for the target year 1999. By the fall of 1996, a set of revised projections reduced the 1999 population target to 170,000 prisoners, a six-year increase of 55,000 and well under half of the original six-year projection.

What can statistical adventures like these teach us, other than the extreme vulnerability of prison population projections (see Zimring and Hawkins 1992, chap. 5)? The pattern observed for prisons—much smaller legal impact because prosecutors and courts avoid Three Strikes penalties—is apparently quite similar to the accommodation seen in criminal trial courts. In each case a large and potentially destructive impact on the demand for government resources was avoided by discretionary actors who undermined the mandatory intentions of the substantive law. But there is an important difference between the long-term prospects for trial courts and those for the prison system.

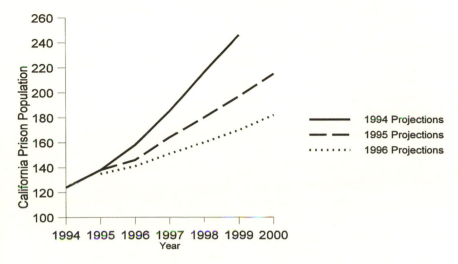

Figure 8.3. Three Different Corrections Department Projections of California Prison Populations.
Source: California Department of Corrections, 1994–1996.

The demand for a criminal trial occurs at the front end of processing in the criminal justice system. Unless extraordinary delays occur, this year's trial burden will pass through the system and leave little, if any, residual demand on the courts in future time periods. By contrast, the effect of long mandatory prison sentences on prison resources is cumulative over time, and in the case of third-strike sentences it is cumulative with a vengeance. Assuming a constant rate of 25-year-to-life third-strike offenders admitted to the prison system, the cumulative burden is 20 times as large in the twentieth year of operation as it is in the first. That is, the system will contain 20 years' worth of sentenced offenders at that juncture compared to only 1 year's worth shortly after the law goes into effect, and the 20:1 ratio of the total correctional burden may actually understate the degree to which the regime increases correctional costs. Because many of those habitual felons sentenced under Three Strikes would have served time in any event, the marginal difference between Three Strikes and non–Three Strikes demands on prison resources will be greatest in the later years of the mandatory sentences. The largest gap in total prison resources will occur relatively late in the game.

Figure 8.4 illustrates this phenomenon by assuming a constant

monthly flow of new cases at 100 per month, quite close to the current average, and contrasts the rate at which three-strike offenders
are admitted to California prisons with the number of such offenders
in prison for the first 20 years of the statute. No releases are possible
before the end of year 20. At what point releases start thereafter and
in what volume is not currently known. What the data and projections demonstrate is the sharp and steady growth in the inventory of
third-strike prisoners over the first two decades of California's Three
Strikes law. There are two potential escape routes from the numbers
in figure 8.4 other than legal change. First, the introduction of new
prisoners could decline further if that section of the law falls to even
lower levels of prosecutorial and judicial use than currently obtain.
There are no indications of this as yet. The volume and rate of third-
strike sentences starts low and stays low, but the volume of new
commitments for a third strike is stable through the middle of 1999.
Second, we have made no adjustments in the projections for inmates'
deaths. As the third-strike population ages, death rates will increase,
although they will probably stay small throughout the first two decades of the law.

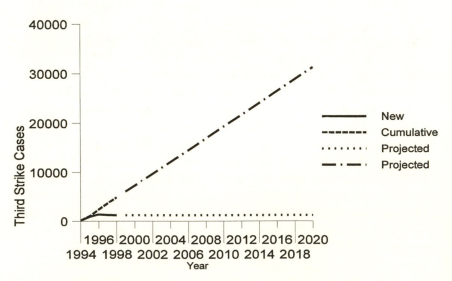

Figure 8.4. Third Strike Prison Population, 20-Year Projection.
Source: California Department of Corrections, 1999 (Pre-1999 Three
Strikes admissions and inventory; projected admissions are a steady
state projection).

Second-strike offenders have a much larger impact on the size and composition of California's prison population than third-strike offenders in any plausible short- or middle-term projection of the law's effect because nine times as many offenders are sentenced under the second-strike provisions. But this volume is also harder to project over the long run because most of these offenders are released much earlier than third-strike offenders can ever be. Figure 8.5 shows year-end totals for second-strike offenders for the calendar years 1995 to 1998. Between 1995 and 1998, the population of second-strike offenders increased from 13,500 to 39,000. The growth in this category represents more than 100% of the total growth in California's prison population over the three years (26,000 second-strike offenders versus 24,000 total).

Our findings in chapter 5 show that most of these two-strike imprisonments would have occurred even without the 1994 law, although for shorter terms. Whereas some offenders can be released

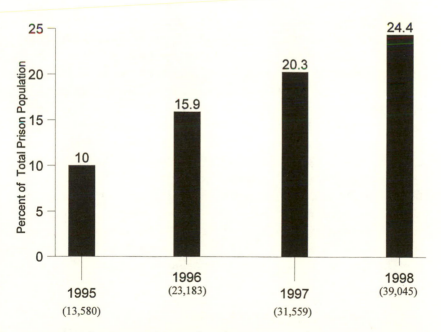

Figure 8.5. The Impact of Second-strike Cases on California Prison Population, 1995–1998 (December 31 Population).
Source: California Department of Corrections, 1999.

from second-strike sentences after two or three years, the number of new second-strike admissions was overwhelmingly larger than the number of releases throughout the first five years of Three Strikes. The second-strike group increased as a share of the total prison population from 10% in 1995 to over 24% in 1998 and was still expanding by more than 4% of the total prison population per year by the end of 1998. Even if the growth rate levels off abruptly in the near future, the second-strike group will probably represent one-third of California's prison population by the end of 2002. The rate of future growth in this population is difficult to project. Many more second-strike offenders will be released, and the net effect of additional commitments becomes a multifactorial guessing game.

However, it turns out that we know a lot more about the impact of prison populations under Three Strikes than the early history of official correctional projections would suggest. The high and inaccurate projections of the early years are misleading in two respects. First, because the sentences that are accumulating under Three Strikes are both mandatory and determinate at the minimum term, our capacity to project their future claim on correctional resources will improve dramatically with the passage of time. If we again assume a constant rate of third-strike sentences per year, after 15 years of experience with the legislation, three-quarters of all the third-strike offenders who will be serving time in year 20 will already be in prison during year 15. Projecting that part of the prison population is not formidably difficult. Second, the population impact of these long terms is smallest in the earliest years of the law's administration. The cumulative impact of 1,200 25-year-to-life sentences each over a 20-year period would be substantial even though that number of prison admissions in a single year is almost invisible in a California-size system (see figure 8.4). With respect to the trial courts, the experience under the Three Strikes law can be justifiably characterized as a crisis that was avoided. As for the prison system, the proper interpretation of the early experiences with Three Strikes is that a crisis has been deferred. Californians will pay dearly for their Three Strikes sentences, but they will pay on the installment plan.

The Politics of Criminal Justice

The Three Strikes initiative had four near-term effects on the politics of criminal justice in California. First, the controversy helped to re-elect an incumbent governor, who turned into a born-again law-and-order candidate early in the 1994 election. Second, the new statute brought to political prominence the Fresno photographer, Mike Reynolds, who had directed the California Three Strikes campaign from its inception. Whereas Governor Wilson was associated with many issues, Reynolds was a single-issue celebrity with a much larger stake in the continued importance of crime in California politics.

Third, a precedent was created of using the threat of an initiative to induce legislative action. Three Strikes was not the first time that matters affecting sentencing and criminal justice were subject to electoral initiatives. Proposition 8 had passed a multipart "victims' rights" initiative in 1982 that was serving many of the same constituencies that later supported Three Strikes (McCoy 1990). But Three Strikes was the first "outsider"-drafted legislation to pass the legislature and become law, months before citizens were to vote on it in initiative form. Using the prospect of an initiative as the basis for making demands on the legislature was a brand new wrinkle in California politics.

Fourth, Three Strikes created a demand for more crime proposals. Although it was a fabulously successful example of outsiders' influence on criminal justice legislation, its ratification as an initiative in November 1994 by the voters was not an unmixed blessing for its authors. Once the law was passed and validated, its authors had worked themselves out of a job. Furthermore, once a proposal that was meant to be a partisan wedge to divide political parties is accepted on a bipartisan basis, its advocates had to shop around for new issues that would force political enemies to the other side of the question. No matter how major the change that is adopted, when proposals quickly become both legislative and bipartisan orthodoxy, they cease to function in the political sphere to define partisan differences and to motivate partisan passions. Far from being able to savor victory at leisure, the advocates of Three Strikes were deprived of an important political vehicle by its broad political acceptance. If Mike Reynolds and the other outsiders who nurtured Three Strikes were to stay active and relevant in California politics, they needed new vehicles to maintain criminal justice as a front-burner issue. If Pete Wilson's political opponents accepted Three Strikes, the pressure was on the governor to find a "get tough" proposal that Democrats would not support.

The recent history of California politics proves that bipartisan success necessitates new bones of contention. The same day Governor

Wilson signed the Three Strikes legislation in March 1994, he proposed a one-strike program to allow life terms for selected sex offenders after a single conviction. Shortly after his successful initiative campaign, Reynolds made a public presentation of a "10-20-
Life" proposal, which would compel additional and consecutive 10-
year sentences for the use of a firearm in a felony, 20-year additional
sentences if the firearm were discharged during the commission of
the felony, and additional 25-year-to-life terms if a victim were in-
jured or killed. The last thing that either Mike Reynolds or California's law-and-order Republicans want to see is crime disappearing as
a partisan political issue. A deemphasis of crime in the political
process would marginalize the crime advocacy groups. From that
perspective, a perfect "Three strikes and you're out" bill, once
passed into law, would be an embarrassment to its progenitors. The
career of the 10-20-Life proposal in the mid-1990s involves all four
elements of the political legacy of Three Strikes and thus deserves
sustained attention.

The Saga of Assembly Bill 4

The search for new criminal justice proposals to be used in political
campaigns began, literally, on the day that California Governor Wilson signed Three Strikes into law. But although the number of "get
tough" proposals proliferated, no single one attracted the substantial
hard-line coalition that had united behind Three Strikes in the early
months of 1994. Having just signed legislation that included every
substantive change that was in the Three Strikes initiative, Governor
Wilson introduced a new proposal for life imprisonment for sex offenders, which he referred to in his remarks at the signing ceremony
as a one-strike program. This proposal attracted very little attention
in the spring and summer of 1994 as the gubernatorial campaign developed. None of the major groups involved in Three Strikes had a
need for diversifying their political portfolios in the middle of 1994
because the Three Strikes initiative was still to be voted on in the November election. The last thing Mike Reynolds needed in the summer and fall of 1994 was a criminal justice issue to distract voters
from the initiative version. One-strike life terms for sex offenders
died quietly.

If a new criminal justice initiative was the last thing that Reynolds
needed in the summer of 1994, however, it had become his highest
priority by early winter. The overwhelming electoral endorsement of

Three Strikes simultaneously presented Reynolds with his greatest triumph and threatened to remove him as an important presence in California political life. Without an issue of potential importance in the election, the father of Three Strikes could maintain a certain degree of celebrity but no real political power. Unless Reynolds were to run for office himself, new issues would be necessary to ensure his relevance in the electoral process.

The new focus that Reynolds selected was an initiative campaign to provide long mandatory sentence enhancements to persons convicted of using firearms in serious or violent crimes. First introduced at a press conference in January 1996, the initiative proposal would add on a consecutive 10-year sentence for offenders convicted of carrying or possessing firearms while committing a violent or serious crime, provide a 20-year add-on if a gun were fired in the course of a serious or violent crime, and add on a mandatory 25-years-to-life if the gun caused injury or death (Cousart 1996). When compared with the Three Strikes initiative, the firearms plan shows both continuity and contrast. Its currency of law reform is mandatory lengthy prison terms, as it was in Three Strikes. The substantive sentencing provisions in the new plan were organized around a sound-bite slogan 10-20-Life, just as the earlier proposal had been molded around "Three strikes and you're out."

But the jurisprudence of 10-20-Life was a marked contrast to the approach in Three Strikes. The special danger targeted in the latter was the career offender, and even the least serious theft required a 25-year-to-life term if the defendant's record contained two strikes. In the language of chapter 7, the 10-20-Life proposal is offense-based rather than offender-based and extended the same mandatory long term to defendants (including juveniles) regardless of their previous criminal record. But the large doses of mandatory punishment that were prescribed in the 10-20-Life proposal applied only to offenses in which the presence of a firearm or its use signified an immediate threat to human life. When Three Strikes and 10-20-Life are considered jointly, the two proposals might be regarded as complementary, as long as the only general principle being served is the beneficial effect of long and mandatory terms of imprisonment for serious crimes or criminals. Whatever the specific problem being addressed, hefty doses of penal confinement is the answer of choice.

The continual emphasis on mandatory consecutive penalties suggests that criminals are not the only enemies contemplated in the Three Strikes and 10-20-Life worldview. Both proposals are pack-

aged to make it clear that discretionary power is to be avoided because government officials (particularly judges) are not to be trusted.
In this regard, one of the great attractions of the initiative process to
the Reynolds group is that it bypasses the processes of representative democracy. It is probably not incidental that even after the success that Three Strikes enjoyed in the California legislature, Mike
Reynolds chose to design his second major political salvo as a campaign aimed primarily at voters. If part of the appeal of a campaign is
mistrust of government, there is good reason to search for political
means that minimize the necessity for consorting with the enemy.

Whatever the appeal of direct democracy, the political and economic support that are required to qualify an initiative for a popular
vote in California is a formidable barrier for most citizen action
groups. More than 400,000 valid voter signatures are required to
place a proposal on the ballot, and the economic resources necessary
to generate that mandate are more than considerable. The 1996 campaign for 10-20-Life lacked the financial and political support of the
National Rifle Association, which had been critical to Reynolds in
the early days of Three Strikes. By May 1996, it was publicly acknowledged that 10-20-Life could not meet the deadline for the 1996
November election with a sufficient number of signatures (Podger
and Howard 1996).

Two developments rescued the 10-20-Life proposal from obscurity
after it failed to qualify for the 1996 initiative ballot: the sudden importance of gun control as a California legislative issue in 1997 and
the strategic decision of Democratic leaders in the legislature to
coopt, rather than to oppose, the proposal for further mandatory sentences. By 1997 the Democratic party had recaptured majorities in
both houses of the California legislature, and Democrats in the
assembly were pushing high-profile proposals to restrict assault
weapons and to ban the sale of those handguns defined as "Saturday
night specials." For Republicans, mostly opposed to any further restriction on the sale or possession of firearms, debates about gun control create a need to propose legislation that simultaneously does not
inconvenience gun owners yet holds some potential for reducing gun
violence. Increasing mandatory sentences for gun crimes is one such
strategy, and Republican legislators were quick to introduce the 10-
20-Life proposal as their alternative to gun control.

The need to provide a rhetorical alternative to firearms control
may inspire politicians to introduce mandatory prison term legislation, but the requirements of rhetoric do not usually involve the ne-

cessity of passing such laws. A legislative stalemate in which neither the mandatory punishments nor the restrictions on firearms became law would usually be considered a satisfactory outcome by anti–gun control forces, who are a legislative minority. For a variety of reasons, however, Democratic legislators decided to coopt and amend the 10-20-Life proposal rather than to oppose it. One motivating factor may have been the desire to pass gun control legislation and put real pressure on a Republican governor to sign it. Passing the mandatory minimum legislation would preserve the Democrats' tough-on-crime credentials and thus put some pressure on the governor to rise above partisan actions. A second important motivation was to avoid the threat that the 10-20-Life proposal would qualify for the statewide ballot in 1998, just in time for the *next* gubernatorial election.

For all these reasons, representatives of the Democratic majority entered negotiations to amend the 10-20-Life proposal that had been a faithful reproduction of Mike Reynolds's version when introduced into the assembly by Republican Representative Bordonaro. The amended version did not alter either the long terms of imprisonment or the provisions that made them consecutive and limited good-time reductions to a maximum of 15%. Instead it seems that the principal objective of the Democratic negotiators was to reduce the number of cases that would qualify for this mandatory treatment. The major change was the deletion of assaults committed by firearms from the statutory coverage unless the offender was a prisoner or the victim a law enforcement officer. Because a substantial majority of all crimes committed with firearms are assaults, this single change cut back the case coverage of Assembly Bill 4 to a fraction of its former scope.

A deletion of the assault category is tactically brilliant but strategically quite problematic. What sets firearms crimes apart from other types of violent crimes is the higher probability of the victim's death or life-threatening injury, and what distinguishes the scaling of the bill's mandatory minimum punishments is the larger danger to the victim that is present when there is injury (25-years-to-life) or a firearm is discharged (20-years-to-life) than is the case when a firearm is merely used in a crime (10 years). From this perspective, however, a firearms assault would seem a poor candidate for deletion from the statutory provision because aggravated assault carries a much higher death risk than any other common violent crimes (Zimring and Hawkins 1997, fig. 4.11, p. 69). The effect of removing assault was to create a law with a broad constituency and no rationale.

In one respect, however, a 10-20-Life proposal without assault is more in the spirit of Three Strikes than Mike Reynolds's original gun crime proposal. The removal of assault will concentrate the law's impact on robbery cases rather than the range of domestic assaults and barroom fights that fit less neatly into a conception of criminality that emphasizes the division between ordinary citizens and violent criminals.

Assembly Bill 4 was passed by both houses of the California legislature and signed into law in September 1997. However, Governor Wilson vetoed the ban on the sale of Saturday night specials that had also been passed by the legislature, using the familiar argument "Common sense dictates that the best way to prevent gun crimes is by first removing from society the criminals who use guns in the commission of a crime" (Wilson 1997a, p. 64).

The legislative success of the bill caused the same occupational crisis for Mike Reynolds as did the passage of the Three Strikes initiative. Pushing for an initiative version of 10-20-Life that would include more offenses was obviously foolish. The original proposal fell far short of qualifying for the 1996 ballot, and no important hard-line constituency was dissatisfied with the version of the plan that had become law. Indeed the enactment and administration of the bill's penalties were not prominent political events in the California of 1997—an extraordinary contrast with the emotional intensity and media visibility of "Three strikes and you're out." In an era of declining crime rates, the public's attention span for mandatory imprisonment was evidently much shorter in California than the Democrats in the state legislature had feared. Thus, 10-20-Life may have passed as a bluff.

Mike Reynolds solved his personal occupational crisis by taking the campaign for 10-20-Life on the road to other states with an evident receptiveness to this innovation in law-and-order politics. As of 1999, no major proposal for further mandatory imprisonment was on the political horizon in California. But even if there is a long pause in law-and-order politics, the political legacy of Three Strikes is anything but stability in the administration of criminal law. As long as those engaged in electoral politics sense that there is a political advantage in proposals for mandatory punishments, new proposals will come forward on a regular basis. In the short term, Three Strikes encouraged further proposals with the sweet smell of electoral success.

If electoral politicians are tempted by the political opportunities of "get tough" proposals, those who make their living in the single-issue politics of California criminal justice must constantly work to destabilize law and practice or resign themselves to unemployment. A candidate for governor can emphasize law and order this week and highway construction next week, but the head of a victims' rights group or a law-and-order lobby does not have a diversified portfolio. The significance of the single-issue politician depends on continual political turmoil in his or her area of interest. As a structural matter, therefore, the existence of a large single-issue crime constituency will operate as a destabilizing influence on criminal law and its administration. This was the clear lesson in California of the first three years under Three Strikes, and the story of Mike Reynolds's recent career suggests that any pause in law-and-order politics in California is in part attributable to efforts to export many of its components of revolutionary change.

Conclusion

The politics and operations of criminal justice in the early years of Three Strikes are certainly not business as usual by any standard. But the criminal justice system did both accommodate and subvert the intentions of those who drafted the statute. The net result was a substantial change in sentencing practices in the direction of increased severity administered at the discretion of prosecuting attorneys and judges, rather than a regime of functioning mandatory punishment.

A crisis in the operation of trial courts was avoided in second-strike cases by prosecutorial plea-bargaining concessions that kept the rate of trials in such cases under 10%. A crisis in the operation of trial courts was avoided in third-strike cases by highly selective enforcement by prosecuting attorneys. Defendants did request jury trials quite frequently when prosecuted on third-strike charges, but prosecutors persevered in only a small fraction of eligible cases. Our three-city study estimated a ratio of eligible second-strike defendants to eligible third-strike defendants of slightly over 2.5:1, but the ratio of second-strike prison sentences to third-strike prison sentences was 9:1. It appears that the basic thrust of the second-strike provisions of the law was accommodated in practice, whereas the mandatory intentions of the third-strike provisions were ignored.

The record of the California Supreme Court when construing ambiguous phrases in the new statute is mixed. In the early years of Three Strikes, when the competition was solely between the usual canons of construction in criminal cases and the "get tough" agenda of Three Strikes, the Supreme Court created a series of "get tough" constructions that were not infrequently problematic. But the court's insistence in *Romero* that the trial courts retained the power to ignore the aggravating impact of prior strikes in the interest of justice was of more practical importance in creating a flexible administration of Three Strikes than all the court's law-and-order holdings combined. When compared with the behavior of other statewide officeholders, the performance of California's Supreme Court justices in the first five years after Three Strikes seems to be courageous.

The short-term impact of the Three Strikes era on California prisons was not substantial. The proportion of second- and third-strike defendants who were imprisoned after the new law did not increase sufficiently to immediately change the rate of increase of the prison population. The aggregate prison population continued to increase at rates close to those experienced in previous years, and the initial projections of the Three Strikes impact made by the California Department of Corrections were ludicrously high. On the other hand, a steady stream of very long prison sentences will be leaving a residue of additional prisoners behind bars for much longer terms, and this process will reach its maximum impact 15 and 20 years after 1994. The only way to avoid such an outcome would be to further reduce the percentage of cases eligible for third-strike treatment that actually receive it. The 100 or so persons classified as third-strike felons who reach California's prisons each month are already a tiny fraction of those eligible for such treatment. But that flow of third-strike offenders will have to be cut even more, or else tens of thousands of inmates will become a permanent residue in the California correctional system beginning in the first decade after the millennium.

The passage of Three Strikes has, meanwhile, energized a single-issue politics that has destabilized the legal principles and operating practices of the criminal justice system. The long shadow of "Three strikes and you're out" has already prompted the passage of a new package of mandatory minimum sentences for offenders who use firearms. And although the legislators cut back on the number of cases in this new wave of mandatory sentences, the reduction in caseload came at the price of any semblance of principle in the legislation.

The rigidities in Three Strikes and its progeny will be undermined by the exercise of prosecutorial and judicial discretion. But to depend on these discretionary diversions is in fact to widen the gap between the law in theory and the law in practice and to increase the awesome and unreviewable discretionary powers of prosecutors. In the first years after Three Strikes, the criminal justice system has continued to operate in the state of California, but at a greater distance than ever before from the provisions of the substantive criminal law.

Part IV

IMPLICATIONS

NINE

The Changing Politics of Criminal Punishment

In this chapter we will provide two complementary historical perspectives on the story of Three Strikes and extract lessons about the political science of crime policy. First, we will put Three Strikes within the historical context of criminal justice policy in California and in the United States, searching for continuity between this development and trends in crime, imprisonment, and criminal justice policy. Second, we will assess what the development of Three Strikes can teach us about the changing determinants of government policy toward crime and criminals in the United States.

Three Strikes represents an extreme example of two common elements in American criminal justice policy, the means of policy formation and its substantive direction. The means that generated Three Strikes was direct democracy, the most direct form of popular participation. The substantive ends were sharply higher terms of imprisonment. The distinctive features of the 1994 story are the extent to which each pattern was a more extreme form of a tendency common during an earlier period in policy-making. What can these patterns tell us about how the current politics of criminal justice are driven and how far the trends toward populism and punitiveness will extend?

The first section presents hard data on changes in crime and punishment in the quarter of a century that preceded Three Strikes. The second section briefly outlines perspectives on the politics of punishment derived from recent American history. The third section discusses a link between broader trends in government and politics and the politics of criminal justice. The path of this chapter is from descriptions of objective trends toward the range of theories about government action on criminal justice policy.

Trends in Crime and Criminal Justice

This section presents data on three dimensions of criminal justice in California: the population, rates of crime, and rates of prison and jail occupancy. We begin with the state's population, which figure 9.1 shows for each year between 1952 and 1995. The second half of the twentieth century was a period of explosive growth in California's population for four decades, followed by a slight pause in the early 1990s. During the period from 1950 to 1990, the population more than doubled, and by 1970 California replaced New York as the most populous state in the union. Although the growth rate was somewhat steeper in the early years of the postwar expansion, its magnitude was never larger than in the 1980s. This explosive growth in population was the central social and government characteristic of California after World War II. The state's principal occupation was growth, and the constant phenomenon of increasing population interacted with all other social and institutional changes to produce qualitatively different outcomes. During the 1980s, for example, the officially documented population of the state expanded by 30%. With no other change in the crime rate or crime policy, that expansion alone would generate a substantial increase in the volume of crime and in the scale of the criminal justice system's response through arrests, trials, incarceration, and supervised releases. When expanding population interacts with increases in crime rates or punishment, a significant pattern of compounded growth results.

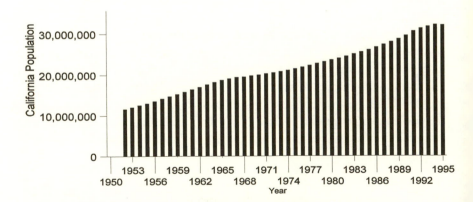

Figure 9.1. California's Population, 1952–1995.
Source: U.S. Census Bureau, Population Division, Population Distribution Branch.

Moreover, the 30% increase in California's population during the 1980s was not only made up of new residents but also represented a shift in the kind of groups that were arriving there. Unless there is a long-term consistency in the social and geographic origins of new migrants, high levels of growth through migration introduce a different mix of ethnic and nationality groups from the population base of the state. All during the second half of the twentieth century, the sense of difference that was associated with fresh immigration was augmented by ethnic, linguistic, and cultural contrasts between old residents and their new neighbors. This phenomenon was particularly characteristic of California after the mid-century because of the exceptionally high rate of growth that persisted in the West, where California was the major population center.

Crime

Figure 9.2 compares rates of homicide per 100,000 population in the United States for the period 1971–1995 with homicide rates for California. The California pattern clearly parallels national trends, with fluctuations first down and then back up in a cyclical fashion for more than two decades. The high homicide periods both nationally

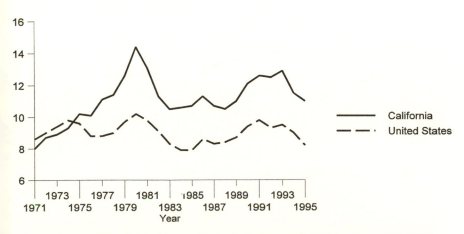

Figure 9.2. Homicide Rates, United States and California, 1971–1995. Source: U.S. Department of Justice, FBI, 1971–1995.

and in California occured around 1974, 1980, and 1991, with significant declines in the early 1980s and then again after 1992.

When the six index crimes traditionally targeted by the Federal Bureau of Investigation (FBI) are the subject of the analysis, the crime trends in the United States and in California show a cyclical pattern again, but there is also some continuation of a general upward trend until the early 1990s. Figure 9.3 contrasts the trends in index crime for California and the United States as a whole but does not begin its reporting period until after the change in the definition and measurement of larceny, which took place in 1973.

In general, the statewide trends in California are representative in both magnitude and direction of nationwide changes. In one sense, however, such a comparison obscures one difference: Whereas rates per 100,000 population are the most appropriate measure of the individual risk of becoming a victim of crime, higher densities of population may result in a higher rate of exposure to observing crime or knowing its victims even when the rate of crime per unit of population remains constant.

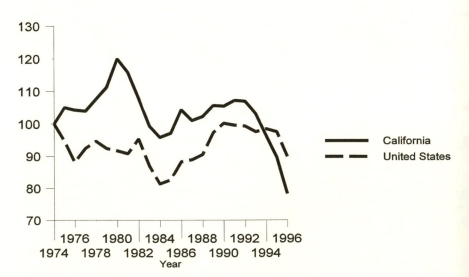

Figure 9.3. Trends in Six Index Crime Rates, United States and California, 1974–1996 (1974 = 100).
Source: U.S. Department of Justice, FBI, 1974–1996.

A close examination of the temporal pattern of California crime carries both good news and bad news about crime as a civil problem in the time period immediately surrounding Three Strikes. On the one hand, there is nothing in an analysis of either lethal violence or crime generally to suggest that rates are either higher in the early 1990s than in earlier periods or that California's crime was significantly different from national patterns. But the bad news in the early 1990s is that reported rates of lethal violence and crime in general were not significantly lower than at any previous point in recent history. The hope-inspiring downturn of the early 1980s had been completely neutralized by increases in the late 1980s. The fact that very high crime rates may be regarded as a chronic rather than an acute phenomenon might lead to higher rather than lower levels of anxiety and anger. And the similarity in the California and national trends may simply suggest that a nasty mood about crime and criminals might also be found broadly in the United States of that period. Indeed, everything that we know about the United States in 1994 suggests that California had no monopoly in anger about crime and criminals (see Zimring and Hawkins 1991, p. 129).

There is one further feature of the California scene that might have increased the frustration of the early 1990s. The return to chronically high levels of crime and violence in the late 1980s occurred in spite of an extraordinary expansion in the rates of imprisonment throughout the 1980s. For those who had faith in the efficacy of large doses of imprisonment to reduce crime rates, the upturn may have been more unacceptable, more infused with a sense of urgency because it was unexpected.

The Growth of Imprisonment

Figure 9.4 compares trends in rates of imprisonment per 100,000 population for the United States as a whole and for the state of California between 1960 and 1995. Rates of imprisonment in the United States declined through the 1960s and reached a low in 1972; then they went upward without interruption every year thereafter. By the mid-1990s the rate of imprisonment, controlling for population change, had more than doubled. The pattern in California is slightly different in its timing and more dramatic in the rapid pace of growth and the magnitude of change. The uninterrupted increase in California did not begin until the very end of the 1970s. There was a downturn briefly in the prison population in 1977 and 1978 that was

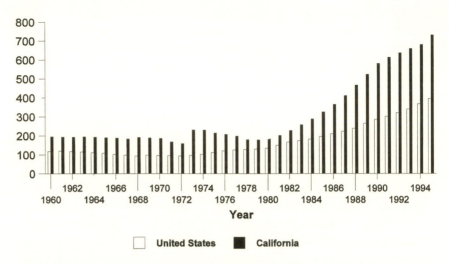

Figure 9.4. Rates of Imprisonment, United States and California, 1960–
1995.
Source: U.S. Bureau of Justice Statistics, 1998, Tables 6.36 and 6.37; California Department of Corrections, 1996.

caused by the release of a large number of prisoners who benefited
from the shift from indeterminate to determinate prison terms; they
had already served more prison time than the new system would
have imposed (see Messinger and Johnson 1977; Zimring 1983).
When the rate of imprisonment did go up on a sustained basis after
1979, the California incarceration rate expanded further and faster
than the rates of other metropolitan states.

One other feature of the growth of imprisonment in California is
missing from the trend outlined in figure 9.4—the interaction of expanding rates of imprisonment with a substantially expanding state
population. During the 10 years after 1980, the prison system grew
more than fourfold in total persons confined. By 1991, the state of
California had by far the largest prison system in the Western indus-
trialized world (see Zimring and Hawkins 1994). By the early 1990s,
some state systems, like those of California and Texas, were much
larger than not only the limited jurisdiction of the U.S. federal prison
system but also the total prison systems of major European countries
such as Germany, Italy, France, and Great Britain (Zimring and Hawkins 1994). Four characteristics of the prison expansion that any
comprehensive, theoretical explanation must address are illustrated

in figure 9.4: First, the large and uninterrupted expansion of the use of imprisonment, observed since the mid-1970s, was a national trend and not a development peculiar to California. The pace of growth in California is larger than the percentage growth documented in the national aggregate, but the similarities between them are far more important than the differences. So the features of the environment that are driving prison populations to historic heights are national in scope. Unprecedented penal severity in the last quarter of the twentieth century is not merely a "left coast" phenomenon. Second, the extraordinary growth of imprisonment is a very large shift in system behavior that is far removed in time from the 1993 and 1994 campaign for Three Strikes. National aggregates for imprisonment had been increasing for 5 straight years and stood at record levels 15 years before the California electorate voted on the statute.

Third, the growth of imprisonment in both California and the United States is noncyclical in recent decades. Consecutive increases rather than short cycles of up-and-down movement have become the rule in prison populations. Nationally, rates of imprisonment have increased for 26 consecutive years as of this writing, and the uninterrupted growth streak is 20 years in California. Because crime rates have exhibited cyclical fluctuations throughout the period since 1960, the noncyclical character of the prison population performance means that trends in imprisonment rates have not tracked trends in crime rates with any regularity in recent years. Crime increased dramatically while prison population rates drifted downward in the United States before 1972, and then rates of imprisonment began an uninterrupted upward trajectory that has not moderated during sustained periods of a decline in crime in the early 1980s and middle 1990s. When the trajectory of imprisonment rates is unrelated to fluctuations in the crime rate, it is a plausible inference that changes in policy play a major role in explaining the former.

Fourth, the sustained increases in rates of imprisonment over the past decades were not consistently related to longer terms of imprisonment or changes in penal legislation. No Three Strikes style of mandatory sentences and no steady trend toward longer periods of time served were linked to the large expansions in prison populations up to the late 1980s. By far the more important contribution was a larger number of offenders going to prison rather than increases in the average term of imprisonment. Chapter 7 demonstrated that the major sentencing change in California went into effect in 1977, and this law contained no sentencing provisions intended to promote expansion in the prison population. That is, the huge growth in the 1980s took place without any major changes in sentencing law (Zimring and Hawkins 1992). What changed, all over the state and all through the 1980s, was sentencing *practice,* not legislative directions for crime and punishment.

Having reviewed some trends in American crime and imprisonment, we believe, first, that the passage of Three Strikes is embedded in a set of long-term trends that must themselves be understood if we are to satisfactorily explain why California adopted that kind of law in 1994. If imprisonment trends are an important indicator, and we think that they are, then the Three Strikes legislation is part of a process that had been operating for almost two decades before the law was passed.

Second, we conclude that the same processes that were at work in California were responsible for radically changing levels of serious punishment throughout the United States. Thus, looking for the origin of Three Strikes in California is properly viewed as searching for the manifestation of a larger national trend in one particular state. The fact that a majority of American jurisdictions had passed some version of Three Strikes by 1997 is further evidence of this effect. Most of the forces that launched Three Strikes in California were present as well in many other states.

Third, whereas the language of the Three Strikes statute was confined to defined types of criminal recidivism, the larger and longer terms had as their subject crime and criminals without any sustained special emphasis. The general themes seem more important than the specific subtopics when the long-term trends are examined. Three Strikes in this sense was reflecting general sentiments on criminals.

Fourth, one further aspect deserves special mention. The sharp expansion of penal confinement has not yet been widely emulated in other Western nations in recent times. Table 9.1 compares imprisonment trends in the Group of 7 (G-7) nations, a "convenience sample" that we collected for a previous study over the period 1960–1990. The United States stands alone in this comparison not only in its very high rate of imprisonment in both reported periods but also in its growth rate, far more than twice as great as any other of G-7 nation. Although David Garland (1996) has argued that trends in the United Kingdom are in the same general direction, the pace of growth has been much slower there, and the 1990 rates of confinement (94 per 100,000) reported are not very far removed from those of France (82 per 100,000) or Germany (78 per 100,000).

Table 9.1. Imprisonment Rates (per 100,000), G-7 Countries, 1960 and 1990

	1960	1990	Percentage Change
United States	118	292	+148
United Kingdom	58	94	+62
France	59	82	+39
Canada	35	45	+29
Germany[a]	85	78	−8
Italy	79	57	−27
Japan	66	32	−51

[a]Data for March 1961.

Source: Home Office, 1961 and 1991 (United Kingdom); Istituto Nazionale di Statistica, 1961 and 1991 (Italy); Ministere de L'Economie et Des Finances, 1961 and 1991 (France); Statistics Bureau, 1961 and 1991 (Japan); Statistics Canada, 1961 and 1991 (Canada); Statistisches Bundesamt, 1962 and 1991 (Germany); U.S. Department of Justice, Federal Bureau of Investigation, 1961 and 1991 (United States); World Health Organization, 1961 and 1991 (all nations).

It may well be that other industrial democracies may follow the lead of the United States in the future, but the contrast in punishment may be an important clue in searching for the roots of Three Strikes. Whatever has been driving the distinctively punitive responses in the United States has not yet had that impact in the other developed nations.

Three Strikes and Politics of Crime

Whereas the structure of Three Strikes in California was unique, much of its political process was typical of the politics of crime in the mid-1990s. This statute is an extreme form of crime and recidivist legislation, but the federal government and 25 other states passed some similar form of legislation during the period between 1993 and 1996. Moreover the themes that were emphasized in these campaigns—public fear and anger over crime, lenient treatment of criminal offenders, the need for victim's rights, and so on—played important roles in the passage of the truth-in-sentencing legislation in many states and a comprehensive federal crime-control bill in 1994. Although the political pressure may have been somewhat more intense in California after the Polly Klaas tragedy, the nature of public opinion about criminal justice in California in 1994 was typical of the political sentiments nationwide.

Contemporary press accounts of the California campaigns mention high crime rates, high levels of public fear and anger, and the belief that criminal punishments were unduly lenient. However, objective data on crime rates show that levels of violent crime had been fluctuating around peak rates achieved in 1974 and 1980. There was nothing new about the crime levels of the early 1990s, but the chronicity of the problem may very well have been one of the things that fueled public anger. Also, media coverage of crime may serve as a stimulus to fear and anger that is independent of variations in crime rates. A single case like the Polly Klaas kidnapping may excite widespread feelings of insecurity because high-status victims in relatively secure environments are also vulnerable to predators. Even a single event of that kind can provoke insecurity and anger in millions of homes.

But whereas fear and anger may be linked to each other in a public response, they are very different emotional states with very different distributions across populations at any given time. One important question is: What elements other than the rate of crime influence levels of public fear? Another key question is: What factors in a social and political landscape translate fear into anger?

The Dual Agency of Fear

Our own comparison of the Three Strikes campaign in California with developments in other states during the same period suggests two conclusions about the relationship between public attitudes and political activity. First, public opinion has a dual role in the political process. It is misleading to think of public anger and fear as solely an *input* in the political process—that is, a set of largely external forces that cause political activity—and equally misleading to regard public attitudes about crime as solely an *output* of the political process, in the sense that public attitudes are a result of political activity rather than a preexisting cause of action by politicians and legislators. The level of emotional arousal, the kinds of emotions that members of the public feel about criminal justice and criminals, and the importance of crime to individuals are important influences in the political process, but the relationship is a simultaneous equation because the treatment of crime and criminal justice in the political process affects the level of feeling, the type of feeling, and the importance of criminal justice as a government issue. Public attitudes are both a cause and an effect of the politics of criminal justice.

Second, high levels of public feeling about crime and criminal justice may be a necessary condition of political action, but it is far from a sufficient condition for major changes. The homicide rate was no higher in 1994 than it was in 1974, and presumably citizens were just as fearful at that earlier time, but the enormous rise of violent crime in the United States over the decade 1964–1974 had surprisingly little impact on the legislative process or the administration of criminal justice. The major federal legislation during the period, the two gun-control acts passed in 1968, was closely linked to the assassinations of Robert Kennedy and Martin Luther King, Jr. (Zimring 1975, part I). There was little pressure for structural change in state penal codes and no upward pressure on state prison populations until after 1973. Crime rates rose and prison populations fell. It might well be that the upward push on prison populations that began in the mid-1970s can be regarded as a delayed reaction to increasing rates of crime in the late 1960s. But why the long delay?

One reason that fear of crime was associated with substantial political activity in the mid-1990s is that the character of public opinion had changed. It could be said that people felt equal levels of fear in 1994 and 1974 but that public attitudes about what governments should do in response had changed substantially. We think that this interpretation is plausible, but it also begs a number of important questions. How and why did public opinion change? It is important to remember that the political process can play an important role in citizens' attitudes toward and expectations about crime policy. Undoubtedly there was a different climate about government policy in the mid-1990s. We suspect that much of the transformation in public opinion was caused by the way in which political actors talked about crime in the intervening years. The different opinions of the 1990s were as likely to be an effect of political rhetoric as its cause.

It is also important to remember that although the aggregate pressure for political action on crime was substantial nationwide, the amount of legislative response varied enormously. By late 1998, the federal government reported the imprisonment of a total of 35 offenders under its 1994 version of Three Strikes, whereas California had imposed second-and third-strike mandatory terms on a thousand times as many offenders (compare Campaign for an Effective Crime Policy 1998 with California Department of Corrections 1999). What accounts for this enormous difference? And might the answer to that question be more important in practical terms than finding out what political forces cause a jurisdiction to pass some version of a bill that calls itself "Three strikes and you're out"?

The Political Science of Contingency

Here are two important questions about the contingencies that influence changes in criminal justice policy: (1) What factors transform citizens' feelings about crime into changes in government policy? (2) What factors in politics or government determine the form and content of changes in government policy? The first question asks, in effect, why did both California and the federal government pass Three Strikes laws in 1994? The second question asks: Why was it that California passed a law designed to have an impact a thousand times that of the federal statute?

The first issue we address here is what factors other than the intensity of citizens' concerns about crime will determine whether democratic governments will change criminal justice policies. We can explore this question by comparing periods of high and low change in crime policy in the same locales and by comparing government systems that exhibit high levels of change in policy and governments that do not. By all such measures, the United States in 1994 was operating in a period of high government activity on the crime front, and the Untied States in cross-sectional comparison with other democracies would be regarded as an exceptionally high-activity locale after 1975.

But what elements of a society and government predispose the system to change policies in response to citizens' concern about crime and criminals? We nominate four factors as predictors of levels of government activity:

1. Widespread agreement on the appropriate means of the government's response to crime
2. Confidence in the crime-reducing efficacy of the tools available to the government
3. The importance of crime as a topic at the level of government that makes crime policy
4. The responsiveness of criminal justice agencies to political pressure.

These factors predict whether or not government policy will change but not necessarily the extent of that change. A review of the

circumstances in the United States in 1993 and 1994 will demonstrate the favorable disposition toward government action on all four
dimensions.

Consensus on Government Policy

One of the puzzles in both Britain and the United States is that
citizens' belief that criminals are treated too leniently actually increases when prison populations and other objective indexes of the
seriousness of punishment are increasing. We showed that public
support for the proposition that punishment was too lenient increased
during the sharpest and longest increase in imprisonment in American history (Zimring and Hawkins 1991). Mike Hough and Julian
Roberts (1999) reported that the percentage of the British public that
thought that the treatment of criminals was too lenient had increased
to 92% from 67% between 1981 and 1996. Meanwhile, the British
prison population was increasing 50% in the five years after 1991
(p. 12).

What seems like a paradox may actually be an artifact of changing
public beliefs. If there emerges over time a widespread consensus on
the part of the citizenry that more imprisonment is an appropriate
government response, increasing majorities will report that the current levels in particular jurisdictions are inadequate. If there is substantial division in a population about the appropriateness of long
prison sentences for burglars, that division will be reflected in
smaller majorities of the population who believe that the punishments for burglars are too lenient. If agreement grows that extensive
imprisonment is an appropriate response to burglary, the percentage
of the population dissatisfied with the sentences currently given to
burglars can be expected to grow. At the same time, the existence of
widespread consensus that imprisonment is appropriate is an important predictor that government policy will change. A growing consensus that increases dissatisfaction also increases punishment.

This scenario is one example of a more general relationship between public opinion and government action. If the public feels
strongly that crime is a problem but there is no substantial agreement
on the correct government response, the likelihood of government
action will be decreased by the lack of consensus on the type of action that the government should take. If public attitudes change over
time in the direction of a larger consensus on the right way to respond to crime, that makes government action more likely; this rela-

tionship also makes political actors who wish to produce changes in government policy into salesmen for the appropriateness of particular types of government responses. Creating consensus becomes an important task in the politics of change.

The absence of consensus in the late 1960s and early 1970s might explain the relatively low levels of change in government policy, and the larger agreement on a punitive response in the mid-1990s explains high levels of policy change, including the Omnibus Crime Control Bill of 1994 (see Windlesham 1998), the hard-line policy on youth violence (Zimring 1998, chap. 1), truth-in-sentencing provisions in state law, and "Three strikes and you're out." The need for a consensus on crime control might also explain why a time lag may be necessary in many circumstances to broker consensus on appropriate responses.

Confidence in the Efficacy of Government Action

The prediction here is the following: A strong belief by citizens that measures available to the government can significantly reduce crime will be associated with higher levels of policy change than will occur when citizens are skeptical about whether there is much that the government can do. Belief in the efficacy of government action is of course linked to widespread agreement about appropriate responses to crime, but consensus and optimism about efficacy are different aspects of public opinion. Large majorities of the population may believe that harsh punishments for criminals are appropriate for serious crime, whether or not they have much impact on the crime rate. That certainly seems to be the prevailing public attitude about capital punishment in the United States in the 1990s.

When the consensus on the appropriateness of policy coexists with belief that actions by the government can make the streets safer, the prospects for substantial changes in policy are very bright. There is, of course, a positive correlation between ideological consensus and instrumental optimism about the effectiveness of crime control. If everybody believes that imprisonment is the right thing to do, this will be associated with the opinion that imprisonment prevents crime. But it is also quite possible that high degrees of consensus about appropriate punishment exist in periods when citizens are not very confident about its instrumental efficacy. For reasons that are easy to understand, periods of rising crime rates tend to be associated with low levels of optimism that government programs can substantially reduce crime rates (Zimring and Fagan 2000). It is probably no coincidence that Robert Martinson's (1974) argument, that "nothing works" in rehabilitation programs, and George Kelling and Anthony Pate's (1977) study, demonstrating the ineffectiveness of doubling police car patrols, were published in the mid-1970s, just after a decade of uninterrupted expansion of crime. In the middle of a relentless crime wave, it is hard to imagine that yet another round of government responses can stem the tide.

Periods of sustained decline in crime are associated with citizens' optimism about the ability of governments to make the streets safer. Declining crime rates create a real-world precedent for the kind of decline that citizens wish to see produced by government initiative. All other things being equal, the role of a decline in fostering optimism about the efficacy of government efforts produces something close to a paradox: Political action on crime may be more likely in periods of decline (when citizens have confidence in the efficacy of government initiatives) than in periods of increase (when confidence in the efficacy of government action is lower). This sort of hypothesis might help to explain the gap that sometimes exists between periods of high public anxiety and periods of extensive political and government change. The effort to pass laws can more easily be justified when citizens believe that legal change can generate palpable improvement in crime rates.

Citizens' confidence in the ability of government may be a more important predictor of support for large and costly programs than for smaller and principally symbolic changes in legal structure. The intensity of public anxiety may itself be a sufficient cause of punitive and inexpensive responses to crime. But the disposition to spend large amounts of the public purse on anticrime programs may depend more on levels of belief that money will have a measurable impact on public safety.

Criminal Justice as a Government Priority

If a government unit's attention is spread over a wide variety of different and important responsibilities, those who hope to change crime policy will need to compete with other important policy areas. If the number of important policy domains is smaller, the prospects for government action in the crime area increase substantially. If this thesis holds true, two elements in the United States in the 1990s predicted higher levels of government action than in other countries or in earlier times.

The first characteristic that distinguishes the United States from many other countries is the federal system of government and its historic placement of responsibility for criminal justice among state and local governments. The national government has plenary authority over a host of important problems ranging from national defense to foreign affairs to economic policy and beyond. But it plays a relatively small part in the administration of criminal justice, with fewer than 15% of all police and administrative responsibility for less than 10% of all prisoners (Zimring and Hawkins 1996).

The 50 state governments that dominate the administration of criminal justice have a far smaller portfolio of other important concerns, a short list that includes major responsibility for education and roads and shared power with the federal government in a number of areas like health and welfare policy. This smaller portfolio means that criminal justice looms large on the horizon of state governments, and it receives attention in the form of legislation and other policy changes. In most Western nations, the larger responsibility for crime and justice rests with the national level of government, so criminal justice concerns must more frequently compete with foreign affairs, national defense, and so on. When the critical level of government is the national government, the smaller relative importance of crime in relation to all other issues predicts a lower level of attention and a lower propensity for policy changes. When criminal justice responsibilities reside in national government, the crime problem is one child in a large family. When the responsibility for crime and justice is concentrated in state governments, the issue moves far closer to the status of an only child.

The relative importance of crime as a government issue will also vary over time, and much of that variance will be produced by developments in noncrime issues. There is nothing like a world war to distract a government's attention from, say, purse snatching. Similarly, periods of economic crisis tend to crowd matters like criminal justice out of the inner circle of immediate concern. The most recent illustration of this phenomenon took place in 1991 when a national economic recession displaced public concern about drug abuse as the nation's number one problem. The converse is that a "war on drugs" or a sustained crusade against crime is far more likely to develop in an era of peace and prosperity, when the relative importance to government of crime and criminal justice is highest. Crime panics may be more frequent when the rest of the news is not troubling.

The Responsiveness of Criminal Justice Policy to Electoral Control

It seems plausible that those government systems whose penal policy can be easily influenced by legislation and voters' behavior are more likely to experience high levels of political activity around the topic of criminal justice than systems in which politics and even legislation have little impact on the actuality of practice. The extreme case is the totalitarian regime, where both the procedures and substantive content of criminal justice policy cannot be touched by either legislative action or citizens' voting, and thus it would be unlikely to experience high levels of political activity concerning criminal justice issues. If those institutions that are available to citizens and elected representatives have little or no power to affect penal policy, there would be little incentive to expend energy or resources on the creation of legal changes that would have no practical effect. In government systems where judicial and administrative officials are responsive to the electorate's sentiments and demands, we expect that the incentive to legislate change would be greater. In that sense responsiveness to populist action creates an environment in which a larger volume of political and legislative action is to be expected.

The importance of government responsiveness in predicting the level of political activity may depend on the type of change in criminal justice that citizens want. If the public desire is chiefly for symbolic denunciation of crime and criminals, the ability of legislative actions to achieve operational change may not be important, and the relationship between government responsiveness and the level of political and legal change may be a weak one. If the criminal law's "bark" is more important than its "bite," citizens will be satisfied with any political activity that makes the right kind of loud noises. If, however, practical results are an important motivation, the relationship between the power of politics to influence penal policy and the volume of legal change produced will be a strong one. Our own guess is that symbolic and denunciatory agendas are sufficiently strong to guarantee a steady stream of advocacy and legislation that may be of little operational effect. On this basis we would predict a weaker relationship in the political system between the level of political and legislative activity on criminal justice and its capacity to influence operational outcomes.

There may be another reason that the demand for legislative activity on criminal justice matters may be relatively inelastic in terms of a practical payoff. If the public's concerns with crime-related matters cannot be displaced to other political topics, the level of the practical payoff available from legal change may not even be strongly related to the level of political reward that comes from policy proposals and political appeals. If votes and popular approval can be obtained by focusing on the crime issue, the potential for an impact on the operations of the criminal justice process may be a secondary matter. If the objective of a law-and-order campaign is to get elected, rather than to influence criminal justice, incentives to conduct such campaigns are principally located in the political rather than the government domain.

With all these contingencies, it is by no means clear that the ability of the political system to change operational outcomes in criminal justice has a consistent and major influence on the amount of political activity devoted to criminal justice or on the number of legislative changes by political action. Where the responsiveness of operational policy to political influence will make a big difference, however, is not on the level of legislative activity but instead on substantive criminal justice policy.

Determining the Impact of Politics on Government Action

Among the more sobering anecdotes in the recent political history of criminal justice in America is the contrast in Three Strikes legislation already mentioned. The U.S. Congress passed a "Three strikes and you're out" law in 1994 that has had a direct legal influence on the criminal sentence of 35 offenders in its first four and a half years. The state of California passed such a law in 1994 that has had a direct legal influence on the criminal sentences of more than 40,000 offenders in the same span. This stunning difference raises questions about whether the two laws should be regarded as examples of the same phenomenon. The economist Herbert Stein (1998) made a comparison that we believe applies to these extreme examples: "Now these developments do have some things in common just as a beheading and a haircut have some thing in common. But the differences are so great that to discuss them as part of the same continuum is misleading and confusing" (p. 8).

The contrast between the federal and California versions of Three Strikes demonstrates the operational importance of variations in modes of legislation with the same title and ideological appeal. There is more difference between the operation of the California and federal plans than there is between the federal program and no recidivist legislation. Details of the coverage and definition are crucially significant in predicting the impact of legal change on the system's operation.

But what circumstances predict the significant variations in legislative detail and implementation that make all the difference in the world? The contrast between the federal law and California's suggests six factors that have significant influence on the operational scope of symbolically motivated crime legislation: (1) the intention of the drafter of the legislation, (2) the amenability of legislative proposals to processes of political compromise, (3) the susceptibility of the criminal justice operation to legislative change, (4) the opinions and priorities of power holders in the operating system, (5) the presence or absence of an active single-issue lobby dedicated to the promotion of a particular legislative change, (6) and the level of the public's trust of government.

Different Intentions Produce Different Results

Chapter 2 discussed the contrasting agendas of those who drafted the California and federal versions of Three Strikes and highlighted the sharply opposed false impressions that each proposal was designed to create. The federal proposal was designed to "talk tough" but produce a minimal impact on the operation of the justice system, and the historical record suggests that it has succeeded brilliantly. The federal pattern of "loud bark, small bite" is the usual type of puffing that one encounters in crime legislation, with restricted definitions and multiple discretions not to proceed being two important devices used to reduce the scope and the operating costs of law-and-order legislation.

By contrast, the people who drafted California's Three Strikes laws wanted to force a maximum impact and did not always pursue that end in an easily visible fashion. The proposal was called "Three strikes and you're out," and yet a mandatory penalty escalation applied to any felony after a single strike in an offender's prior record.

The mandatory punishment for a second or third strike applied to *all* felony convictions, not merely to those for a violent crime or a serious felony. Every decision point in the structure of Mike Reynolds's version of Three Strikes attempted to provide for the highest level of mandatory sanctions and to have them apply to the maximum number of felony cases. The record of prosecution and punishment under Three Strikes suggests that the hard-line architects succeeded in drafting their statute for maximum effect.

The point of this comparison is a simple one: The intentions of those who draft legislation are a very important element in predicting its impact on the system. As much as broad definitions and mandatory language may be watered down in practice or extenuated by judicial construction, the ambition of a competent draftsman will be reflected in the degree to which a legislative change will produce larger or smaller changes in performance. The contrasting ambitions of the federal and California drafters may not fully explain the thousand-to-one difference in policy impact, but it is an important part of the explanatory process.

Opportunities to Compromise

The possibilities for compromise in the normal legislative process are an important moderating influence on the impact of legislative changes that emerge from negotiation. One natural method of obtaining a large legislative majority is to reduce the extent of the change being demanded. In this usual course of events, the existence of five different Three Strikes proposals in the California legislature in February 1994 would have resulted in passage of one of the less extreme proposals rather than the legislation with the broadest projected impact.

But the path of Three Strikes in California was not a normal one. When California's governor and the legislative leadership dared each other to back down from supporting the most extreme version of recidivist legislation, the result was that the most radical of the proposals was enacted. This peculiar twist in the Three Strikes story both demonstrates the importance of the role that compromise plays in the ordinary political process and illustrates the extraordinary and differential impact of legislative proposals that are not subject to legislative horse trading. The legislative version of California's Three Strikes is a rare example of nonnegotiable proposals in the legislative process. However, the initiative process, deciding criminal justice proposals by putting them on a statewide ballot, is almost universally an up-or-down vote on a single proposal that voters can accept or reject but cannot change. Once a ballot initiative has been certified by the voters, the opportunity to negotiate has passed; this tends to produce somewhat more radical shifts in policy than will emerge from a legislative body that is doing business as usual.

The greater flexibility of the legislative process can be directly observed in the career of 10-20-Life as a legislative proposal in California, as discussed in chapter 8. The substantial reduction in the coverage of the new penalty structure and in the number of cases that would be generated by the mandatory minimum is exactly the sort of watering down that we would expect from the process of legislative consideration. This suggests that a shift in emphasis from the give and take of representative democracy to the yes-or-no politics of electoral initiative will be associated with an increase in the extremity of changes proposed and to some extent an increase in the extremity of changes enacted by the process of direct democracy.

The Accessibility of Policy to Political Influence

We have predicted only a weak relationship between the accessibility of elements of policy to direct political control and the amount of crime legislation proposed and passed by legislatures. We would predict a strong relationship, however, between the accessibility of policy decisions to political control and the amount of direct influence that is exerted by crime legislation and initiatives. In a system of government in which administrative bodies such as parole boards determine the release dates of offenders, the influence of punishment legislation on the time served in prison by individual offenders will be much weaker than in a system in which parole has been eliminated and determinate sentencing set by legislation has a direct influence on the time that an offender will serve. Of course, new laws can always remove the powers of agencies such as parole boards and by that process make criminal justice policy more accessible to a democratic government. If parole powers are an obstacle to the comprehensive restructuring of punishment, the democratic process can always remove those layers of insulation that separate the sentiments of the population from individual punishment decisions.

It is still true that whatever layers of insulation exist between popular opinion and the details of criminal punishment are an important predictor of the scope and practical impact of "get tough" legislation. If the system has been structured so that legislation can have a direct influence on time in prison without altering the normal allocation of power in criminal sentencing for adults, the influence of legislation on practice will tend to be greater. If there are a large number of mediating institutions, such as parole boards and institutions that award or restrict good time, the impact of most of the laws that are passed on penal practice will be weaker.

If this theory proves true, the determinate sentencing reform of the mid-1970s helped lay the groundwork for the maximum impact of Three Strikes on California's criminal punishment policy in the mid-1990s; it removed a tradition of nonpolitical influence on time served that was an important layer of insulation between the political process and punishment levels in individual cases. In the federal system, by contrast, the creation of a Federal Sentencing Commission certainly did not stop Congress from passing mandatory minimum legislation during the high point of the "war on drugs." But the creation of a sentencing commission created an institutional enemy of mandatory minimum legislation that may have reduced such sentences in both legislation and practice. The existence and influence of a sentencing commission has become an obstacle to the broadest reach of mandatory penalties in the federal but not in the California system.

The Attitude of Enforcers

In a criminal justice system devoted to unreviewable prosecutorial power, there is no such thing as a mandatory minimum punishment because prosecutors are free to avoid the mandatory provisions of any penalty. Prosecutorial power is only an extreme case of the discretionary power to avoid legislative edicts that were designed to be mandatory in effect. The power of criminal justice officials to moderate and negate even mandatory legislation means that the support of powerful functionaries within the criminal justice system is an important predictor of the degree to which radical changes in legislative pronouncements are reflected at street level. Chapter 5 showed that the second-strike cases outnumbered third-strike cases by a factor of slightly more than 2:1. But second-strike criminal sentences outnumbered third-strike criminal sentences by a ratio of 9:1. Since the mandatory language of Three Strikes is equally absolute for both classes of cases, the difference in the degree of *actual* enforcement is a graphic demonstration of the importance of the attitude of enforcers on the actual impact of legislative change.

Indeed, these two branches of Three Strikes are almost a controlled experiment. Legislative and voters' support for the two wings of Three Strikes were identical, and so was the timing of the effective date of the legislation. The 3.5 to 1 difference in enforcement is at the same time a powerful indicator that prosecutors and judges were more favorably disposed toward second-strike than toward third-strike penalties and a dramatic illustration of the magnitude of enforcement difference that can be produced by a difference in prosecutorial support. We would not argue that the aggregate 3.5 to 1 difference is anywhere near the maximum difference in enforcement that different official attitudes can produce. But it is large enough by itself to reflect the extreme vulnerability of mandatory legislative ambitions to the discretionary powers of criminal justice officials.

The Presence of Special Interests Dedicated to Broad Changes in Policy

Legislators and voters are both interested in a large number of different policy areas and have limited attention spans for particular issues. The single-issue special-interest group has by definition an unlimited attention span for the details of government policy in its particular area of concern. When such a single-issue lobby exists and has influence in the political process, this will create a tendency for legislative action in its topical concerns. If this general tendency is important, it might explain the broader impact of Three Strikes in a state system like California's, which has a variety of single-interest criminal justice lobbies, than in a federal legislative environment, where single-issue criminal justice lobbies are rare. All other things being equal, the existence of action-oriented single-issue lobbies in the legislative process will increase the impact of legislation on practice.

The Implications of Mistrust

Mistrust is of substantial importance in determining the scope of penal legislation and is also significant in comprehending the links between Three Strikes and the political environment and history of California. The level of trust in government has a direct influence on the scope of penal legislation. When those who trust government officials wish to get tough on criminals, they can create large discretionary powers and explicitly delegate the decision in individual cases to officials who administer the criminal justice system at the retail level. Actual punishment decisions can then be made one case at a time. When citizens distrust their government, discretion and delegation become a target. In an atmosphere of mistrust, making judges and parole officials more powerful is not regarded as a reliable way to increase punishment for the truly serious offenders who are the motive for the reform. Distrust of government action is characterized by mandatory rather than discretionary penalties for broad categories of crime so that the truly appropriate candidates for punishment cannot escape their just deserts.

California's Three Strikes is a textbook case of how the politics of distrust expands the class of offenders covered by extreme measures and substitutes mandatory for discretionary punishment in individual cases. To extend a 25-year-to-life minimum sentence to any felony reconviction deliberately creates a broad category in which all its members receive enormous punishment. The mandatory elements of the statute do not serve a theory of punishment so much as respond to a distrust of the discretionary exercise of government authority. In this sense, California's Three Strikes is not merely another kind of habitual-criminal legislation; it is rather one step in a campaign to take decision making out of the hands of as many government officials as possible. At its core, then, Three Strikes represents a jurisprudence of mistrust rather than any particular theory of punishment.

Precedents in the Politics of Mistrust

That part of Three Strikes provoked by the politics of mistrust has important links to historic precedents in criminal justice, in taxation, and in the populist assault on the size and mission of government that dominated American politics for the last quarter of the twentieth century. The criminal justice ancestor of Three Strikes is the Determinate Sentencing Law of 1976, hostile to the extensive discretion of judges and parole boards in sentencing (see chapter 7). The reformers who wrote *Struggle for Justice* (1971) certainly did not intend to provide a fundamental premise for the extravagant mandatory prison terms of Three Strikes, but mistrust of individual government actors is nonetheless a common structural characteristic of the two approaches.

Another ancestor of Three Strikes is the tax revolt mounted through the initiative process in California in the late 1970s. Proposition 13, limiting property taxes, and associated with the Howard Jarvis and Paul Gann campaign to limit government growth, was a breathtaking mixture of appeals to pecuniary interests and mistrust of government units grown fat and powerful. The broad categories and mandatory language of Three Strikes were lineal descendants of the inflexible and invariable arithmetic of tax and spending limitations.

These are also important links to the broader politics of neoconservative populism that came to power in the America of the 1980s. Ronald Reagan was a popular president whose electoral victories were produced by running against the government structures that he presided over. To the extent that mistrust of government leads to extremes in the application of penal sanctions, there is no irony at all in the large expansion of prison population that occurs when antigovernment populism is a dominant political attitude. Soaring prison populations are a manifestation of mistrust in government because the unwillingness to delegate power in individual cases makes attempts to increase punishments in the system depend on blunt instruments.

Mistrust as a Political Strategy

We suspect that criminal justice is not merely one arena among many where mistrust of government affects the kind of legal change advocated. Instead, we believe that crime and punishment are core concerns of those seeking to increase mistrust in government and to benefit from the high levels of mistrust that already exist. Making citizens feel unsafe and suggesting that government agents take the side of offenders, rather than victims, are common methods of undermining trust. Those who wish to promote regimes of mandatory punishment have a natural incentive to undermine confidence in government expertise, sincerity, and honesty. A corollary of this is the prediction that environments with relatively high trust in government will produce penal reforms that are far less drastic. Trust in government is a natural precursor of delegation, and delegations on an individual case basis are the natural alternative to sweeping and mandatory reclassification.

When some of the predictions discussed in this chapter are combined with our theories of mistrust, we see that the ideal environment for a Three Strikes campaign is not an acute social or government crisis but rather periods of relative stability and prosperity when citizens' dissatisfaction and unease are nevertheless high. It is not when the economic system or the apparatus of law enforcement breaks down that citizens are most vulnerable to appeals for Three Strikes but rather during periods of free-floating anxiety, when fear and insecurity are not closely connected to concrete problems within personal experience.

The mid-1990s was a vintage period for the politics of mistrust all over the United States. The Three Strikes phenomenon produced new versions of habitual-criminal legislation in the majority of American states. To be sure, most of them were not as emphatically mandatory or otherwise antigovernment as the California version. The "loud bark, small bite" pattern of federal law was more typical. But so-called truth-in-sentencing provisions in state and federal legislation in 1994 were paradigm cases of distrust-driven design. The truth-in-sentencing approach is not to alter the nominal sentences of imprisonment available for specific offenses but rather to sharply increase the percentage of a prison sentence that must be served before an offender can obtain release at the discretion of the parole or prison authorities. The twin targets of truth-in-sentencing are criminal offenders and lenient government officials.

Yet another chapter in the recent politics of mistrust has been a campaign by the National Rifle Association to pass state legislation that requires local law enforcement officials to issue permits to carry concealed weapons without special requirements. These "shall issue" laws cut back on the discretionary power of sheriffs and police chiefs. Distrust of government is central to the organized opposition to firearms control in the United States.

The list of factors we deem relevant to the amount and direction of criminal punishment is an inadequate account of the causes of Three Strikes for at least two reasons. First, the factors are incomplete. The important political forces that we have discussed are themselves effects of multiple causes. If mistrust of government is predictive of a particular form of penal legislation, what factors in the social and political life of California increased mistrust in the 1980s and early 1990s and why? Each of the factors mentioned has multiple antecedents that are important in understanding the social and political roots of changes in criminal punishment. Any account that ignores those earlier antecedents rightly risks being regarded as superficial.

The political factors discussed are also an incomplete explanation for Three Strikes because they identify tendencies that do not amount to a sufficient cause of that particular legislation. The particular form of the Three Strikes initiative is itself as much a product of accident as of trends that can be identified, even in retrospect. Accidental drafting choices, the coincidental occurrence of a major crime during a gubernatorial political campaign, and many other un-predictable events (discussed in chapter 1) played a significant role in determining the passage of the law. All of the structural and attitu-dinal factors could occur many times in a slightly different California without resulting in a legal change of the magnitude and shape of Three Strikes.

Some Political History Retold

A theoretical discussion of the politics of criminal punishment has potential uses in the explanation of history and in the prediction of future developments, a task we defer to the last chapter of this book. Here we wish to summarize very briefly some lessons about how California's version of Three Strikes fits into a pattern of politics and policy reforms in contemporary American criminal justice. To what extent is the political process that produced this reform represen-tative of the current American scene? To what extent is California's Three Strikes law peculiar in its origins and implementation? What in the political and government process of the last quarter of the twentieth century has been driving the expansion of imprisonment-based criminal justice?

The structural characteristics in California that predict increased punishment for criminals were utterly typical of circumstances found across the United States in the 1990s. Several factors, ranging from federalism, economic prosperity, and the end of the Cold War to a growing consensus for a hard line on crime control, conspired to make punitive responses to crime into a high political priority. With the exception only of the Polly Klaas kidnapping, every other ele-ment that would predict a high probability of "get tough" legislation in California would also predict a high probability of "get tough" legislation everywhere else. In its susceptibility to punitively ori-ented law reform, California was far more typical than peculiar.

California was, however, peculiar in its vulnerability to extreme versions of punitive law reform. The initiative process was a major force in this regard because it granted the power to draft the terms of proposed legislation changes to single-interest groups. Then the threat of hard-line crime policy as a defining issue in a gubernatorial campaign made the state's legislative assembly swallow the Three

Strikes initiative whole, without any of the negotiations and compromises that are characteristic of the legislative process in plural
democracies. The breadth of the Three Strikes law was thus outside
the range of legal changes that could ordinarily be expected to
emerge from the political process.

Three Theories of Change

The sharp changes in levels of imprisonment in California are universally acknowledged to be a result of shifts in the importance of
public opinion in the creation of penal policy, but it is not clear what
aspects of public attitudes toward crime and criminal justice have
generated the pressure for shifts in policy over the three decades that
begin in 1970, when the policy changes took place. Three quite different explanations are possible.

First, there is the theory that the content of public opinion about
the punishment of felons has changed over the past generation, so
that citizens who used to believe in nonincarcerative sanctions for
burglars now favor imprisonment. When most people search for patterns of change in public opinion, it is a toughening of attitudes or
increased hostility to criminals that is first mentioned. It turns out
that empirical support for half of this theory (the current demand
to imprison offenders) is much stronger than for the other half (that
the public's earlier sentiment was not a hard-line attitude toward
the punishment of felons). Public hostility toward criminals is a historical constant in stable democracies and is usually associated with
support for punitive treatment of convicted offenders, although there
is evidence that the public support for prison is higher in the United
States currently than in other Western nations. The significant issue
is whether the public attitudes toward increasing punishment are a
recent change, which can explain the recent expansion of punishment, or a long-standing condition.

A second theory is that although the content of public attitudes
toward crime and criminals may not have changed much, their
salience as a political issue has increased over the last generation.
Public sentiments about the proper punishment of burglars may have
been negative all along, but this issue was not as important to citizens in 1970 as in 1990. There is some empirical support for this
theory. A Gallup poll asked, "What do you think is the most important problem facing the country today?" periodically over the past

fifty years. A crime item was nominated by 4% of respondents in 1965 but by 27% in 1995 and 17% in 1999 ("Week in Review" 1999, p. 4). There are also up-and-down fluctuations in the degree of public concern over the whole time period. The political impact of increased salience of the crime issue is that citizens are much more likely to act on punitive sentiments they may always have felt. When crime becomes important, negative sentiments are more likely to mobilize political action and thus to influence policy.

The causes of fluctuations in the salience of crime as a public issue are an understudied question. To some extent, high rates of crime should increase the importance of crime concerns, although rates of life-threatening crimes may be more important here than rates of property offenses (Zimring and Hawkins 1997). Of equal importance are the status of other potential social concerns; crime takes a backseat to economic crisis or war but rises to higher importance during periods of peace and prosperity. There are indications, too, that media coverage and political emphasis affect the salience of crime as a public issue (Beckett 1997).

The third theory of change emphasizes the structures that transform public opinion into policy. The changing nature of the mechanisms in government that make punishment decisions may have made citizens' sentiments into a more powerful influence because of their increased *proximity* to punishment decisions. In California, the elimination of a parole authority in 1976 removed a powerful non-elected and expert body from the determination of prison terms and left sentencing in the hands of an elected legislature. As a matter of structure, this put the determination of prison terms only one step away from public opinion, much closer than before, and the notion that expertise is important in such decisions was undermined by replacing parole decisions with legislative judgements. Penalties became just another political decision. Furthermore, the creation of narrow terms of imprisonment in the determinate sentencing law of 1976 constrained judicial discretion and set a precedent for the fixed terms imposed by such legislation as Three Strikes and 10-20-Life.

The decline in experts' influence and the shift of power into institutions more responsive to democratic pressure are developments that would predict more punitive policies even if nothing else changed. But when they occur at the same time that crime is becoming more salient as a political issue, the compound effects of the new structures and new concerns can be substantial. Thus structural

changes in California helped to create the environment that produced the 1994 reforms. We would not argue that the earlier attack
on parole power and judicial discretion was a sufficient condition for
creating a law like Three Strikes, but it may have been a necessary
condition.

TEN

Democracy and the Governance of Criminal Punishment

The Three Strikes story is remarkable in that it involves lawmaking by the mass participation of registered voters. The details of a complex legislative proposal were placed on the ballot and voted up or down by a majority of the eligible voters who participated in the election. Is this process a good idea for legislation on penal policy? If not, why not? To what extent should popular will set criminal penalties? How should the governance of penalties be organized in modern democratic governments?

This chapter addresses the question of what should be the appropriate means for setting penalties in a political democracy. This is both a fundamental and a neglected topic. To do even preliminary justice to questions of this depth requires an attempt to provide a series of contexts in this chapter much broader than the specific circumstances of the Three Strikes initiative. We will first define terms and describe the allocation of power in the punishment-setting process according to the proximity or distance of each element in the decision from democratic oversight. We will then address three questions about nonpolitical definitions of excessive punishment. The third section of the chapter will inventory the range of possible objections to the method of setting penalties in the Three Strikes initiative, and the different remedies that might be used to address each one. Were the problems associated with Three Strikes inherent to all democratic methods of choosing punishment or were they produced by the particular processes used in California? We will then provide a basis for comparison by considering the attenuations of democratic control imposed in liberal democracies on the governance of central banks, which set interest rates. There is a rich tradition of antipopulism here, and some effort to provide justification for the insulation of substantive policy from direct democratic control. Finally, we will consider some proposed methods for insulating punishment decisions from any problems of process and substantive bias.

Methods of Choosing Punishment: Key Terms
and Typical Patterns

Criminal punishment is a special function of government with distinctive distributions of power and authority in every modern state. In most systems, two separate levels of decision making produce individual penal outcomes: general provisions and particular applications. *General provisions* include rules on what types of unpleasant consequences will be used and which types of offenders will be eligible for which types of punishment. These rules are often broad generalizations, usually promulgated by legislative bodies. The *particular application* of these rules to a convicted offender determines what kind and amount of punishment will be imposed in the case of a particular person. For felony crimes, state authorities decide whether prison, probation, or capital punishments should be authorized and what types of offenses and convicted persons should be eligible for each authorized punishment. State authorities also determine which authorized punishment should be used in each individual case that is eligible for punishment. Rule makers will first determine whether prison will be available as a criminal punishment, for what duration, and for which offenders. Government officials will then apply these general rules (and usually a great deal of discretion) in determining what punishment will be imposed in particular cases. The general provisions on punishment can all be made by a single government body or distributed among a variety of different government agencies. In the United States, general provisions on punishment can come from legislatures; sentencing commissions; and in some recent cases, voters.

The power to determine individual punishments can also be distributed among different government authorities. Both sentencing judges and parole authorities are in the business of making particular applications of punishment provisions. They jointly determine the time of incarceration where both function. The usual pattern is for a significant separation of powers in government between the authorities that promulgate general principles and those that make particular applications. Indeed, these two functions are often allocated to different branches of government. The wholesale branch of rule making is normally lodged in legislative bodies, whereas the retail task of assigning punishments in particular cases is usually found in the judicial branches of government.

The focus of this chapter is on where the power to punish is and should be located in democratic systems of government. Our working definition of a democracy is a system of governance in which those who exercise government power are subject to the electoral control of citizens by majority vote. In such systems, the majority vote of citizens will have influence over the rules of punishment in a direct or indirect fashion, but the extent of this power and the circumstances of its exercise will depend on how the means of expressing power and the choice of punishments in general rules or particular cases are separated.

Four links between democratic processes and punishment rules lead to different degrees of voters' influence. The first and most direct link is *direct democracy*, in which the punishments available and imposed in particular cases are selected by the majority vote of participating citizens. We know of no case in which the penalty was selected by a plebiscite, but two existing systems move pretty close to some form of direct democracy. First, juries, small groups of citizens selected as representatives of larger communities, still function as life-or-death penalty selectors in most of those states that retain a death penalty. This is seen as one method of direct involvement of the citizenry in the particular application of punishment. Second, a democratic majority may select a general rule that requires a single punishment for the entire class of cases covered by the general provisions. Where citizens enact such a mandatory punishment by a majority vote, they are attempting to choose individual punishments by legislating the same unvarying result for all legislatively defined crimes of a particular type. In this version of direct democracy, the voters legislate without providing any mediating institutions.

The second form of democratic control is *representative democracy*, the selection of general rules and particular applications by elected representatives. Rather than choosing rules (as in direct democracy), the voters in a representative system choose the persons who will exercise rule-making power. Citizens select legislators who promulgate the general provisions of penal law. When the general provisions have mandatory penalties, the particular applications have also been selected by representative democracy, so in formal terms the selection of individual penalties takes place only one step removed from majority vote. In another method of representative democracy, judges who choose punishments for convicted offenders are elected by majority vote. The general provisions of the penal law can be determined by one branch of government (such as the legislature) and the particular application by another (such as judges), but each set of decisions is only one step removed from direct voter control. Separation of powers in these circumstances is not the equivalent of creating a wide gap between public sentiment and penal choice.

The third link between democracy and penalty choices is a system of *delegation*, which creates at least one additional space between a majority of citizens' votes and the punishments imposed. In a system of delegation, an elected legislature or executive delegates the power to set punishment rules or to make particular applications to govern-ment actors who have not been elected. Such actors include ap-pointed judges and parole boards, sentencing commissions, and cor-rectional officials frequently given the power to reduce prison terms with good-time determinations. The difference between represen-tative democracy and delegated power is the lack of a direct link between an elected official and a particular rule or decision. The elected official has no direct responsibility for a particular outcome in a delegational system.

The fourth link, delegating power to government actors, is struc-tured to reduce the power of electoral majorities to influence punish-ment rules and outcomes. This is what we call *insulated delegation.* Strategies have been devised to create government actors less subject to democratic influence than normally appointed officials. Long terms of office (including life tenure for judges) and staggered terms that do not coincide with the electoral cycles of the persons who ap-point the power holder are two common methods of insulation. If the border between ordinary delegations and these insulated delegations of power is crossed only when systems are deliberately designed to reduce electoral influence, the prevalence of the practice is not wide-spread. But if we count all the administrative and judicial systems that function as insulation, the apparatuses in modern government that shield executive and judicial decisions from even legislative control take a great variety of forms and are responsible for the ma-jority of all government decisions. So although the boundary of insu-lated versus simply delegated decisions may be problematic in some cases, the concept is of both theoretical and practical importance.

The systems have been listed in order from the most to least democratic. When we use this vocabulary to describe the distribu-tion of decision making in punishment systems, we find that the most important contrast is between general provisions (which are typically wide bands of authorized punishments) and the power to make particular applications. Democratically elected legislatures usually select general provisions of penal legislation but leave to judges and expert administrative bodies the details of policy and the particular decisions in individual cases. This division of authority is utterly typical of modern government and is in no sense peculiar to criminal punishment. But the modern habit of keeping the generalities of legislative penal law very general indeed has created an allocation of responsibility that often locates individual decisions in institutions effectively removed from representative democracy, whether in the judicial branch (where conscious insulation from democratic controls is quite common) or administrative bureaucracies like parole boards and prison systems (where low-visibility decisions are made without substantial legislative oversight).

As a matter of practice, the punishment decisions in complex modern democracies are made one or more steps removed from electoral controls. Table 10.1 displays the pattern of decision making in the United States at the federal level and for the other six members of the G-7 nations. We use the G-7 group as a convenient sample of modern democratic governments, which we have profiled before in another context (Zimring and Hawkins 1997, chap. 2). The predominant modes for determining punishments cluster neatly among the G-7 nations. No nation uses direct election to determine general pe-

Table 10.1. Punishment Decisions by Level of Democratic Control in the G-7 Nations

	General Provisions	Particular Applications
Direct democracy		
Representative democracy	Canada, France, Italy, United Kingdom, Germany, Japan, United States	
Delegated authority	United States (sentencing commission)	United States (sentencing commission)
Insulated delegation		Canada, France, Germany, Italy, Japan, United Kingdom, United States (federal judges)

nal policies; all nations except the United States instead use representative democracy (the United States at the federal level delegates most general policies to a sentencing commission). All of the G-7 nations use insulated judicial officers to administer punishments at the retail level, with judicial discretion quite wide in most systems and rather more narrow in the U.S. scheme.

Although the table provides a good summary of the predominant power distribution in punishment, it misrepresents the allocation of power wherever mandatory punishments are enacted as part of the general provisions of the penal law. If a mandatory penalty takes effect, the result is a conflation of the power to set general policy and the power to determine punishments in particular cases. The body that sets the general standard also seeks to control the particular application, and what table 10.1 tells us about this conflation process is that it relocates the control of retail punishment much closer to the electorate. When the U.S. Congress takes discretion out of the hands of both federal judges and the sentencing commission in favor of mandatory penalties, the body that sets the penalty is a legislature selected by representative democratic processes rather than nonelected judges and commissioners who are insulated from removal or discipline by democratically elected officials.

The degree of democratic power over punishment is sharply different in the 50 states of the United States, as shown in table 10.2. Most American states follow the G-7 pattern—elected legislatures that make general policy for criminal penalties—but since 1980, 16 states have created what are called sentencing commissions to set guidelines that have varying amounts of legal influence on the options of sentencing judges. The guidelines issued by sentencing commissions in 8 states go beyond mere advice to constrain the discretion of sentencing judges. These are the states we list as providing insulated delegation for general provisions of punishment (16% of the total). But if this group of states has set one aspect of punishment policy further removed from democratic control, the majority of American states has pushed criminal punishment closer to popular review by providing for the initial election of trial judges (27 states) or periodic election review for judges selected by state executives (11 states). Those states that use election of judges for initial selection have a much more powerful democratic influence than the states that use only retention election because the inertial forces that govern the political process once a judge is an incumbent will make judicial removal by election a pretty rare event. But even retention review is a

Table 10.2. Percent Distribution of American States by Types of Control Over Criminal Punishment

	General Provisions	Particular Applications
Direct democracy	—	—
Representative democracy	84	76
Delegation	—	—
Insulated delegation	16	24
	100%	100%
	(50)	(50)

Sources: Review of statutory materials by Sarah Kermgard, Earl Warren Legal Institute.

very substantial contrast to the notion of a professional and independent judiciary.

Popular Choice: Three Preliminary Questions

The issue around which this chapter is organized is whether many forms of democratic choices result in levels of punishment that are excessive. We will here address a necessary prerequisite to this question, the need for a standard of appropriate punishment that is independent of popular choice. We will first consider whether all punishment desired by a majority of a community is necessary and nonexcessive for that reason alone. We will next consider a series of definitions of excessive punishment that are sufficiently distinct from popular views, thereby setting a standard for judging whether punishments chosen by a majority of a community's voters might nonetheless exceed the community's needs or the offender's just deserts. The final part of the analysis considers two contrasting versions of the social cost of punishment—one including and one excluding the suffering of offenders.

With that discussion as background, we will discuss a variety of different aspects of democratic choices that might generate excessive punishments. Using the Three Strikes account as a foundation, we will consider the potential problems in binary choice initiatives, in mandatory minimum punishments, and in using the choices of a majority of voters to prescribe the punishments.

Popular Will and the Necessity of Punishment

When stories like Three Strikes are the basis for criticism of populist punishments, the implication is usually that such punishments tend to be more severe than necessary and in that sense excessive. In punishment of street criminals, vox populi is rarely accused of undue leniency. Yet the notion of popular punishment being excessive seems close to a contradiction in terms. The key issue is the role of community norms in determining the amount of punishment that the community needs to exact because of an offender's harmful intentions and actions. If a majority of the community thinks that 15 years is appropriate for auto theft, has it not demonstrated that a penalty of 15 years is necessary to the morale and stability of the community?

Not quite. One of the core benefits of punishing criminals is the reassurance to law-abiding members of the community that standards of justice have been served and that criminal offenders have not benefited from their transgressions. But not all punishments that community members would approve are necessary to secure the benefits of imposing a deserved punishment. As Norval Morris (1974) argues, it is best to see deserved punishments as a range—anything below the lowest punishment will offend the community's sense of justice, and anything above the highest will seem to community members to be excessive. But any punishment between the minimum and maximum will serve the community's need for the imposition of a just penalty. Community support for larger punishments than meet the minimum threshold may also exceed the punishment necessary in a particular case even if a majority of the community would not be disturbed to see the higher punishment imposed. Minimum desert is about the level of punishment a community needs to witness, given the occurrence of a crime, not about the level of punishment members of the community may want or will accept. It is therefore more than possible that citizens will support levels of punishment larger than those necessary to serve the full range of community benefits, including its retributive stake in exacting a deserved penalty.

If the difference between necessary and popular retribution is the major reason that a community's consent to punishments does not create its own self-executing justification, the possibility of citizens' error is a second basis for not using majority support as an automatic validation for elected levels of punishment. Citizens may support higher penalties in the belief that deterrent benefits or incapacitative effects are larger than is actually true. This occurred with Three

Strikes, if the attorney general of California was typical of the man in the street. This mistake may render the punishment supported excessive, given the true state of the punishment's effects.

So the importance of desert is a key item in the calculus of punishment's costs and benefits and complicates the measure of the latter. Desert is also an intangible element in the equation, not the sort of factor that fits into a mechanical formula with ease. But if the punishment inflicted on offenders is regarded as a social harm unless justified by the benefits it generates, the majority's approval of levels of punishment will not foreclose an inquiry about whether a particular punishment is excessive.

The Meaning of Excessive Punishment

If an offender's suffering is to be regarded as a harm, at least when it exceeds the bounds of necessity, the definition and measurement of excessive punishment are of central importance. It turns out that there are at least three clearly distinct definitions of excessive punishment, two of which are closely related to the Three Strikes statute: cruelty, proportionality, and instrumental necessity. When a commentator speaks of excessive punishment in the sense of cruelty, the assertion is that some punishments should not be administered by a civilized state regardless of the crime. Torture, for example, is regarded as unsuited to a civilized government for any offender, and similar arguments have been made and accepted about the death penalty in many Western nations (Zimring and Hawkins 1986, chap. 1). In the United States, the Eighth Amendment's prohibition of cruel and unusual punishments is thought to cover such excessive punishments, with no need to refer to the offender's crime or degree of culpability. When judged on grounds of cruelty, a punishment stands alone and is not measured against the harm done or intended by criminal defendants.

In contrast, in considering just deserts or proportionality, comparing the size of the penalty to the nature and extent of the offender's wrongdoing is the heart of the matter. The central complaint of proportional excessiveness is that the punishment is more than the offender deserves, given the nature of the wrong. One measure of proportional excess is punishment that seems extreme when compared to the punishments exacted for other, greater crimes. If crimes of equal or greater seriousness are treated more leniently, one can decide that the punishment imposed does not conform to the hierarchy of greater punishments for greater offenses, which should inform the scale of penalties in a just penal code. This type of argument is made in the publicized Third Strike case in which theft of a piece of pizza generated a 25-year-to-life sentence (because any petty theft is a felony in California if committed by a person with a prior felony theft conviction, and any felony generates the mandatory third-strike minimum). However, in administering the Eighth Amendment prohibition of cruel and unusual punishments, the United States Supreme Court has not been generous to arguments based on violations of proportionality. Long mandatory sentences for drug possession and life terms for habitual offenders have been upheld against Eighth Amendment challenges, although one challenge was upheld, in *Rummel v. Estelle* (1980). The measurement of proportionality is obviously neither mechanical nor precise, and no claims of exactness have been made on this topic.

The last major class of excessive punishment claims is what we call functional or instrumental excessiveness—when it is alleged that a particular level of punishment is more than is required to produce desirable levels of deterrence, incapacitation, or general prevention. Although theoretically distinct from claims of proportionality, in practice there is much overlap because it is argued that particular punishments are excessively harsh and achieve no measurable increment in deterrence or retribution, and are thus excessive on instrumental grounds as well. Some of this mix was seen in arguments about the death penalty in *Furman v. Georgia* (1972; see, e.g., White's, Marshall's, and Brennan's opinions).

In theory, optimal levels of deterrence and incapacitation might be determined and the effect of threats could be precisely measurable, but no persuasive demonstration of the measurement of optimal levels has been realized in practice, and we are skeptical that one is in prospect. For some purposes of punishment, such as deterrence, it is possible to imagine not only declining levels of marginal deterrence but also marginal increments of punishment without any marginal increment of deterrence at all. By contrast, substantial increments of additional imprisonment will always yield some additional incapacitation, so the argument of excessiveness in relation to incapacitation is that the incremental benefits are too small to matter. The allocation of the burden of proof in matters of marginal increments will usually determine which side will win the argument. Whoever has the burden will usually fail to discharge it. Typical arguments will use a mix of different types of excessiveness and standards of measurement that it is charitable to call inexact.

Two Measures of Cost

The idea that punishment in excess of that necessary to achieve legitimate social ends is an undesirable result assumes that the pain felt by offenders is an important component of the social cost of punishment. If not, unnecessary punishment is only socially harmful if the material resources necessary to deliver the punishment are substantial, as in the case of penal confinement, or if innocent parties suffer. Should the offender's pain count toward the social cost of punishment? If so, the problem is that the same suffering seems to count both as a debit and a credit, contributing toward deserved punishment and thus being a tangible benefit of the process, yet counting toward the cost of punishment as well. Is this double-entry bookkeeping an inconsistency?

Our vote in this case goes with the moral appropriateness of double-entry bookkeeping. Even though the need to cause an offender some harm is one of the justifying positive elements of criminal punishment, the harm that is inflicted is nonetheless also a social cost that counts against the practice whenever it occurs. The good that punishment achieves, including retribution, is an important part of restoring balance and order to a community where a crime had its primary impact. But to the extent that offenders suffer, this is a negative impact that weighs against further punishment. A just and necessary punishment does not eliminate the social harm of an offender's suffering, but it can do more good than the harm it causes. That the harm generated is also a benefit makes for a more complex scheme of accounting, but there is no contradiction. The only alternative is social indifference to offender's excessive suffering, a condition that would call into question the notion of excessive punishment. As two of us argued some years ago:

> The harm suffered by offenders as a result of the extra measure of punishment administered for deterrent motives must be recognized as a cost, not insubstantial, to the community as a whole. If the community should gain satisfaction from punishment as an expression of retributive feeling, no joy should come from punishment in excess of that required to express collective feelings of outrage. Our own reading of the Kantian

principle is that the offender is a citizen, and the community's decisional process exists to protect his welfare as well as that of others.

Incidentally, Bentham [1843–1859], who has often been accused of crude utilitarianism, was quite explicit on this point. "It ought not to be forgotten" he wrote, "although it has been too frequently forgotten, that the delinquent is a member of the community, as well as any other individual . . . and that there is just as much reason for consulting his interest as that of any other. His welfare is proportionately the welfare of the community—his suffering the suffering of the community." (Zimring and Hawkins 1973, p. 42)

Theories of Distortion

One way to construct a catalog of potential problems is to list the range of possible complaints about the way in which Three Strikes in California made policy. The concerns include a variety of procedural and substantive matters, which call for substantially different solutions. So there is a practical benefit, as well as theoretical value, in keeping the different types of potential problems separate.

From the perspective of concern about excessive punishment, three categories of problems are associated with the development of Three Strikes in California: structural characteristics of the initiative as a method of selecting punishment policy, the use of mandatory minimum penalties to make the general provisions of penal law determine the penalties applied in particular cases, and elements in popular opinion that generate biases toward the selection of excessive levels of punishment.

Characteristics of Initiatives in California

Two structural elements of California's version of the initiative might contribute to excessive punishments: the reduction of choice to a single special-interest-authored yes-or-no vote, and the provision that amendments to the state constitution passed by initiative cannot be altered except by supermajority in the legislature. Of the three classes of potential bias we will discuss, complaints about characteristics of the California initiative process are of the smallest general importance and will get less attention from us for this reason.

Any initiative in California is a yes-or-no proposition in which the terms have been drafted by the proponents and the only alternative typically available is a vote to do nothing. When the public appetite is large, careful drafting can push the terms of a proposition beyond those that most citizens would prefer as long as a majority would prefer the more extreme position to no action. The choice that faced voters in November 1994 was 25-years-to-life for any third strike or no change in California law. Even citizens who would have preferred a proposal restricted to violent crimes or lesser mandatory terms might prefer the extreme change to no change.

By contrast to this take-it-or-leave-it plebiscite, the legislative process is typically an arena with multiple proposals and almost inevitable compromises. Chapter 1 showed that it took an unusual game of chicken between a governor and a legislature to push the most extreme form of Three Strikes through the legislative process. In the ordinary give-and-take of the legislative process, one of the four less substantial proposals would have emerged, probably further reduced in impact by legislative compromise. This is one reason that the Three Strikes laws in 25 jurisdictions have in aggregate less than one-tenth the sentencing impact of California's law.

One method of finding middle-range alternatives that may better reflect public preference is the Swiss system, which allows the government to put alternative proposals of the scheme into an initiative once an initiative is on the ballot (DuBois and Feeney 1998). This provision would not have made any difference in Three Strikes after the legislature had accepted Governor Wilson's ultimatum, but the counterproposal mechanism would reduce the tactical use of extreme positions in other political circumstances.

The second problem of California's initiative politics is the capacity of proposed constitutional changes to restrict the ability of the state legislature to modify initiative rules even when the change was passed by simple majority. In the case of Three Strikes, the initiative provides that the terms of the law can be changed only by two-thirds majority of both houses of the California legislature. DuBois and Feeney (1998) argue that the most direct reform to address this problem is to abolish the nonlegislative constitutional initiative. The problem is that the ability to limit legislative power in this way is a nice fit with a distrust of government, which was a principal appeal of both the tax limits of the 1970s and the mandatory punishment terms of Three Strikes. The ability to restrict future legislative change is rendered difficult to revoke by the same political circumstances that make it particularly dangerous.

If these peculiar features of California law had not been in effect in 1994, the state would probably have passed a set of persistent offender penalties closer to the pattern of other jurisdictions, or its Three Strikes provisions would in any event be subject to easier legislative modification. So the contributions of California initiative law to the saga of Three Strikes is not trivial.

Excessiveness and Mandatory General Policies

The single policy tool in the Three Strikes arsenal is mandatory minimum punishments prescribed for a whole class of offenders. Whereas most organizations of government create separate mechanisms to decide general penal principles and policy and to make particular decisions in individual cases, the mandatory term is an effort to conflate these two decisions into a single general rule that applies to every particular case. Adding specific penalties to legislation gives the emphasis on punishment a more specific focus, and making punishments mandatory has appeal when judges and parole boards are distrusted. But broad mandatory penalties are almost always a currency of penal hyperinflation.

Any mandatory punishment established as a general rule in legislation or initiative form involves three separate processes that tend to push the punishment upward: (1) the aggregation of punishment to a single standard governed by the imagined worst case; (2) the tendency to make binding determinations of prison time early in the process and ignore the opportunities for dual-currency reductions in prison terms; and (3) an exclusive focus on the crime and other aggravating factors, which generates higher penalties than would obtain if the offender and his or her claims were considered individually before the punishment was set.

Aggregation Errors in Generality

The statutory provisions of the criminal law define only general categories of prohibited behavior. A statute will define robbery, for example, and may provide two or three different grades that reflect different levels of danger and injury. Typically, there will be a wide range of behavior within each offense. When a wide range of potential punishments is available for each legal category, the retail process of individual determination can attempt to match each particular offense and offender to an appropriate punishment. Mandatory provisions narrow the range of punishments available: The extreme example is the third-strike penalty in California that provides essentially the same punishment for all felonies, from petty theft through attempted murder. Choosing any single punishment to cover a wide range of different offenses of differential seriousness will create aggregation errors—many offenses will be given the wrong punishment—but these errors will not be randomly distributed. To force the choice of a single punishment will cause selection to be on the high side because of the felt need to provide for the worst case within each category. When forced to choose between overpunishing nondangerous offenders and underpunishing the most serious offender in a single class of offense, we believe that most people will elect the right punishment for the worst case even at the risk of overpunishing others. But this choice is only an accurate indication of a citizen's preference under forced choice. We believe that the aggregate amount of punishment a citizen will choose when restricted to a single standard will exceed the total level of punishments the citizen would select individually for each offender in the class. This worst-case bias is one reason that special interests who wish to increase punishment are rational to choose mandatory minimum terms as the vehicle to achieve it.

Mandatory punishments attached to broad categories of crime not only push punishments upward but also blur proportionality distinctions between categories of offenders. The average robbery is a lot more dangerous than the average burglary—the death risk from robbery is 50 times as great as from burglary in the United States (Zimring and Hawkins 1997, p. 69). But the difference between the worst-case burglary and the worst-case robbery is probably much less than the gap between averages for the two crimes. If this holds, single punishments that are based on the worst-case preferences will not reflect the differences in seriousness between different types of crimes that are found in typical cases.

Dual Currency and the Bias of Front-end Time Setting

One of the most curious characteristics of criminal sentencing in the Untied States is the large and persistent gap between the announced length of prison sentences imposed at trial and the actual length of time served. For prison time, the criminal justice system seems addicted to barking louder than it bites. The most famous example of early release was the parole power that could be exercised to release an offender after only a fraction of the nominal sentence was served. The formal justification for parole was rehabilitation—the parole board could make judgments about the inmate's progress in prison programs and the danger he or she might present to the community. Discretion for early release was based on the expert's ability to predict dangerousness and confirm rehabilitation.

Or was it? In the mid-1970s, California and Illinois both passed penal reform measures that expressly repudiated parole and the rehabilitative justification for imprisonment (Zimring 1983, pp. 105–107), but both states adopted statutory systems with substantial good-time credit discounts from the actual term sentenced (California Penal Code §2931). This persistence during a repudiation of the foundations of parole provides a forceful demonstration that discounts between nominal and actual prison terms are deeply set in American criminal justice.

The most obvious explanation for the gap is what we call the dual-currency phenomenon, which invites efforts to redetermine the time in a prison sentence after the immediate need for strong condemnation and symbolic communication has passed. A review of the two functions of penalties will illustrate the importance of the phenomenon.

A good example of dual-currency sentencing was reported in newspaper accounts some years ago about a builder in Spain who was convicted of fraud and theft charges involving many badly built houses, causing substantial harm to a large number of buyers. The developer's sentence at trial was about 2,000 years of imprisonment, a period of calendar time five times as great as the total span of modern European history and between 50 and 100 times the life expectancy of a healthy person of middle years. Whereas this Spanish sentence was long enough to be something of an international novelty, there is widespread use of judicially imposed sentences vastly in excess of individual life spans throughout the Anglo-American legal world. Prison sentences of 100 years, 200 years, and more are not uncommon in some American state systems; and the sentence of "life plus 99 years," which achieved some prominence in American popular culture, was not infrequently authorized under penal law.

The judge who pronounced the 2,000-year sentence was using the terms of a prison sentence to underscore the seriousness of the offender's crime and the severity of the loss associated with his acts; the judge was selecting a term of imprisonment that was designed to denounce and stigmatize the defendant's crime. The penalty was probably multiplied so that each of the many victims was palpably considered in the sentence. Thus, the Spanish judge was engaged in an exercise that is a common and legitimate aspect of criminal sentencing, which can select punishments to serve symbolic, as well as operational, functions. There will frequently be a conflict between the appropriate punishment for instrumental crime control, like incapacitation and deterrence, and the punishment that will most effectively convey the symbolic denunciation of the defendant and his or her act. In such circumstances, the decision maker who places more weight on the symbolic rather than the instrumental use of punishment will usually give a larger sentence than one more concerned with operational matters.

Several features of twentieth-century criminal procedure have functioned to some extent as methods of accommodating differing levels of emphasis for symbolic and instrumental concerns. Allowing large discounts between levels of imprisonment imposed by sentencing judges and actual time served in prison is one method of accommodating the need to make dramatic statements without being compelled to require lengthy confinement. Separating a judge's power to sentence an offender to prison from a parole board's or correctional authority's power to decide how long offenders actually stay there allows the parole board to make instrumental decisions removed in time and visibility from the commission of the crime and the proof of the offender's guilt. A penal system that barks louder than it bites may in fact be more efficient than one that attempts to average symbolic and instrumental concerns into a single punishment value.

There is, however, a direct conflict between a mandatory sentence that means what it says and the power to discount or redetermine prison terms long after the initial sentence has been announced. To the extent that mandatory-sentencing schemes reduce the power to change prison terms, they push toward a single sentence that will somehow take account of both the symbolic and operational requirements of the criminal sentence. This sort of averaging can be expected to increase the length of time served in prison for two reasons. First, when the symbolic needs at the time of trial and sentencing are higher than the felt operational needs later on, averaging the two together for a single binding sentence will result in more time served than if a back-end adjustment or discount could have set the actual sentence at the lower operational level or closer to it. Of course, if discounted sentences are themselves compromises rather than dominated by operational values, the compromise feature of a mandatory minimum may not result in a further increase in the sentence.

But the fact that a single sentence is settled at trial or in legislation is a process of front-loading the decision to give more emphasis to the symbolic character of the sentence, to the need to underscore the community's condemnation of the offender's crime and the high importance placed on the suffering of the victims. A single trial-based or statutory penalty will be weighted toward symbolic values and tend to be higher than an adjustable sentence in time served.

Some of these tendencies have been apparent in the legislative and administrative careers of determinate sentencing. California based its middle-term sentences in 1977 on average time served but doubled them and provided a good-time discount. The effort was to reproduce the bark-and-bite pattern of prior regimes. The federal sentencing commission sharply reduced discounts in its sentencing guidelines to about 15% of its new nominal sentences. But the guidelines also expanded the use of prison and provided some upward movement in time served as a result (Hofer and Semisch 1999; Tonry 1996, p. 82). And even these increased sentences were overtaken by Congress with mandatory drug sentences that sharply increased time served.

Some state sentencing commissions have tried to impose single standards of time served that are based an operational values. North Carolina and Minnesota are prominent examples of this, but they are also the exceptions that prove the rule about mandatory minimum sentences passed in the legislative process. The commissions are archetypes of policy being made by delegation to institutions insulated from democratic control.

No contemporary discussion of dual currency could be complete without some discussion of "truth in sentencing" as a criminal justice reform movement of the 1990s. This widespread movement culminated in provisions in the 1994 federal crime legislation to encourage states to require violent offenders to serve 85% of their initial sentences. Rather than recognizing an issue of dual currency, the assumption of the reform appears to be that the initial sentence is the correct one and the adjustments that are made are corruptions of criminal jurisprudence.

One point that should be emphasized is the contradictory assumption of state sentencing commissions and determinate sentencing schemes, which usually base sentences on historical time served, on the one hand, and the truth-in-sentencing reforms, on the other hand. The former place a great weight on adjusted sentences as precedent and thus honor the adjustments made and the operational values. The truth-in-sentencing approach appears to regard the legislative or judicial sentence as the right standard, although the federal law also places high presumptive value on judicial sentences that are based on the sentencing commission's guidelines, which were themselves based on adjusted sentences in past practice. So the truth-in-sentencing standards of the 1994 federal law contradict themselves on the value of operational adjustments for appropriate levels of punishment, approving back-end adjustments that were incorporated in commission guidelines but rejecting back-end adjustments made by parole boards.

This discussion may be imposing more principle on truth in sentencing than is really operating. The approach may simply be a tactic to expand time served by closing the gap between nominal and actual prison time, pushing the actual toward the nominal, and the sole reason that the initial sentences are preferred is because they are higher. If so, the preference of the truth-in-sentencing proponents for single-standard sentences should be a confirmation that they believe an upward drift in actual punishment will accompany all but the most disciplined and insulated of single-standard sentencing schemes.

The Crime-centered Focus of Mandatory General Standards

When an individual offender is sentenced by a judge with substantial discretion to choose the type and amount of punishment, data are available on a wide variety of relevant issues: the crime and its effects on victims, the offender's past record and future prospects, and the offender as an individual with a unique history and future prospect. People who favor mandatory punishments are making a more abstract judgment, as well as seeing the circumstances relevant to punishment through a narrower lens: there are data on the crime and its impact on the community and nothing else except a general and always negative impression of the criminal. The decisional environment is untouched by the human dimensions of the subjects of punishment, and this is an additional bias toward increasing the level of punishment imposed.

The upward bias in bloodless, general rules of punishment is a corollary of whatever pressure toward mercy that results from the presence of a defendant and his or her desire to avoid harsh punishment. This surely must be one of the primary forces that leads to the judicial sentencing decisions critics characterize as soft-hearted. And the obvious cure for this ameliorative pressure is to remove the people that make penalty decisions from contact with the people to be punished.

The three upward influences that characterize mandatory sentences are overlapping and interactive. The absence of a particular crime and particular defendant encourages worst-case images of the paradigm case, filling the void left by no concrete image of the offender and the offense in a particular case. The lack of real offenders and situations also invites the emphasis on symbolic aspects of condemnation and punishment.

It is not possible to distinguish these processes in operation, and it would therefore be difficult to measure the individual contribution of each. Instead, we can only offer our judgment concerning the joint impact of these three influences on the penalty level, and that impact is very substantial. We would not be surprised if the same citizens would support penalties more than twice as high in any abstract general standard than for real people with discretionary choice of type and amount of punishment in typical cases. Social psychologists might be able to measure this impact, but we are not aware of any attempts to do so.

Procedure and Substance in Democratic Decision Making

The only way that voters or representative legislatures can control choices of punishment is by eliminating or greatly narrowing discretionary options in particular cases. Either the legislature and electorate are content to provide general priorities and frameworks for individualized choices by delegated government actors, or general judgments on punishment levels must constrain discretion in individual cases. (The use of juries—a microcommunity—to make individual punishment decisions has fallen into disrepute for a variety of reasons, except for the death penalty.)

Because direct democracy in setting punishments depends on mandatory general standards, there are grounds to disfavor democratic controls simply on the basis of the procedures they entail. If individualized determinations of punishment are preferable to binding general rules, on grounds of either operational efficiency or proportional justice or both, the democratic determination of punishments is problematic for procedural reasons that are independent of any substantive biases of the general public. The conflation of general and individual penalty determinations is an inevitable collateral cost to plenary democratic control, and that cost can be considered substantial enough to disqualify the move toward detailed democratic controls.

Populist Bias in Choice of Penalty

The inevitable link between democratic control and procedures that remove individualized decisions about punishment make any discussion of substantive bias in popular penalty choices a matter of conjecture. If general standards themselves affect penalty choices, the behavior of voters in case studies like Three Strikes could be partly or wholly the result of the procedural problems already discussed. The influence of citizens' opinions may be difficult to measure outside their decisional context, and the policy significance of these attitudes may be rendered moot by the procedural costs of bringing them to bear on individual decisions. Much of what has been complained about as populist bias might be an artifact of the procedures that express popular will.

But the procedural biases of binding general standards are probably not the whole story. The substantive tendencies that seem most likely in public decisions about criminal punishment track the procedural problems mentioned and might not be a strong independent force if members of the general public were involved in less general and less abstract choices. The essential element of the way in which public opinion applies to questions of penal policy is that citizens tend to express not a preference for specific penalties but an attitude toward criminals, a nonproportional hostility that tends neither to make distinctions among types of crime nor to express clear preferences for particular patterns of punishment. In choosing between more severe and less severe punishments, the citizen will usually choose the former, simply as a way of expressing hostility toward those who commit a crime. These negative attitudes create only a general predisposition—the average citizen does not think about a scale of punishments as a set of graded relationships between different types of crime. Voting for penalties is most importantly a way of voting against crime. When that general attitude is applied to a specific set of penalty choices, the more severe choice is the more emphatic vote against crime. At that level of generality, when thinking of criminals as a general category, there is no natural limit to this nonproportional hostility. It is only when specific situations involve an individual with a face and a story that punitive sentiments might encounter an upper limit.

The tendency for citizens to open-endedly support higher penalties when choosing between alternatives does not mean that the specific preferences expressed are important to the voters. There may be a large gap between the specific penalties citizens might choose and the levels of punishment the same citizens will tolerate if others in government choose them. We believe that this is one fundamental characteristic of punishment in modern Western democracies. A corollary is that as more elements of punishment policy move closer to democratic control, punishment levels for common criminals will tend upward.

The tendency for members of the public to vote only their attitudes toward criminals may be dependent on the citizen's role, as well as on the way in which the issue is made into a choice. Turn a complaining cab driver into a sentencing judge and his or her sensitivity to questions of desert and proportionality in individual cases might be just as strong as the judge sitting in the next courtroom. Because the questions voters can decide are limited in form, we cannot know how much of the upward bias is a product of the character of who is making the decision and how much is a function of how the issue is presented.

One other limit haunts the effort to analyze governance of punishment and the choice of excessive penalties—the problem of defining and measuring excess. Most mandatory punishments lack a sense of proportionality, and the most extreme seem to fit this meaning of excessive. The threshold of instrumental excessiveness is more elusive.

But perhaps we need not measure the excessiveness of particular penalties to reject the prospect of direct democratic control. It may be that the necessary procedures so invite excessive outcomes that this problem is a sufficient reason to discourage the practice. That is, if there are disciplines and perspectives that should be involved in choosing sentence ranges or particular case punishments that are missing from achievable democratic processes, the procedural tendency toward excess could become a basis for avoiding direct democracy without the further measurement of excessiveness. Thus one possible definition of expertise in punishment choice is the discipline necessary to consider all the aspects that a balanced punishment decision should consider.

Some Conclusions

From the standpoint of either proportionality or the instrumental functions of criminal punishments, we cannot identify optimal levels of punishment for particular crimes, let alone a scale of such punishments for the wide range of different behaviors prohibited by modern penal codes. Even so, it is apparent that the combination of mandatory penalty rules and the democratic selection of penalty levels will err on the high side, as well as treat crimes of different levels of severity in troublesomely similar fashion. We expect that experts who would disagree with one another about optimal levels of punishment would nonetheless agree broadly about the problematic tendencies of mixing popular sentiment and mandatory penalty rules.

Two different preventive approaches can be attempted, either singly or in combination. One is to shift the power to set punishments to government actors protected from direct democratic controls. This can be done even at the level of setting general standards with bodies like sentencing commissions. Although sentencing commissions do make rules for much narrower categories of offenses and offenders than general laws like Three Strikes, the range of punishments they may leave to an individual judge can be rather small. The hope is that expert choices of narrow ranges will be closer to the correct punishment for the categories covered. A second approach is to maintain a wide discretion for the particular application of the law at the individual level. To some extent, this is an alternative to the insulated expert commission with tight standards. But both approaches may be desirable in concert. Problems like dual currency and worst-case standards are threats to mandatory standards even in the hands of expert bodies. There may be strong reasons to consider institutional methods of creating discretion in individual cases and sentence adjustments after substantial portions of a long prison sentence have been served.

But how and when should a democracy protect itself from public opinion? And do we know enough about the problems associated with governance by popularly chosen mandatory minimums to justify the resort to techniques of insulated delegation? The last two sections of this chapter approach this issue indirectly—giving our version of the story of independent central banking in the United States, a prominent twentieth-century example of insulated delegation by design, and examining some current criminal justice reforms by using the language and concepts developed earlier in the chapter.

The Justification of Independent Central Banks

In modern times, central banks are the most prominent example of the explicit design of government institutions to insulate decision making from democrative control. In every Western democracy, the policies on interest rates and other conditions of monetary policy are made by institutions created by the state and universally believed to be exercising state power. But a strong normative preference for what is called independence has meant the deliberate design of central banks to minimize their responsiveness to popular preferences and to the legislative bodies created by representative democracy. The extensive literature on the case for and against independence is of substantial value to those considering the issue of governance in topics without a legacy of analysis, topics such as punishment.

What sets central banking apart from the other administrative agencies that have taken power in the twentieth century was not the delegation of power from democratically to nondemocratically responsible actors but rather the explicit distrust of democratic influence that produced a proliferation of techniques of insulation. Those who design central banks go beyond what we called delegation to administrative bodies and have elevated what we called insulated delegation to an art form. Techniques of distancing from democratic control have been put in place, including an ideology of independence for the central bankers, staggered terms for bank governors, professional qualifications and nonpolitical identifications for those appointed, long terms in office, and negative judgments of attempts by government officials to exert influence on the governors.

In the United States, the Federal Reserve system created in 1913 delegated power to a complex system involving a mix of the Federal Reserve Board, the Federal Open Market Committee, and directors and officers of regional banks. All other independent agencies are subject to congressional audit and appropriations, but the Federal Reserve is not—it is supported by income from its own operations. This particular insulation from accountability to Congress is mentioned as an important part of the design by a friendly analyst: "The system's audit and budget procedures were essential elements in its unique organizational structures. The arrangement enabled it to be a buffer between the electorate and the government, and thereby to exercise discretion within the government to do what from a political viewpoint was unpopular" (Clifford, 1965, p. 393). An unsympathetic observer sums up the same arrangement as follows:

> The Federal Reserve system is accountable to no one; it has no budget; it is subject to no audit and no Congressional committee group can truly supervise its operations. The Federal Reserve, virtually in total control of the nation's vital monetary system, is accountable to nobody—and this strange situation, if acknowledged at all, is invariably trumpeted as a virtue. (Rothbard 1994, p. 3)

The virtue of independent monetary authorities is considered a fundamental feature of International Monetary Fund (IMF) reform packages imposed on borrower nations in the 1990s; in Murray Rothbard's (1994) phrase, independence is literally "trumpeted as a virtue," and a necessary virtue for IMF support. Rothbard detects a dissonance in this enthusiasm for independence: "It is curious how many self-proclaimed champions of 'democracy' whether domestic or global, rush to defend the alleged ideal of the total independence of the Federal Reserve" (p. 5). Why is this so?

Three separate justifications were historically put forward for the insulated status of central banks:

1. The need for special expertise in monetary policy.
2. The conflict of interest that would bias a government toward setting low interest rates to minimize its own debt service expenditures.
3. The bias of democratically responsive institutions toward policies that produce undesirable levels of inflation. (Clifford, 1965, p. 34)

The first two reasons for autonomy are only partial explanations for the special status of a central bank in American national government. Fear of the inflationary bias of democratic governance is the central justification.

The need for special expertise is a traditional rationale for the creation of administrative agencies within the executive branch of government. By itself, however, the requirement of expertise does not carry any extraordinary need to insulate decisions from accountability to democratic institutions. The substantive mission of the National Aeronautics and Space Administration is, literally, rocket science, but this agency is accountable to congressional audits and its director serves at the pleasure of a democratically elected president. Nobody complains even though citizens and most members of Congress have only a limited understanding of physics. Why, then, is the public's innocence of economics a disqualification for democratic control?

The potential conflict of interest is specific to circumstances of high government debt and does not match the concerns of those attempting to insulate Federal Reserve power from Democratic responsiveness. Low debt service is a special interest of the government, not something that ordinary citizens would worry much about. Indeed, those citizens who purchase government bills and notes would wish a higher return. Although citizens with their own debts would have an incentive to push interest rates lower, that is a different concern than a government conflict of interest.

The real heart of the argument is the inflationary bias of democratic preferences. The usual statement of the problem is that majorities of the public or those who secure power through electoral majorities prefer policies that promote inflationary outcomes, policies such as easy access to credit and low interest rates. In this view, it is not that the public prefers inflationary outcomes but rather that such outcomes are a necessary result of policies with other desirable features, policies that command majority support.

And what is the harm of such policies? On that question, the political economists who support insulation are far from unanimous. One argument is that these policies lead to hyper-inflationary circumstances, which leave nearly everybody worse off. In this view, public support is almost completely the result of lack of understanding of the eventual cost of policies that produce short-term rewards. This view of the undisciplined outcomes of popular monetary policies is that they dis-serve the majorities that support them. The bias toward such policies in majority-rule environments is attributable to the ignorance of economic effects on the part of all who support them.

A second argument is that inflationary monetary policies are on balance inefficient even if the redistributive impacts of such effects as job creation and economic growth create winners, as well as losers. This is the usual position attributed to market economists who criticize the lack of discipline in central banks that are responsive to majoritarian pressure (Barry 1991).

A third argument holds that high levels of inflation are wrong and are to be avoided on grounds that are independent of efficiencies in the market economy. There is in the history of the hard money/soft money debate a view of expansionary monetary policy as a harm in itself rather than a set of policies that might lead to harmful effects. In this view, the problem of democratic influence on monetary policy is inflation itself, not the harmful effects that inflationary policies might lead to. The gold standard was to many of its proponents a moral principle, a bedrock of economic order, rather than merely an instrumentally justified discipline on the growth of a money supply.

This moralist position has not been the formal justification for the insulation of central banks. What is less clear is whether vestiges of the moralist perspective may have influenced the consequentialist arguments that do currently stand as the mainstream justification. Certainly the rhetoric of some modern political economists, linking inflation to moral decline in a permissive society, are closer in tone to an earlier generation of gold standard moralists than to the dispassionate neutrality of an economic analyst who will criticize the preferences of others only if they hamper efficient markets. There are also overtones of the competing interests (in the short term at least) between debtors and creditors and between the unemployed and the propertied that form something of a subtext in the antimajoritarian ethos of central banking (Buchanan and Wagner 1977).

Three lessons from the central bank story might help us frame our consideration of the governance of punishment.

1. *The insulation of central banks was based on a substantive preference in monetary matters rather than on a general theory of the need to qualify representative democracy.* The consensus that created independent central banks was the need for restraint in monetary policy. From this pragmatic concern, rather than from any theory or set of findings about the performance of different types of government agencies, the need for insulation was inferred. So those who created the Federal Reserve were primarily dedicated to a monetary policy and searched for an institutional configuration that would facilitate their preferred outcome. This may be characterized as working backward, but that seems to be an accurate history of the architecture of central banking. When the institutions were put in place, there was general consensus that anti-inflationary decisions require political insulation but no real consensus on why that might be (compare, e.g., Buchanan and Wagner 1977 with Miller 1998).

The obvious analogy in punishment policy is that the real motive for insulated delegation is moderation in penalty levels. This sort of

working backward from a preference for avoiding long and mandatory prison terms is common in criminal justice reform efforts.

2. *Once in place, insulated institutions can have long and stable
careers in political democracies.* Supported by an ethic of independent professionalism, the U.S. Federal Reserve has already had an
87-year career with no sustained attack on its principles of decision
making or its insulations from political control. In no sense can this
stable institutional history be read as explicit public consent to non-
democratic monetary policy, but it is not fanciful to characterize the
unchallenged functioning of the Federal Reserve as a version of implicit consent to the extraordinary status of the institution. The norm
of independence has kept political actors from seriously questioning
the existing institutional arrangement. Market-oriented observers
might be tempted to read into this record an inference that the Federal Reserve accommodates majoritarian sentiments when making
policy to avoid political conflicts, but the evidence for this is slight.
Deliberate provocations may be avoided, but an ethic of independence is also a powerful factor in the largely unquestioned persever-
ance of independent functioning by the Federal Reserve during a historical period when populist sentiments are in ascendance.

A distinction is necessary between the conditions of political support and popular acceptance necessary to build institutions that will
make decisions insulated from democratic review and those necessary to maintain insulated institutions once they are operating. Inertia
is a powerful ally in the organization of government power, and there
have been no serious challenges to the independence of the Federal
Reserve in the modern era. This does not mean that establishing a new
institution with insulated status would be easy or achievable. Furthermore, changing a set of decisions that was previously within democratic influence to a structure insulated from such review would be even
harder than creating an insulated status from scratch. Removing democratic controls in a visible way is an uphill battle in which none of
the significant inertial forces at work support the shift. So creating a
Federal Reserve–like status where significant legislative controls had
previously existed is a prospect not enhanced by a careful reading of
the history of the Federal Reserve in the United States.

A similar set of institutional tendencies applies in criminal justice. A tradition of independence is probably much easier to maintain than to invent, and explicit displacement of democratic control
is a particularly hard sell.

3. *A theory of required expertise can serve as a sufficient basis for*

insulated institutions in government and in public opinion. A consensus that professional expertise is necessary to make monetary policy has been the justifying principle for the independence of the Federal Reserve, and from the perspective of the public, this has been a commitment to expertise much more than a commitment to a particular restraint as a policy. The central importance of faith in the expertise of the responsible officials illustrates the potential impact of the loss in publicly acknowledged expert status for judges and parole agencies in the criminal justice system, which was one prelude to the increases in imprisonment in the 1970s and 1980s. If an ethic of expertise is one necessary element in the construction of insulated decision-making structures, the current reputation of judges and correctional officials will make a criminal justice ethic of expertise a difficult task. To put the comparison the other way around, if the expertise of central bankers was not accepted by the general pubic and political actors, the insulated status of the institutions they administer would be in grave doubt. In this regard, the special political status of the Federal Reserve in the United States is as much public relations as political economy. As former Federal Reserve Board Chairman William McChesney Martin put it, "At some point economics becomes theology—you have to introduce the element of faith" (Clifford 1965, p. 36).

The lesson here for criminal justice reform is the importance of a commitment and respect for expertise, which is itself a justifying ideology for the insulated delegation of punishment power. The rejection of traditional authorities in sentencing will leave the system vulnerable to political control without the creation of new justifications for expertise.

Some History Retold

We have examined the separation of powers in various systems of criminal justice, comparing systems in industrial democracies and the 50 states of the United States. Here we will concentrate on the analysis of how government systems have evolved over time in the United States. The focus is first on California over the two decades between the advent of determinate sentencing in 1976 and the regimes of mandatory minimum sentencing of Three Strikes and 10-20-Life. We will then contrast these developments with an account of sentencing commissions in Minnesota and in the federal system. Discussing the recent history of criminal sentencing in California is covering events and legislation that have already been analyzed in chapters 7 and 9. But the point of this retelling is to use the vocabulary and theories of this chapter to provide new insight to a thrice-told tale about California, as well as to explore an alternative method of achieving some of the reform objectives that created determinate sentencing a generation ago.

California entered the 1970s with an allocation of power in criminal punishment only slightly different from the predominant pattern in the United States. The legislature defined crimes and provided a series of indeterminate sentences for felonies, with authority delegated to judges and the parole authority. Judges were given the authority to choose between prison and nonprison sanctions, and the authority to determine the amount of time the offender would serve was given to the parole authority. This pattern was typical in the United States, except that judges in other states had greater influence on the minimum and maximum prison sentence and thus more power over how much time an offender would serve.

The mechanical impact of the 1976 determinate sentencing law was to leave the judge's in-or-out power undisturbed but to replace parole determination with a series of legislatively proscribed terms. Thus the power of the parole authority was assumed by the legislature. The authority of sentencing judges was not reduced by this legislation in any direct way, and the ability to choose a term might actually have increased the judge's impact on the time served by those defendants the judge sent to prison. The 1976 reform attempted to preserve the discounting of nominal sentences that was in the power of parole boards by creating 50% good-time sentence reductions. The approach was meant to improve the offender's position by reducing the disparity in prison sentences and eliminating the uncertainty about release dates that parole power produced. All other elements of pre-1977 prison terms were supposed to remain as they had been.

The means taken to achieve these ends created a number of structural and symbolic precedents for the advent of Three Strikes. The first result of removing parole was to eliminate punishment decision making by an administrative agency with delegated power and to give that power to an elected legislature. The second impact of the 1976 reform was to create a new currency of punishment—the presumptive determinate sentence—and to give to an institution of representative democracy the power to issue that currency and change these new sentences at will. The 1976 reforms made the state legislature into the central bank of just deserts, with institutional supremacy over judges in determining the particular prison term for each felony in the penal code.

The creation of the new category and its assignment to the legislature undermined the two claims of expertise that had separated criminal punishment in California from democratic power. The obvious victim was parole expertise, the central target of the reform. The claims that such agencies could determine the dangerousness of an offender or the prisoner's response to rehabilitation was rejected by the legislative reforms as both unproven and irrelevant to the measure of appropriate punishment. So the insulation from democratic control that parole represented was deliberately removed, yet without any reference to the ability of a legislature to set punishment. The legislature won this power by default.

The 1976 reforms in California also undermined the claims of judges to special expertise, first, by subordinating the judicial role in setting prison terms to tight legislative guidelines. The 1976 law redefined the dominant factors in setting penalties and failed to give judges much power beyond the in-or-out decision. The old allocation of power between judges and parole could be viewed as a division of authority between expert bodies on the basis of comparative advantage. Once the in-prison behavior of offenders is downgraded in the jurisprudence of imprisonment, the claim of the sentencing judge to increased power seems obvious. But the authority of judges was instead subordinated to a nonexpert body, a legislature that became the reigning expert on what term of imprisonment best served the purposes of criminal punishment for a class of offender. Second, the 1976 legislation undermined the status of judges by moving the emphasis from individual determinations of appropriate prison terms to generalizations about categories of offenses that could then be mechanically applied in individual cases. Because of its drafters' fear of disparity in sentences for similar offenders, the legislation sought to determine appropriate prison terms for whole categories of offenders, with small adjustments up or down for aggravation or mitigation. This preference for the wholesale over the retail denigrates the importance of the judicial domain.

There were, it should be noted, important adjustments to legislatively determined sentences for entire categories of felons in the 1976 law. Judges might have been tightly constrained once they decided on prison as a criminal sanction, but the choice between imprisonment and probation was a matter of judicial discretion. This is no small power in a system where felony convictions produced more nonprison sentences than imprisonments, the situation in California in the mid-1970s. Moreover the nominal prison terms in the legislation were reduced for good-time credit. But neither of these important sentencing provisions was rooted in a theory of expertise or penological function. These were the silently constructed characteristics of the new law, without either an institutional or intellectual foundation. The discretion to avoid imprisonment was a potential embarrassment for a system that was supposedly reducing disparity by standardizing the prison terms of the minority of felons who were sent to prison. No express theory of judicial competence went with this power; indeed it was unmentioned.

Good time was designed as an all but automatic discount rather than a discretionary manifestation of correctional expertise, and the reformers who had just undermined the claims of parole boards to legitimate authority over release were not about to give prison administrators a cloak of expertise. That was a matter of just deserts alone, which left the good-time adjustment as transparently arbitrary. Why not 30% or 70%? Why have any discount at all? The 1976 reforms rejected the ideology of rehabilitation and replaced it with a set of practices that was not closely linked to ideologies or normative traditions. No criminal justice officials gained status in the 1976 reforms, and the only government officials who gained power were legislators and prosecutors. In retrospect, the determinate sentencing reforms left California vulnerable to the extreme form of Three Strikes from the start.

Sentencing Commissions as Insulated Delegations

The reforms that produced sentencing commissions in a number of states and in the federal government began in the same historical period that produced determinate sentencing in California, and the preoccupying concerns of the reformers involved the same mixture of doubts about rehabilitation and sentencing disparity. The determinate sentencing laws were clustered in the period from 1976 to 1980, whereas the sentencing commissions were launched in 1980 in Minnesota and adopted by federal law in 1984.

Although there are substantial variations in sentencing commissions, the eight or nine systems which give legal authority to a sentencing commission's guidelines are all administrative or judicial agencies with delegated power to establish guidelines that sentencing judges must acknowledge and follow in making individual decisions. Whereas California and other determinate sentencing jurisdictions created legislative sentencing structures, the jurisdictions with sentencing commissions delegated the authority to a new institution in government that was removed from the legislature and regarded as independent and expert. So whereas the determinate sentencing systems destroyed the institutional structure of parole and replaced it with legislative mandates, the laws for sentencing commissions replaced one expert institution with another (Knapp 1987).

In the latter jurisdictions, there was a new agency at the front end of the system to replace the older parole authority that had operated at the back end. These new systems produced some of the same conflation of general and individual stages of sentencing when their guideline ranges were narrowed to reduce the opportunity of individual judges to treat similar cases in grossly different ways. To the extent that narrow guidelines produce the tendencies toward excess discussed earlier, their force on the front end of the sentencing process will tend toward unnecessarily high sentences.

But the systems that replaced parole with a new independent institution have been more successful in fighting off legislative assaults than have those determinate systems that created new sentences with no new institutional forces. The federal sentencing commission was overcome by mandatory minimum drug penalties early in its career, but some state systems, such as Minnesota, have fared much better. What makes this particularly interesting is the lack of any justifying ideology to support the legitimacy of sentencing commissions. Parole boards were supported by an ideology of rehabilitation and prediction of dangerousness (Morris 1974, chap. 2), but the sentencing commission is a nakedly pragmatic institution with an expertise that is not linked to any larger theory of criminal punishment. That this openly pragmatic portfolio might be enough to defend the new institution from legislative incursions is remarkable, although the saga of the central banks suggests that a long tradition of pragmatic restraint may itself become a justifying ideology of independence and requires no thicker theology to survive.

If the institutional presence and patina of expertise of many state sentencing commissions has insulated the systems in which they operate from aggressive legislatures, the way in which such commissions now operate in the United States raises both political and structural problems. They are politically vulnerable to legislatively imposed penalties, as well as to pressure to increase penalties to avoid legislative conflicts. Both of these processes have been prominent in the career of the U.S. sentencing commission (Tonry 1996, chap. 3).

The major structural weakness of a strong sentencing commission is that it must provide fairly narrow sentencing guidelines. But narrow guidelines generate costs not unlike the inefficiencies of mandatory minimum sentences. If the symbolic need for longer sentences is honored, sentences longer than operationally necessary are imposed because there are minimal back-end adjustments. But if the symbolic need for long sentences to underline the condemnation of criminal acts is ignored, the system becomes more vulnerable to citizens' dissatisfaction and to legislative override. Narrow sentencing guidelines are also problematic measures of the particular harm that an individual offender has inflicted on the community and on degrees of culpability. Instead, complex sentencing grids tend to emphasize easily measured matters, such as dollar loss or amounts of prohibited drugs, that cannot be persuasively tied to large increments in punishment for entire classes of differently situated offenders (Tonry 1996, pp. 13–24).

The best use of a sentencing commission would be to issue broad guidelines and policy statements that left wide areas of discretion for sentencing judges in particular cases. The way to avoid undue disparity in prison terms is to have some back-end adjustments, especially for long sentences, imposed by an authority on a case-by-case basis and informed by general statistics collected by the courts or by the sentencing commission. The same commission that issued guidelines could do these case-by-case determinations, or they could be assigned to a separate, complementary agency. The conflation of the general and the particular is not a necessary part of the design of a sentencing commission.

Indeed, the fine irony of reforms in both determinate sentencing and sentencing commissions is that the best way to cure the disparate sentences of traditional parole is with the same adjustment powers exercised at the same point in the process by an agency with a different agenda. Something very much like parole with different marching orders could improve both systems, but the reputation of parole was too tied to its prior functions for law reformers ever to consider a multipart system that involved a parole-style function. That would have been, in 1980, akin to a temperance union that was in favor of "the hair of the dog that bit you" as a cure for a hangover.

The public relations success of sentencing commissions as credible repositories of expertise suggests the large role that institutional factors and intangible questions of social status will have in protecting punishment policy from populist overrides. Just as central banking is a matter of public faith, so, too, is setting the punishments for convicted offenders. New institutions like the sentencing commission are one part of the answer; restoring faith in the authority and expertise of sentencing judges is another.

The particular history of California in the 1970s sheds important light on two dimensions of the circumstances that led to Three Strikes and 10-20-Life. The contrast of California's reforms with those based on sentencing commissions for the same complaints shows the special vulnerability that will be created when all the institutions that make criminal justice policy are put in disrepute and no new institutional actors are invested with public trust. Viewed in this way, the democratic endorsement of Three Strikes in 1994 was not a preference of citizens for fixed penalties over other theories of punishment, it was a choice made in a vacuum. The system that California put in place in 1976 never had articulate defenders because the common ground for its supporters had been opposition to a previous regime. The division of authority in the state after 1976 was in the service of no ideology, and the courts had no articulate supporters in the executive or legislative branch. When distrust in government becomes political orthodoxy, and it did in California, direct democratic control may appear as a last refuge rather than an optimal allocation of powers.

ELEVEN

Legacies and Lessons

The concerns of this final chapter are more specific than the subjects raised in chapter 10. There, the Three Strikes experience served as a stimulus for an exploration of the governance of punishment in democracy. Here, we wish to focus more closely on the law's impacts and implications that appeared in the 1990s. The legacies we refer to are the changes in procedure and legal outcome that Three Strikes has produced and is likely to produce in the future. The lessons are the insights that are available to students of penal law from the brief history of Three Strikes. Many of these lessons are, as yet, tentative because its immediate legislative history is less than a decade old at this writing—which provides even more reason to record what seem to be the implications of this unfolding chapter of penal law while memories and evidence are still fresh.

The legacies of the specific law that we have studied are concentrated in the state of California. The lessons that can be drawn from its origins and aftermath are of general importance and will receive most of our attention in this concluding chapter. Our discussion in these last pages is more self-consciously editorial in both topic selection and in tone than in earlier chapters.

Four Legacies

The concrete changes produced by Three Strikes in California can be reported under four headings: the law itself, its operational impact, the Three Strikes legend in California, and the effect on the politics of criminal justice.

The Law

The initiative passed by the voters in November 1994 is no ordinary legislative pronouncement but rather a set of rules protected from legislative revision by requirements of super-majority support. This restriction was widely thought to be the only provision that separated the statutory version of Three Strikes, which took effect in March 1994, from the initiative version of Three Strikes which was passed by the voters in November 1994.[1]

The rationale for restricting legislative revision is not difficult to discern: It is distrust of government. Whereas democratically elected legislators serve as a bridge between popular will and the instrumentalities of government, it is the association of the legislators with the "otherness" of formal government that motivated the decision to circumscribe the legislature's amending capacity. Just as a distrust of judges-as-government justified the mandatory minimum of both the legislation and initiative, the distrust of legislators-as-government justified the curtailment of legislative amendment.

The Three Strikes law in effect in the year 2000 provides minimum terms of imprisonment that must be sought by prosecutors and imposed by judges whenever persons convicted of felony crimes have one or more strike conviction on their criminal records, unless not doing so by prosecutors or, by the terms of the California Supreme Court's decision in *People v. Romero* (1996), by sentencing judges is "in the interests of justice." The formal legal framework of Three Strikes in California now provides that each of the two institutional actors who control sentencing decisions have discretionary power on a unilateral basis. In both theory and practice then, it is not possible to estimate the degree of enforcement mandated under the legislation. The rules of Three Strikes are subject to the independent discretion of both prosecutors and judges.

The Operating System

As our study of arrests and punishments in the aftermath of Three Strikes demonstrated, the systems that quickly evolved under the new statute were highly discretionary and much less of a direct challenge to the traditional authority of prosecutors and judges than the rhetoric of the political campaign would have suggested. Only as much of the program as local prosecutors wished to enforce could be launched. This led to a wide variation in the levels of enforcement in

---

[1] The legislation passed earlier in the year restricted change in parallel language, but the legislature in all probability lacks the power to restrict future legislatures. Only the initiative put Three Strikes safely beyond the power of a legislative majority.

different places, notable in our study by the much lower prosecution rate in San Francisco than in San Diego.

In addition to the substantial variation in enforcement, the two different provisions for sentence enhancement have been implemented with sharply different degrees of fidelity to the language of the statute. Statewide, the odds that a case that qualified for a second-strike mandatory sentence would receive it were three and one-half times as great as the chance that a case that qualified for a three-strikes enhancement would receive that. This meant that the silent partner in the penal package became the dominant influence on rates and patterns of imprisonment. Ninety percent of the prison sentences imposed under the authority of the Three Strikes law were second-strike sentences of twice the nominal term normally available for the current charge and three times the actual time served when release restrictions were factored in. Only 10% of the sentences imposed under Three Strikes were the 25-year-to-life terms mandated for any felony conviction when two prior strikes had been established (California Department of Corrections 1999).

The dominance of the second-strike category is a natural product of the wide discretionary powers available under the Three Strikes legislation. The second-strike penalties are less drastic increases from prior prison sentences than the third-strike minimum and therefore more likely to fit with the priorities of local prosecutors. The second-strike punishments are also more closely linked to the seriousness of the defendant's current offense than the one-size-fits-all three-strikes minimum of 25-years-to-life. To the extent that proportionality in punishment is a value of importance to prosecutors and judges, the second-strike sentencing scheme is much more likely to result in adherence.

The wide gap between mandatory language and discretionary application is the major explanation for the way in which the new law was accommodated by the court and correctional systems in California without major crisis. It had been predicted that the court system would grind to a halt under the weight of demands for jury trials made by those who faced high mandatory penalties (Feeley and Kamin 1996). In the case of second-strike offenders, however, there was ample room for plea bargaining because altering the charge for which the defendant would be convicted changes the mandatory sentence required by the law. So demands for jury trials could be kept under control for this class of cases, and these were the great majority of prosecutions under the new statute.

For the three-strikes category, the 25-year minimum did produce a rate of jury trials ten times as great as the standard for felony cases, but a systemic breakdown was avoided because only a very small fraction of potential cases became actual cases. The impact on court resources of even a 50% incidence of demand for jury trials will not be overwhelming if only 1 case in every 10 that were eligible received full-scale prosecution.

The same combination of second-strike plea bargaining and three-strike nonprosecution lightened the impact of the new legislation on the prison system. The number of second-strike commitments quickly became quite large, but the level of sentence for this category was not hugely different from the terms imposed prior to Three Strikes. The Three Strikes sentences were discontinuously large when compared with prior practice, but only about a hundred such offenders a month have been added to the prison population in the first years of Three Strikes. Although the number of three-strike offenders present in California prisons will increase dramatically over the first two decades of the new system, the short-run impact of the law has been less than a 10% net increment in a prison population that was already over 130,000 when the law was passed.

So Three Strikes in California has been absorbed and accommodated in the criminal justice system in ways that appear to compromise the systemic ambitions of a statute dedicated to distrust of the exercise of discretion by government officials. Have these processes of compromise and accommodation scandalized the political constituencies that gave birth to Three Strikes? They have not, and this absence of acrimony is an important element in the narrative history of the statute. There have been no investigative reports and exposés. Only the California Supreme Court's holding in the *Romero* case inspired any protest by the lobbyists responsible for Three Strikes and by their supporters in the state legislature. Even there, a threat to reverse this decision by generating another voter initiative was soon abandoned ("Three Strikes Initiative Circulated" 1996). Although the constituencies that produced Three Strikes were active in California politics during 1996 and 1997, the operational status of the law was not one of their priorities.

The Legend

A curious and revealing legislative struggle occurred in California during 1999, more than five years after the Three Strikes legislation took effect. After a heated debate, the California legislature enacted a law providing for a publicly funded study of Three Strikes (Senate Bill 873, 1999). The chief sponsors of the proposal were liberal Democratic legislators who were opposed to Three Strikes in principle and who wanted to build a case for weakening its regime. The study was their inspired attempt to seize the rhetorical high ground. After all, who could be opposed to studying the effects of the law?

Both the study's proponents and those opposed to it saw the proposal as an assault on what we call the legend of Three Strikes, a story of crime policy in California only tangentially related to actual history but one of large importance in California politics. The essential elements of the legend are threefold: first, that punishment policy in California prior to Three Strikes was lenient and irresolute; second, that the law was a broad shift in policy from *soft* to *hard* on crime and criminals in general; third, that crime rates, which had been increasing up to the time that the statute was enacted, then turned downward as a consequence of the new law. The central role of the 1994 legal changes in this version of history explains why the attorney general's report (discussed in chapter 6) refers to the "Three Strikes era" in California crime and punishment. The 1994 law has for many been recast as the watershed reframing of punishment in the state.

The controversy surrounding the study proposal is evidence that both sides regard it as an attack on the legend of Three Strikes. The liberals hoped that study results would debunk myths about the law's effectiveness and create an environment in which the terms of the statute could be modified. The opponents of the proposal consider the legendary status of Three Strikes to be a considerable asset. Why open the presumed effectiveness of the legislation to study? Orthodox beliefs function most effectively when they are not questioned.

If those supporting the study believe that any negative findings on the deterrence of the 1994 legislation would undermine its public support, they may be soon disappointed. Citizens' support for Three Strikes could be the opposite of an instrumental justification, in which people believe that the legislation is appropriate only because they suppose it is effective. Instead, it is often the case that belief in the effectiveness of a penal statute is rooted in the citizens' conviction that the law is appropriate. Since the penal measures *feel* right, they must be working well. That is the usual causal ordering for a belief in orthodoxy.

Empirical evidence that might call into question the deterrence of

Three Strikes will be of little effect in undermining support for the statute, for two reasons. First, the belief that penalties must deter because they are morally justified is a very hard faith to shake with counterevidence because the subject wants to believe. Thus the belief can be maintained against formidable assault. Second, even if deterrence is disproved to the satisfaction of the orthodox, belief that Three Strikes is appropriate policy can still survive. It should be remembered that incapacitation rather than deterrence was the primary justification for the 25-year-to-life terms (Green 1995; Podger 1993), and claims of substantial general deterrence came after the fact. There is no indication that this add-on justification has become a sine qua non for continued public support. Remove the case for deterrence, and considerations of retribution and incapacitation will still provide support for Three Strikes orthodoxy.

So it is probably not a concern about the belief in deterrence that motivated resistance in the legislature to the study proposal. It is rather that hostility to and doubt about an orthodox belief system is in itself an insult to the believer and the belief. The doubts about Three Strikes are not resented because they may lead to political difficulties; they are in and of themselves a denial of the normative beliefs that supporters hold. It is the heresy itself rather than what further harm it might accomplish that provokes the anger of Three Strikes supporters. It is the insult that constitutes the injury. Under such circumstances, the governor of California, Gray Davis (1999), waited more than a month and then vetoed the legislation, concluding that "an additional study is unlikely to produce much, if any, useful information that is not already available."

The Politics of Crime

The veto of a study bill is another indication that the 1994 law and the processes that produced it have created a political landscape notably inhospitable to reversing Three Strikes. Single-issue politicians concern themselves with criminal justice proposals and no others. With the sole exception of associations of defence attorneys, the single-issue politicians in criminal justice form an alliance for penal severity that regards the Three Strikes law as iconic orthodoxy. The professional prosecutors associations are not viscerally tied to the Three Strikes legend, but their members are in no way constrained by the terms of the 1994 law and so do not have any incentive to change it.

In these political circumstances, the path of least resistance for reducing the role of Three Strikes in criminal sentencing will be discretionary disuse of the law's provisions by prosecutors and judges. The contrast between statutory provisions and operational reality has always been greatest for the three-strike section of the legislation because of the gap between its provisions and prosecutorial notions of appropriate punishment. This will continue. It is also much easier for prosecutors to operationally nullify provisions in Three Strikes than for judges to do so. The discretion not to prosecute is all but invisible, whereas the judicial set-asides of the penalties after prosecutors seek them are both visible and controversial. But if prosecutorial discretion is the main engine in reducing the impact of Three Strikes, substantial geographic diversity will continue in California, pushing the state even further down the path of decentralized power.

Two further developments in the politics of criminal justice in California and elsewhere deserve mention. The first of these political legacies is a loose coalition of interest groups united in support of expanding the use of imprisonment as a criminal sanction. Motives for this emphasis vary among the coalition's partners. The prison guard's union has an obvious economic stake in the expansion of the basis for its employment, whereas victim advocacy groups embrace the prison because it is the most severe of widely available punishments. One striking element in the career of this coalition is its timing—after the largest increase in imprisonment in California's history rather than before. Between 1980 and 1991, the prison population of the state grew almost fivefold, and this was before any organized coalition for prison expansion came into existence (Zimring and Hawkins 1992).

The second political legacy is an assumption that virtually all issues of punishment policy can be reduced to a zero-sum competition between crime victims and criminal offenders. Whether the question is prison terms for burglars, registration of sex offenders, or recreational facilities in state prisons, the notion of a zero-sum competition asks the voter to decide the issue by choosing between offenders and their victims. The implicit assumption is that anything that is bad for offenders must be beneficial to victims. As a matter of utilitarian reasoning this approach has little merit, but as political rhetoric it is both versatile and appealing. Once every policy question becomes a status competition, the appropriate result is a foregone conclusion. Instead of calculating costs and benefits, all a citizen must do is choose sides.

The rhetorical versatility of this conception is quite astonishing.

No punishment seems too extreme if anything that hurts offenders benefits victims. There is never an issue of diminishing marginal returns if each new proposal can be cast as the same zero-sum choice, and thus punishment levels never reach a saturation point. Inquiries about cost are beside the point because policy results can be assumed from the intention of the proposal to harm offenders. As long as any such harm to offenders *must* produce benefits to victims, the voters' choice on any question is easy and the process of punitive reformation will be endless.

We suggest that something like the dynamic of a zero-sum assumption has played an important role in the politics of crime in the United States for more than a decade. Whether the particular topic is transfer from juvenile court, good-time reductions in prison sentences, plea-bargaining reductions, or restrictions on the appeal of death sentences, the general framework of sentiment follows a zero-sum pattern. Whether this set of assumptions has always characterized popular sentiment or has come to prominence in recent years we cannot say. But its contemporary importance in the United States is apparent.

Lessons

What can the career of Three Strikes in California tell us about crime policy in the United States? What lessons might there be for students of criminal justice in other industrial democracies? We will discuss three linked patterns that we observed in California and believe to be important matters of broad applicability to criminal justice policy in all modern democracies.

A Tale of Two Statutes

We will begin by again mentioning a dramatic contrast discussed in chapter 2. Both the state of California and the federal government passed versions of Three Strikes in 1994. By the autumn of 1998, a total of 35 persons were sentenced under the provisions of the legislation passed by Congress. By that time, more than 40,000 offenders had been sentenced under the California version of the law (Campaign for an Effective Crime Policy 1998). The public mood and political environment in Sacramento and Washington were not dissimilar in 1994, and the legislative products were given the same Three

Strikes label. But the operational impact of one version was a thousand times greater than that of the other. Our earlier discussion of this contrast dealt with legislative details and political tactics. Our effort here is to explore the characteristics in politics, in government, and in the operation of criminal justice that result in enormous variations in the operational consequences of different forms of the same legal endeavor.

To comprehend the huge contingencies in current conditions is an important ambition for our concluding analysis. What political and government conditions generate two different examples of the same type of law that have operational impacts of vastly different orders of magnitude? The three connected features of current circumstances we would emphasize are the following:

1. The loose connection between symbolic politics and operational outcomes in criminal justice
2. The large operational significance of variations in institutional structure in determining criminal justice outcomes
3. The paradoxical politics of government distrust in current criminal justice policy

Loose Coupling

If the motivation behind public support for enhanced punishment is a symbolic denunciation of criminals and crime, this need to make a symbolic stand may not be closely linked to any particular set of outcomes. It is the message sent about crime and criminals rather than the number of extra years of punishment or the volume of offenders who will be subject to it that is the main point of the law. This circumstance of "loose coupling"[2] between a symbolic message and any level of operational results can produce high variability in the impact of laws that send the same message—35 persons sentenced under the federal law as opposed to a thousand times more in California. As message-sending instrumentalities, these two laws might be more similar than their grossly different systemic impacts would suggest.

Partly because of loose coupling, the bark of much penal legisla-

---

[2]We have pilfered the phrase "loose coupling" from Simon Singer's (1996) *Recriminalizing Delinquency*, but he uses the term in a slightly different way—to refer to all systems that are not hierarchically organized around tightly defined goals (see pp. 19–21).

tion was notoriously louder than its bite. The political system could maximize the symbolic impact of new legislation and minimize its cost by creating a large rhetoric of toughness but with minimal operating results. The federal version of Three Strikes is a typical example of such low-budget crime crackdowns. Whatever else one might say about 35 prison sentences in four years, they generate a very slight burden on the prison budget of the leading industrial economy of the world. And the traditional examples of loose connections between symbolic and operational content were all tough talk but modest action.

The story of Three Strikes in California provides important evidence that the loose coupling between the symbolic and the operational in criminal justice can be used to magnify rather than minimize the latter. California's statute is a rare example of crime legislation that bites louder than it barks, even after the discretionary dilutions in practice are taken into account. One outstanding example is the penalty enhancements attached to persons with only one prior strike offense. It turns out that 90% of the punishment enhancements imposed under the California statute were based on a provision of the law that 90% of the voters probably were unaware of.

Recent examples of programs designed to maximize operational impact can be found outside California, although not with the degree of stealth and audaciousness displayed by adding a second-strike penalty to a Three Strikes proposal. The discussion of dual-currency issues in chapter 10 mentioned a recent round of truth-in-sentencing reforms aimed at reducing the gap between nominal and actual prison sentences through increases in the percentage of the nominal sentence that must be served. This derivative form of minimum sentence was mandated in the 1994 Federal Crime Bill as an approved state policy for violent, but not for nonviolent, felonies. Although the jurisprudential logic of truth in sentencing is obscure, its operational impact is a sharp increase in the actual length of prison sentences for any class of offender covered by such a provision. There is ample evidence that this operational goal, rather than the appropriate allocation of power among agencies that set criminal punishment, was the inspiration for truth in sentencing. So the loose linkage between the symbolism of crime legislation and its operational impact can now be exploited in two directions. The traditional false advertising of hollow crackdowns can now be contrasted with the manipulation of symbols deliberately designed to maximize punishments, often without disclosure.

The reverse variety of loose coupling is a recent arrival in the politics of punishment because no significant constituencies wanted increases in imprisonment until quite recently. The usual rewards for "get tough" politicians were public approval of symbol-laden legislation and perhaps credit when any crime news was good. There was no strong political incentive for heavy operational changes in the punishment system, so largely symbolic legislative results had no enemies in the political process. It is a very recent moment in American political history when constructing more prisons became a political goal with a constituency that was broader than building contractors. Part of this was the identification of groups with a pecuniary interest in the expanding scale of imprisonment, such as the prison guards union in California. A much larger part, however, was persuading the groups that had always been attached to the symbolic elements of law and order to care about the operational consequences of program choices as well. One force external to criminal justice has played an important role in this expansion: the professionalization and sophistication of state-level politics. If there was ever a time when advertising and politics were separate spheres of American life, that period had long since passed by the mid-1990s. The citizen activist now conducts political campaigns with professional public relations and policy analysis.

In the short run, the effect of the loose coupling between symbolic and operational impact has been to increase the variance in the latter—to make it more likely that a Three Strikes law can produce anything from 0 to 40,000 prison sentences. But is this a permanent condition or merely one step in a transition from a largely symbolic politics of criminal justice to a political discourse that is consistently concerned with operational consequences?

There is no doubt that the principal concerns of citizens on criminal justice questions will remain symbolic. The politics of crime and criminal justice are primarily symbolic matters everywhere, and quite likely to remain so. If electoral issues concerned with criminal justice also carry direct operational implications, we expect that the electoral processes of the states and the federal system will be crowded with groups of proposals that carry similar symbolic messages but widely varying operational implications. If "truth in sentencing" is the fashion, for example, we would expect eight different bills called "truth in sentencing" to be introduced with grossly different potential impacts on prison sentences. Despite the fact that the real difference between such proposals will be in their operational implications, it is not likely that this will play a very prominent role in citizens' reactions to them. This prediction amounts to an assertion that what we call the loose connection between symbolic and operational content is an inherent feature of the democratic politics of criminal justice.

If unpredictable and variable outcomes are considered a problem, the bes⁺ hope for avoiding them may be to restrict the direct operational consequences of legislative and electoral pronouncements. If the problem is the loose relationship between symbolic and operational impact, the solution might be to further attenuate the influence of symbolic legislative acts on operational results. But the organization and legislation of a government system to achieve such an uncoupling must be created by the same democratic mechanisms that produce loose coupling and high variability. Under what circumstances will a legislative body restrict its power to affect the level of punishment and the resources dedicated to its delivery?

One lesson of the survey of G-7 nations in chapter 10 is that such limits are the normal legal tradition in modern democracies and are located in nonlegislative instrumentalities, that is, the judiciary and the executive branches. Therefore, in protecting systems from the consequences of loose connections, attention should be transferred from mechanisms of direct and representative democracy to institutions of administrative and judicial governance.

The Significance of Institutional Structure

In one respect, no institutional structure can protect a criminal justice system from democratic preemption because a democratic override of any institutional arrangement is always available as a last resort. But the politics of criminal punishment is dominated by the habits and usual procedures of government rather than by power configurations of last resort. The two institutional configurations that minimize the operational impact of symbolic legislation are the delegation of policy-setting responsibilities to administrative and judicial agencies and the separation of general principles concerning punishment, which are typically promulgated by legislative bodies, from the determination of penalties in particular cases, which are not.

Several characteristics of California government and jurisprudence combined to produce the highly leveraged operating impact of Three Strikes. The initiative device allows outside proponents to draft proposals and thus to dictate the terms of the question to be presented to voters. In theory, this drafting power is all that advocates need to produce a legislative proposal designed for maximum operational impact. But this theoretical power will usually be limited by institutional patterns of criminal sentencing that produce diffusion of the legislative impact. If judges and parole authorities had traditionally played a major role in setting the length of a prison sentence in California, there would have been a conflict between the allocation of power among agencies under the new proposals and the existing sentencing system. But the determinate sentencing statute of 1976 had already allocated that power to a legislative authority, so Three Strikes was more consistent with current practice.

If the ideology and practice of sentencing in California had emphasized individualized determination of the appropriate punishment, a conflict between that approach and the one-size-fits-all logic of Three Strikes would have been evident. But here again prior changes in sentencing law had paved the way for a Three Strikes of maximum impact. If the ideology of sentencing prior to Three Strikes had been based on faith in the expertise of either judges or parole authorities, the conflict between that ideology and the preemptive distrust of official discretion would have been apparent. But distrust of official discretion was already the orthodox belief of criminal justice in California.

The sentencing authority in the federal system was less hospitable to a Three Strikes approach of maximum impact. A sentencing commission had been legislatively established in 1984 and designated as an expert authority on appropriate criminal sentences. Although the product of such a commission came dangerously close to an embrace of nonindividualized determination of punishment, overriding the authority of a commission with a broad set of mandatory penalties would generate tension between Congress and the agency that Congress had created. Congress had done so during the drug panic of the late 1980s. However, the precedent was not considered an attractive model for a Three Strikes initiative by any of the significant institutional influences on the federal legislation.

The institutional pattern that can provide a bulwark against preemptive legislative action is a matter of both function and social status. An allocation of punishment-setting power to specialized actors is much less likely to be preempted than is a punishment-setting power that already resides in the legislature. Moreover, powers held by functionaries with high reputations for expertise are far less vulnerable to legislative override than authority administered by government actors who are not trusted by the public.

One factor that determines trust is a theory or ideology of expertise. If those who hold the power to set terms of punishment are believed to be experts at their jobs, the chances of a legislative preemption are greatly diminished. One feature of California jurisprudence that made the systems vulnerable was that the expert function of judges, gauging appropriate penalties in individual cases, had been undermined as a priority by the 1976 determinate sentencing legislation. That earlier law was an extraordinary combination of the ends and means of law reform. The statute announced that deserved punishment rather than rehabilitation or deterrence was to be the central goal of imprisonment; but the law put the state legislature in charge of calculating deserved punishments for a great variety of crimes. Even if the goal of the reform had been appropriate, the choice of agency to accomplish it could only be regarded as self-defeating. Making the legislature the default determiner of just penal deserts created a vacuum in 1977 that Three Strikes filled in 1994. No institutional structure of sentencing authority is completely safe against a Three Strikes statute. But a multiagency allocation of authority, backed by public belief in the ability of the empowered agencies to do their jobs, is the best insurance against a massive influx of mandatory punishment terms.

The ideological dimension of the system that determines criminal punishment reflects a conception of how particular penalties should be set. Judicial discretion to choose between alternatives must be based on the idea that this is a legal decision. As soon as the choice of penalty is shifted from the individual to the aggregate level, the character of the selection process changes. When agencies like parole boards or sentencing commissions determine norms for time served, the selection seems to be an administrative process, so the expertise required to perform it is presumably administrative. When penalties are determined by legislative bodies, the nature of the task can easily be seen as a political task—that is, after all, the particular competence of legislative bodies.

One implication of this analysis is that sentencing commissions are an incomplete defense against legislative preemption. To the extent that they remove the individual and the legal-jurisprudential aspects from punishment determination, administrative processes can lay the groundwork for a later political takeover of this responsibility. The deterrent to political preemption that such commissions represent is as an alternative expert institution established to occupy the field of criminal sentencing. The strength of this claim may well depend on the credibility of the commissioners' claim to expertise. They are experts on what?

The Paradoxical Politics of Government Distrust

The last lesson we will emphasize here has both broad and disturbing implications. The punishment of criminals is at root an exercise of government power. It might therefore seem reasonable to suppose that citizens' support for harsh measures would increase with increasing levels of trust in government and that support for excessive punishments would decline when levels of confidence in government fell. In this reading, support for harsh punishment would be a disease of excess confidence in state authority.

Yet the fluctuating levels of public confidence in government in California produced almost the opposite pattern. The early months of 1994 were a low point for citizens' trust in state government, but the demand for criminal punishment had never been greater (Jeffe 1994). This is what we call the paradoxical politics of government distrust. There are two explanations for this negative relationship between confidence in government and the demand for high levels of criminal punishment. First, crime seems to be a bigger problem when trust in government is low. That is, dissatisfaction with the current level of government achievement leads to insistence on more government service. Second, distrust means that citizens worry that judges will identify with offenders and treat them with inappropriate leniency. A bad judge in this view is one prone to coddle criminals and thus act against the interests of the citizenry, and mandatory punishment is the way to ensure against such weakness. But the mandatory term is a huge expansion of punishment, rendering excessive outcomes in many cases to ensure sufficiency of punishment in a very few worst-case offenses.

The fear that government authorities will serve the interests of criminals becomes a way of recruiting citizens in a political war against their government. In this view, the criminal and the judge have become the citizens' common enemy. This was the radical subtext of Three Strikes. It is a political development that could hardly be regarded as good news in the United States, but it is nonetheless a prospect of substantial importance. Those who wish to undermine faith in government find that cultivating fear of crime is a promising means of doing so. Thus a further reason to insulate punishment from democratic political processes is to avoid placing a vulnerable area of governance in an arena where it can be used as an opening wedge for broader attempts to undermine the credibility of government.

The close connection between laws like California's version of Three Strikes and what we call the politics of distrust is one illustration of a more general phenomenon—the link between the quality of criminal justice and social and governmental trends that originate outside its boundaries. An angry and distrustful citizenry prefers broad and extreme penal measures rather than individualized penalty decisions. Proportional justice in the punishment of an offender is a value that can only be respected by a government whose citizens trust those who govern. Decency and fairness in criminal justice are an indication of broader government soundness, whereas punitive excess is often a symptom of weakness and instability.

References

Barry, Brian. 1991. "Does Democracy Cause Inflation?" In *Democracy and Power: Essays in Political Theory I*. Brian Barry, ed. Oxford: Clarendon Press.

Beckett, Katherine. 1997. *Making Crime Pay: Law and Order in Contemporary American Politics*. New York: Oxford University Press.

Bentham, Jeremy. [1843–1859] 1802. "Principles of Penal Law." In *Works*, vol. 1, pp. 365–580. J. Bowring, ed. London: Simpkin, Marshall.

Beres, Linda S., and Thomas D. Griffith. 1998. "Did 'Three Strikes' Cause the Recent Drop in California Crime? An Analysis of the California Attorney General's Report." *Loyola of Los Angeles Law Review* 32:101.

Blumstein, Alfred, Jacqueline Cohen, Jeffrey A. Roth, and Christy A. Visher. eds. 1996. *Criminal Careers and "Career Criminals."* Washington, D.C.: National Academy Press.

Buchanan, James M., and Richard E. Wagner. 1977. *Democracy in Deficit: The Political Legacy of Lord Keynes*. New York: Academic Press.

Butterfield, Fox. 1996, March 8. "Tough Law on Sentences Is Criticized." *New York Times*, p. A14.

California Department of Corrections. 1994–1996. *Annual Reports*. Sacramento, Calif.: CDC.

California Department of Corrections. 1999. *Quarterly Movement Summary Report*. Sacramento Calif.: California Dept. of Corrections.

California Department of Justice, Criminal Justice Statistics Center. 1997.

California Department of Justice, Office of the Attorney General, Bureau of Criminal Information and Analysis. 1998. *Crime and Delinquency in California*.

California Legislature, Senate Bill 873. 1999.

California Penal Code §1170(a)(1) (West Supplement 1996).

California Penal Code §667 (West Supplement 1996).

California Penal Code §2931 (West Supplement 1996).

Campaign for an Effective Crime Policy. 1998. *"Three Strikes" Laws: Five Years Later*. Washington, D.C.: Campaign for an Effective Crime Policy.

Carman, John. 1993, December 8. "Haunting Images Cling to Polly Klaas Tragedy." *San Francisco Chronicle*, p. E1.

Carp, Robert A., and Ronald Stidham. 1998. *Judicial Process in America*, 4th ed. Washington, D.C.: Congressional Quarterly Press.

Chaiken, Jan M., and Marcia R. Chaiken. 1982. *Varieties of Criminal Behavior*. Santa Monica, Calif.: Rand.

233

Clark, John, James Austin, and D. Alan Henry. 1997. *Three Strikes and You're Out: A Review of State Legislation.* National Institute of Justice, U.S. Department of Justice, Office of Justice Programs. Washington, D.C.: U.S. Government Printing Office.

Clifford, Albert Jerome. 1965. *The Independence of the Federal Reserve System.* Philadelphia: University of Pennsylvania Press.

College Blue Book. 1995. 25th ed. New York: Macmillan.

Council of State Governments. 1998a. *The Book of the States,* vol. 3. Lexington, Ky.: Council of State Governments.

Council of State Governments. 1998b. *CSG State Directory, Administrative Officials.* Lexington, Ky.: Council of State Governments.

Cousart, Felicia. 1996, January 20. "Three Strikes Author Launches Anti-Gun Violence Intiative." *Fresno Bee,* p. B1.

Douglas, William. 1994, March 18. "Panel OKs Amended '3 Strikes' Bill, Provision Allows Parole After Age 70." *Newsday,* p. 17.

DuBois, Philip L., and Floyd Feeney. 1998. *Lawmaking by Initiative: Issues, Options and Comparisons.* New York: Agathon Press.

Egan, Timothy. 1994, February 15. "A 3 Strikes Law Shows It's Not As Simple As It Seems." *New York Times,* p. A1.

Federal Bureau of Investigation. 1990–1997. *Uniform Crime Reports for the United States—1990–1997.* Washington, D.C.: U.S. Department of Justice.

Feeley, Malcolm M. and Sam Kamin. 1996. "The Effect of 'Three Strikes and You're Out' on the Courts." In *Three Strikes and You're Out: Vengeance as Public Policy.* David Shichor and Dale K. Sechrest, eds. Thousand Oaks, Calif.: Sage.

Fogel, David. 1975. *"We Are the Living Proof . . ." The Justice Model for Corrections.* Cincinnati: W. H. Anderson.

Freedman, Dan. 1994, January 28. "Critics Hit Reno as Top Aide Quits." *San Francisco Examiner,* p. A10.

Furillo, Andy. 1996, August 4. "Impatient Crime-Busters Leave Legislature on Sidelines." *Sacramento Bee,* p. A10.

Furman v. Georgia. 1972. 408 U.S. 238, 92 S. Ct. 2726.

Garland, David. 1996. "The Limits of the Sovereign State: Strategies of Crime Control in Contemporary Society." *British Journal of Criminology* 36:445.

Gilliam, Jerry. 1994, March 2. "Legislators Fear Public on '3 Strikes,' Brown Says." *Los Angeles Times,* p. A3.

Davis, Gray. Letter dated October 10, 1999, and referenced as Veto Attachment to S.B. 873.

Green, Stephen. 1995, January 7. "'Three Strikes' Begins to Jam Courts, Jails in Some Counties." *Fresno Bee,* p. A1.

Greenwood, Peter, C. Peter Rydell, Allan F. Abrahamse, Jonathan P. Caulkins, James Chiesa, Karyn E. Model, and Stephen P. Klein. 1994. *Three Strikes and You're Out: Estimated Benefits and Costs of California's New Mandatory-Sentencing Law.* Santa Monica, Calif.: Rand.

Greenwood, Peter W., and Susan Turner. 1987. *Selective Incapacitation Revisited.* Santa Monica, Calif.: Rand.

Hecht, Peter. 1994, July 10. "Two Grieving Fathers Part Ways on '3 Strikes' Crusade." *Sacramento Bee*, p. A1.

Hofer, Paul J., and Courtney Semisch. 1999. Examining Changes in Federal Sentencing Severity 1980–1998. *Federal Sentencing Reporter* 12:12.

Hutto v. Davis. 1982. 454 U.S. 370, 102 S. Ct. 703.

Japha, Anthony. 1976. *Sentencing Patterns Under the 1973 New York State Drug Laws*. (Drug Law Evaluation Project Report). New York: Association of the Bar of the City of New York.

Jeffe, Sherry Bebitch. 1994, January 9. "Wilson Hoping Crime Will Assure His Job—But What Has He Done So Far?" *Los Angeles Times*, p. M6.

Judicial Council of California. 1996. *The Impact of the Three Strikes Law on Superior and Municipal Courts*. San Francisco: Judicial Council of California.

Kamin, Sam. 2000. The Death Penalty and the California Supreme Court: Politics, Judging and Death. Ph.D. dissertation, University of California at Berkeley.

Kershner, Vlae. 1994, March 3. "Governor Wants '3 Strikes' Plan That Is Toughest, Most Costly." *San Francisco Chronicle*, p. A1.

Knapp, Kay A. 1987. "Implementation of the Minnesota Guidelines: Can the Innovative Spirit Be Preserved?" In *The Sentencing Commission and Its Guidelines*. Andrew von Hirsch, Kay A. Knapp, and Michael Tonry, eds. Boston: Northeastern University Press.

Kurtz, Howard. 1994, October 11. "Political Peddlers' Bitter Bromides." *Washington Post*, p. A1.

Legislative Analyst's Office. 1995, January 6. *Status: The Three Strikes and You're Out Law—A Preliminary Assessment*. Sacramento, Calif.: Legislative Analyst's Office.

Lungren, Dan. 1997, February 24. "Our Tough Law Works." *USA Today*, p. 10-A.

Males, Michael, Dan Macallair, and Khaled Taqi-Eddin. 1999. "California Three Strikes Ineffective." *Overcrowded Times* 10:1, 14–16.

McCoy, Candace. 1990. *Politics and Plea Bargaining: Victim's Rights in California*. Philadelphia: University of Pennsylvania Press.

Messinger, Sheldon, and Phillip E. Johnson. 1977. "California's Determinate Sentencing Statute: History and Issues." In *Determinate Sentencing: Reform or Regression*. Washington, D.C.: U.S. Government Printing Office.

Miller, Geoffrey P. 1998. "An Interest-Group Theory of Central Bank Independence." *Journal of Legal Studies* 27:433.

Ministere de L'Economie et Des Finances, 1961 and 1991 (France).

Morain, Dan. 1994a, January 27. "Assembly Panel OKs Five '3 Strikes' Bills." *Los Angeles Times*, p. A3.

———. 1994b, March 7. "A Father's Bittersweet Crusade, Mike Reynolds Vowed That His Murdered Daughter Would Not Die in Vain; Few Thought He Would Win, But Today He Will See the 'Three Strikes' Bill Signed Into Law." *Los Angeles Times*, p. A1.

————. 1994c, October 17. "Proposition 184 'Three Strikes'" A Steam-roller Driven by One Man's Pain." *Los Angeles Times*, p. A3.

————. 1994d, March 4. "Three Strikes Clears State Legislature." *Los Angeles Times*, p. A1.

Morris, Norval. 1951. *The Habitual Criminal*. Cambridge, Mass.: Harvard University Press.

————. 1974. *The Future of Imprisonment*. Chicago: University of Chicago Press.

Paddock, Richard C. and Jennifer Warren. 1993, December 5. "Suspect's Tip Leads To Body of Polly Klaas." *Los Angeles Times*, p. A1.

People v. Benson. 1998. 18 Cal. 4th 24, 954 P. 2d 557, 74 Cal. Rptr. 2d 294.

People v. Davis. 1997. 15 Cal. 4th 1096, 938 P. 2d 938, 64 Cal. Rptr. 2d 879.

People v. Hendrix. 1997. 16 Cal. 4th 508, 941 P. 2d 64, 66 Cal. Rptr. 2d 431.

People v. Superior Court (Romero). 1996. 13 Cal. 4th 497, 917 P. 2d 628, 53 Cal. Rptr. 2d 789.

Pindyck, Robert S., and Daniel L. Rubinfeld. 1991. *Econometric Models and Economic Forecasts*, 3rd ed. New York: McGraw-Hill.

Podger, Pamela J. 1993, November 16. "Murder Victim's Father Launches Repeat-Felon Penalty Initiative." *Fresno Bee*, p. B-1.

Podger, Pamela J., and Phoebe Wall Howard. 1996, May 12. "Reynolds' Campaign Losing Steam." *Fresno Bee*, p. A1.

President's Commission on Law Enforcement and Administration of Justice. 1967. *The Challenge of Crime in a Free Society*. Washington, D.C.: U.S. Government Printing Office.

Reiss, Albert J. 1986. "Co-offender Influences on Criminal Careers." In *Criminal Careers and "Career Criminals,"* Alfred Blumstein, Jacqueline Cohen, Jeffrey A. Roth, and Christy A. Visher. eds. Washington, D.C.: National Academy Press.

Riccardi, Nicholas. 1994, August 31. "Statewide Crime Rate Is Down in First Half of '94." *Los Angeles Times*, p. A3.

Richardson, James. 1994a, March 16. "Brown Won't Touch 'Three Strikes' This Year." *Sacramento Bee*, p. A4.

————. 1994b, February 12. "Three Strikes Supporters Divided." *Sacramento Bee*, p. A4.

Rothbard, Murray N. 1994. *The Case Against the Fed*. Auburn, Ala.: Ludwig Von Moses Institute.

Rummel v. Estelle. 1980. 445 U.S. 263, 100 S. Ct. 1133.

Schiraldi, Vincent. 1994, June. "Corrections and Higher Ed Compete for California Dollars; Corrections Winning." *Overcrowded Times*, p. 7.

Schlossman, Steven L. 1977. *Love and the American Delinquent: The Theory and Practice of "Progressive" Juvenile Justice*. Chicago: University of Chicago Press.

Shogren, Elizabeth. 1995, December 4. "Population in U.S. Prisons Is Up Record 8.8%." *Los Angeles Times*, , p. A1.

Singer, Simon. 1996. *Recriminalizing Delinquency: Violent Juvenile Crime and Juvenile Justice Reform*. New York: Cambridge University Press.

Skelton, George. 1993, December 13. "Wilson Seizes the Day After Polly's Murder." *Los Angeles Times*, p. A3.

Stall, Bill. 1994, February 28. "GOP Pins Hopes on Crime Issue to Re-Elect Wilson." *Los Angeles Times*, p. A3.

Stein, Herbert. 1998, February 25. *New York Times Book Review*, p. 8.

Stiller, Daniel W. 1995. "Initiative 593: Washington Voters Go Down Swinging." *Gonzaga Law Review* 30:433.

Struggle for Justice. 1971. A Report on Crime and Punishment in America. Prepared for the American Friends Service Committee. New York: Hill & Wang.

"Three Strikes Initiative Circulated." 1996, October 3. *San Diego Union-Tribune*, p. A3.

Tonry, Michael. 1996. *Sentencing Matters*. New York: Oxford University Press.

Turner, Michael G., 1995. "'Three Strikes and You're Out' Legislation; A National Assessment." *Federal Probation* 59:16.

U.S. Bureau of Justice Statistics. *Prisoners in 1990*. Washington D.C.: U.S. Government Printing Office.

U.S. Department of Justice, Federal Bureau of Investigation. 1961, 1971–1997 and 1999. *Uniform Crime Reports for the United States*. Washington, D.C.: U.S. Government Printing Office.

Vitiello, Michael. 1997. "Three Strikes: Can We Return to Rationality?" *Journal of Criminal Law and Criminology* 87:395.

Von Hirsch, Andrew. 1976. *Doing Justice: The Choice of Punishments*. Report of the Committee for the Study of Incarceration. New York: Hill & Wang.

Wechsler, Herbert. 1961. "Sentencing, Corrections, and the Model Penal Code" *University of Pennsylvania Law Review* 109:465.

"Week in Review." 1999, August 1. *New York Times*, p. 4.

Weintraub, Daniel. 1994, March 8. "'Three Strikes' Law Goes Into Effect," *Los Angeles Times*, p. A1.

Weiss, Kenneth R. 1991, February 19. "Budget Cuts Cost Area Legislators 16 Staff Members," *Los Angeles Times*, p. B1.

Welch, Richard S. 1994, February 28. Memorandum to Director of Corrections.

Wilkie, Dana. 1994, October 12. "Prop 184: 3 Strikes Already on Books, Foes Say Its Passage Only Bolsters a Bad Law." *San Diego Union-Tribune*, p. A1.

Wilson, Pete. 1997a, October 5. "Point: Remove Criminals from Society, Not Guns from Innocent Citizens." *San Diego Union-Tribune*, p. G4.

———. 1997b, March 9. "'Three Strikes' Law Truly Makes California Safer." *Los Angeles Daily News*, p. V-3.

Windlesham, Lord David James George Hennessy. 1998. *Politics, Punishment, and Populism*. New York: Oxford University Press.

Zimring, Franklin E. 1975. "Firearms and Federal Law: The Gun Control Act of 1968." *Journal of Legal Studies* 4:133.

———. 1976. "Making the Punishment Fit the Crime: A Consumer's Guide to Sentencing Reform." *Hastings Center Report* 6(6):13–21.

———. 1981. "Kids, Groups and Crime: Some Implications of a Well-known Secret." *Journal of Criminal Law and Criminology* 72:867–885.

———. 1983. "Sentencing Reform in the States: Lessons from the 1970s." In *Reform and Punishment: Essays in Criminal Sentencing.* Michael Tonry and Franklin Zimring, eds. Chicago: University of Chicago Press.

———. 1996. "Populism, Democratic Government, and the Decline of Expert Authority: Some Reflections on 'Three Strikes in California.'" *Pacific Law Journal* 28:243–256.

———. 1998. *American Youth Violence.* New York: Oxford University Press.

Zimring, Franklin E., and Jeffrey Fagan. 2000. "The Search for Causes in an Era of Declining Crime Rates." *Crime and Delinquency* 46: 446–456.

Zimring, Franklin E., and Gordon Hawkins. 1973. *Deterrence: The Legal Threat in Crime Control.* Chicago: University of Chicago Press.

———. 1986. *Capital Punishment and the American Agenda.* New York: Cambridge University Press.

———. 1991. *The Scale of Imprisonment.* Chicago: University of Chicago Press.

———. 1992. *Prison Population and Criminal Justice Policy in California.* Berkeley, Calif.: Institute of Governmental Studies Press.

———. 1994. "The Growth of Imprisonment in California." *British Journal of Criminology* 34:83–96.

———. 1995. *Incapacitation: Penal Confinement and the Restraint of Crime.* New York: Oxford University Press.

———. 1996. "Toward a Principled Basis for Federal Criminal Legislation." *The Annals of the American Academy of Political Social Science* 543:15.

———. 1997. *Crime Is Not the Problem: Lethal Violence in America.* New York: Oxford University Press.

Index

Academic lawyers, criminal justice policy processes and, 13

African American defendants and offenders, 57, 60

American Law Institute, 13

Assault, rate of injuries and deaths attributable to, 48

Assembly Bill 4, saga of, 140–145

Bentham, Jeremy, 192

Beres, Linda, 102

British prison population, 163

Brown, Willie, 12

Burglary, punishment trends before and after Three Strikes for, 76–80

Burke, Edmund, 12

California Adult Authority, 110, 111

California Board of Prison Terms, 115

California Bureau of Criminal Statistics, 38, 67

California Correctional Peace Officer's Association, 5

California Department of Corrections
  crime decline study, 102
  and impact of Three Strikes on prison population, 11, 66, 133–134, 135, 136
  second- and third-strike enforcement under Three Strikes, 63–64, 65

California District Attorneys Association, 6, 11

California Penal Code, 4

California State Department of Justice, 36, 54

California Supreme Court, 125–126, 128, 129
  People v. Benson, 130, 132

People v. Davis, 130, 132

People v. Hendrix, 131

People v. Romero, 131, 132, 146, 218, 220

Campaign for an Effective Crime Policy, 19–20

Caplan, Gerald, 13

Central banks, justification of independent, 204–209, 213

Chicago, crime drop, 89

College and university justice programs, 13

Consensus on government policy, 163–164

Constitution, U.S., Eighth Amendment, 189, 190

Court system, Three Strikes and California's, 125–126
  appellate review, 128–133
  trial courts, 126–128

Crime control, Three Strikes as, 85
  monthly crime trends and Three Strikes, 87–90
  the official story, 85–87
  testing two theories of California's crime decline, 101–103
  two methods of crime prevention, 90–95

Crime and criminal justice trends, 151–153
  crime, 153–155
  growth of imprisonment, 155–159
  Three Strikes and politics of crime, 159–177

Criminal justice officials, power of, 172–173

Criminal justice, politics of, 138–145

Criminal justice system, Three Strikes and structure of California's, 24–26

Criminal punishment, impact of Three Strikes on, 63, 83–84

Criminal punishment, impact of
    Three Strikes on (*continued*)
    contrasting levels of enforce-
        ment, 63–64
    impacts of the Three Strikes on
        punishment, 66–83
    second- vs. third-strike enforce-
        ment, 65–66
    See also Democracy and the
        governance of criminal
        punishment
Criminal recidivism
    California legislature and defini-
        tions of, 31–32
    identification of new classes of
        criminal recidivists, 33

Dangerous-offender approach in
    Three Strikes statute, 53
Davis, Gray, 222
Death penalty, 189
Death sentences, 129
Decline in crime, California's,
    85–105
Democracy and the governance of
    criminal punishment, 181
    aggregation errors in generality,
        194–195
    crime-centered focus of manda-
        tory general standards,
        199–200
    dual currency and the bias of
        front-end time setting, 195–199
    methods of choosing punish-
        ment, 182–187
    popular choice, 187–192
    procedure and substance in
        democratic decision making,
        200–204
    sentencing commissions,
        212–215
    theories of distortion, 192–194
Democrats, California, legislation
    for enhanced punishment for
    recidivists, 5–6
Desert, minimum, 188
Determinate sentencing, 112–115
Determinate Sentencing Law of
    1976, 25, 174, 210, 212
Deterrence, crime prevention by
    general deterrence, 94–95
    how much Three Strikes deter-
        rence is possible?, 95–96

theory vs. practice in general de-
    terrence, 103–105
Deukmejian, George, 128, 129
Direct democracy, 183
Distrust of government, 173–177,
    231–232
Drug offenses, punishment trends
    before and after Three Strikes
    for, 76–80
Dual-currency sentencing,
    196–199
DuBois, Philip L., 193

Early release, 195–196
Eighth Amendment prohibitions,
    189, 190
Electoral control, responsiveness
    of criminal justice policy to,
    167–169
England, habitual-offender laws
    in, 4
Excessive punishment, meaning
    of, 189–191
Expansion, prison, 156–157

Fear of crime, 160–162
Federal Bureau of Investigation
    (FBI), 154
Federal Crime Bill of 1994,
    226
Federal Criminal Code, passage of,
    23
Federal Open Market Committee,
    204
Federal Reserve Board, 204
Federal Reserve system
    creation of, 204–205
    as insulated institution, 206,
        207, 208, 209
Federal Sentencing Commission,
    172, 209, 213, 214
Federal Sentencing Guidelines of
    1987, 23
Feeney, Floyd, 193
Felony arrests in California,
    33–34, 43–45
    before and after Three Strikes,
        117, 118
    median and mean age at arrest
        by Strike status, 56
    time trends for no-strike,
        74–76
    violent felonies, 46–48

Felony convictions
  in California by Three Strikes
    status, 51–52
  second- and third-strike arrests
    resulting in, 67–68
Firearms control, 10-20-Life pro-
    posal, 141–145
Furman v. Georgia, 190

Gann, Paul, 174
Garland, David, 158
General provisions on punish-
    ment, 182
Griffith, Thomas, 102
Group of 7 (G-7) countries
  imprisonment rates for, 158–159
  punishment decisions by level
    of democratic control in,
    185–186, 228
Gun crime, 10-20-Life proposal,
    141–145
Gun-control acts, 161

Habitual-offender approach in
    Three Strikes statute, 53
Habitual-offender laws, 4
Harvard Law School, 13
Heymann, Philip, 15
Hispanic defendants, 57
Homicide arrests, California, 33,
    34, 39, 53–55
Hough, Mike, 163

Illinois, penal reform measures
    passed in, 196
Incapacitation, crime prevention
    by, 91–94
  incapacitation efficiency, 92
  incapacitation impact, 92
Indeterminate sentencing, 110–112
Inflationary monetary policies,
    206–207
Institutional structure and crimi-
    nal justice system, 228–231
Insulated delegations, 184
International Monetary Fund
    (IMF), 205

Jarvis, Howard, 174
Johnson, Lyndon B., 67
Judicial and prosecutorial deci-
    sion making under Three
    Strikes initiative, 26–27

Judicial vacancies, 128
Juries
  Three Strikes and demand for
    jury trials, 219
  use of juries in making punish-
    ment decisions, 200
Jurisprudence of imprisonment in
    California, 109
  current California law, 115–117
  cycles of reform in criminal sen-
    tencing, 109–115
  proportionality and disparity in
    criminal sentencing, 117–123
Juvenile courts, 130–131

Kelling, George, 165
Kennedy, Robert, 161
King, Martin Luther, Jr., 161
Klaas, Polly, 5, 6, 11, 13, 160, 177

"Life-plus 99 years" sentences,
    196
Loose coupling, concept of,
    225–228
Los Angeles
  before and after comparisons of
    deterrence in, 96–97
  before and after Three Strikes
    research design in, 36–37, 38,
    39, 54
  crime drop, 89
  incarceration rates for second-
    strike cases in, 80–81
  incarceration rates in third-
    strike cases in, 81–83
  time trends for no-strike felony
    arrests in, 74–76
Los Angeles District Attorney's of-
    fice, Three Strikes and in-
    crease in criminal trials, 126
"Loud-bark, small bite" pattern
    of federal law, 169, 176, 195,
    226
Low debt service, 206
Lucas, Malcolm, 129

Macallair, Dan, 103
McGeorge School of Law, 13
Males, Michael, 103
Martin, William McChesney,
    209
Martinson, Robert, 165
McCoy, Candace, 139

Minnesota
    federal sentencing commissions
        in, 209, 212, 213
    mandatory minimum sentences
        in, 198
Mistrust, politics of, 173–177,
    231–232
Model Penal code effort, 13
Morris, Norval, 4, 188

National Aeronautics and Space
    Administration (NASA),
    205–206
National Institute of Justice, 13
National Rifle Association
    and absence of expert analysis
        on Three Strikes, 11
    campaign for Three Strikes ini-
        tiative, 5
    lack of support for 10-20-Life
        proposal, 142
    politics of mistrust campaign by,
        176
New York
    crime drop, 89
    drug laws, 24
No-strike defendants
    felony arrests, 43, 46, 49, 51, 54,
        56, 59
    imprisonment and average sen-
        tence for, 69–70
    time trends for no-strike felony
        arrests, 74–76
    trial rates for no-strike cases, 127
North Carolina, mandatory mini-
    mum sentences in, 198

Offender-based vs. offense-based
    jurisprudence, 114, 115
Older felons, 56
Omnibus Crime Control Bill of
    1994, 164
One-strike provision
    one-strike felony arrests, 42–43,
        45–46, 51, 54, 56, 59
    one-strike life terms for sex of-
        fenders, 140

Parole, early release and justifica-
    tion for, 195–196
Particular application concept on
    punishment, 182
Pate, Anthony, 165

Penalty choices, populist bias in,
    201–203
People v. Benson, 130, 132
People v. Davis, 130, 132
People v. Hendrix, 131
People v. Romero, 131, 132, 146,
    218, 220
Politics of crime. See Three
    Strikes and politics of crime
Popular will, necessity of punish-
    ment and, 188–189
Population, California's, 152–153
President's Crime Commission,
    1966, 13
Prison system, California, 133–138
    growth of imprisonment, 155–159
    impact of Three Strikes on
        prison sentences, 73–74
    imprisonment and average sen-
        tence for no-strike defendants,
        69–70
    imprisonment and incarceration
        patterns before and after Three
        Strikes, four offenses, 76–80
    incarceration rates in second-
        strike cases, 80–81
    incarceration rates in third-
        strike cases, 81–83
    large prison population in, 17, 18
    mean and median prison terms,
        70, 72, 73–74
    Three Strikes incapacitation im-
        pact on, 91–94
    See also Jurisprudence of im-
        prisonment in California
Proposition 8, 139
Proposition 13, 174
Proposition 184, 11
Prosecutorial and judicial decision
    making under Three Strikes
    initiative, 26–27
Public opinion
    about punishment of felons, 178
    and government policy, 163–164
    public attitudes toward crime
        and criminals, 178–179
    transforming public opinion
        into policy, 179

Rand Corporation, 86, 102, 103
Reagan, Ronald, 175
Recidivists in urban California
    crime, role of, 41, 58–61

arrests as a measure of crime, 41–43

demographics of Three Strikes eligibility, 55–58

extent of criminal histories, 51–53

recidivism and California violence, 46–48

recidivism, Three Strikes, and crime, 43–46

supplementary homicide sample, 53–55

Three Strikes targets as criminal groups, 48–51

See also Criminal recidivism

Reduction in crime, California's, 85–105

Representative democracy, 183–184

Reynolds, Mike, 145
and 10-20-Life proposal, 141, 142, 143
and Three Strikes initiative, 4, 6–7, 48, 139, 140, 170

Robbery, punishment trends before and after Three Strikes for, 76–80

Roberts, Julian, 163

Rothbard, Murray, 205

Rummel v. Estelle, 190

San Diego
before and after comparisons of deterrence in, 96–97
before and after Three Strikes research design in, 36–37, 38, 39, 54
incarceration rates for second-strike cases in, 80–81
incarceration rates in third-strike cases in, 81–83
prosecutors for third-strike sentencing in, 132
time trends for no-strike felony arrests in, 74–76

San Francisco
before and after comparisons of deterrence in, 96–97
before and after Three Strikes research design in, 36–37, 38, 39, 54
incarceration rates for second-strike cases in, 80–81

incarceration rates in third-strike cases in, 81–83

time trends for no-strike felony arrests in, 74–76

Saturday night specials, 142, 144

Second-strike and third-strike provisions, 219–220
before and after comparisons of deterrence of second- and third-strike defendants, 97–98
enforcement under Three Strikes law, 63–66
impact of second-strike cases on prison population, 137–138
incarceration rates in second-strike cases, 80–81
incarceration rates in third-strike cases, 81–83
punishments for second-strike defendants before and after Three Strikes law, 70–71
punishments for third-strike defendants before and after Three Strikes law, 71–72
second- and third-strike felony arrests, 41–61, 67–68
sentencing for third-strike cases, 116, 119–120
third-strike prison population projections, 135–136
trial rates for second- and third-strike cases, 127–128

Senate Bill 873, 221

Sentencing commissions, 212–215, 230–231

Sentencing, criminal
cycles of reform in, 109–112
dual-currency sentencing, 196–199
institutional patterns of, 228–231
length of sentences and length of time served, 195–196
negative architecture of determinate sentencing, 112–115
proportionality and disparity in, 117–123

Sentencing disparity, 111–112, 113, 119–123

Sentencing policy, Three Strikes label as a poor predictor of, 20

Sex offenders, proposal for life imprisonment for, 150

"Shall issue" laws, 176

Social cost of punishment, 191–192
Special-interest groups, 173
Stein, Herbert, 168
Struggle for Justice, 111, 112, 174
Supreme Court, U.S.
    Eighth Amendment challenges,
      190
    See also California Supreme
      Court
Swiss system, lawmaking initia-
    tives in, 193

Taqi-Eddin, Khaled, 103
Tax revolt initiative, 174
10-20-Life gun crime proposal,
    141–145, 171
Theft, punishment trends before
    and after Three Strikes for,
    76–80
Third-strike provisions. *See*
    Second-strike and third-strike
    provisions
"Three Strikes' Era Drop in Cali-
    fornia Crime Rate" (report),
    86–87
Three Strikes law in California
    characteristics of initiatives in
      California, 192–194
    court system and, 125–133
    as crime control, 85–105
    excessiveness and mandatory
      general policies, 194
    impacts of the Three Strikes on
      punishment, 66–83
    legacies of, 217–232
    legislative and initiative
      processes, 3–24, 27–28
    passage of law, 7, 12, 17, 168
    sentences under, 19, 20, 69–74
    sequence and penalty under, 9–10
    structure of California's criminal
      justice system and, 24–26
    summary of the legislation, 7–9
    See also Second-strike and
      third-strike provisions
Three Strikes law, federal, 169,
    224–225, 226
    sentences under, 20
    serious crime restrictions in,
      19
Three Strikes law in Washington
    passage of law, 4, 17
    sentences under, 19

Three Strikes and politics of
    crime, 159–160, 222–224
    accessability of policy to politi-
      cal influence, 171–172
    attitude of enforcers, 172–173
    compromise, 170–171
    confidence in efficacy of govern-
      ment action, 164–165
    consensus on government pol-
      icy, 163–164
    criminal justice as a government
      priority, 165–167
    dual agency of fear, 160–162
    mistrust, 173–177
    political science of contingency,
      162–163
    presence of special interests
      dedicated to broad changes in
      policy, 173
    responsiveness of criminal jus-
      tice policy to electoral con-
      trol, 167–169
"Three Strikes and You're Out—Its
    Impact on the California
    Criminal Justice System After
    Four Years" (report), 85–86
"Three-time loser" laws, 4
Trial courts, California's, 126–128
Truth-in-sentencing, 176, 199, 227

United States, punishment deci-
    sions by level of democratic
    control in the, 185–187

Victims rights initiative, 139
Violent crimes, violent felony ar-
    rests in California, 43–45
Vorenberg, James, 13
Voting support for Three Strikes in
    California, 37

White and other defendants, 57
Wilson, Pete, 129
    and absence of expert analysis
      on Three Strikes, 11
    and "getting tough" on crime
      initiative, 5
    and preference for Reynold's
      Three Strikes program, 6
    and 10-20-Life proposal, 144

Zero-sum competition, concept of,
    223